White Kids

In *White Kids*, Mary Bucholtz investigates how white teenagers use language to display identities based on race and youth culture. Focusing on three youth styles – preppies, hip hop fans, and nerds – Bucholtz shows how white youth use a wealth of linguistic resources, from social labels to slang, from Valley Girl speech to African American English, to position themselves in their local racialized social order.

Drawing on ethnographic fieldwork in a multiracial urban California high school, the book also demonstrates how European American teenagers talk about race when discussing interracial friendship and difference, narrating racialized fear and conflict, and negotiating their own ethnoracial classification. The first book to use techniques of linguistic analysis to examine the construction of diverse white identities, it will be welcomed by researchers and students in linguistics, anthropology, ethnic studies, and education.

MARY BUCHOLTZ is Professor of Linguistics at the University of California, Santa Barbara.

White Kids

Language, Race, and Styles of Youth Identity

Mary Bucholtz

CAMBRIDGE
UNIVERSITY PRESS

University Printing House, Cambridge CB2 8BS, United Kingdom

Published in the United States of America by Cambridge University Press, New York

Cambridge University Press is part of the University of Cambridge.

It furthers the University,s mission by disseminating knowledge in the pursuit of education, learning and research at the highest international levels of excellence.

www.cambridge.org
Information on this title: www.cambridge.org/9780521692045

First published 2011
5th printing 2014

Printed in the United Kingdom by Clays, St Ives plc.

A catalogue record for this publication is available from the British Library

ISBN 978-0-521-87149-5 Hardback
ISBN 978-0-521-69204-5 Paperback

For Jon

Contents

List of figures

List of tables

Preface

The origins of this book lie in California, where I did my graduate work and where I am now a professor, but the issues I confronted there stayed with me when I took my first academic post in Texas. In both places historical divisions between black and white are obvious, yet they take different forms in each. In California, the construction in the post-World War II era of the three interstate highways that converge in West Oakland (not far from the bungalow in South Berkeley that I rented while I attended graduate school) disrupted the surrounding neighborhood and its largely low-income African American residents. The new throughways formed a transportation corridor that further facilitated so-called "white flight" from Oakland to the surrounding suburbs. In Texas, State Highway 6 (which runs through College Station, home of Texas A&M University, my first employer) divides the small town of Calvert, separating the black descendants of tenant farmers from the white descendants of landowners in ways that are still starkly visible today.

Such dividing lines are a central issue of this book. While it is clear that the binary separation of black and white is as socially and culturally artificial as it is biologically baseless, academic theories of multicultural diversity and post-modern fluidity have had little impact on American racial ideologies, even in states with large and diverse populations such as California and Texas. Roads are imaginary lines that have real consequences for where people go and how they understand their position. Roads can be crossed, they can be jackhammered into dust, but their foundations are laid in the earth and their traces are not easily eradicated. The following pages examine how the imaginary lines of race, so deeply inscribed in American society and culture, shape young European Americans' experience of being white and how this experience is articulated in their social practices, especially their use of language.

This book is the product of many years of work, thought, and discussion, and it could not have been written without the generosity of many people. Above all, I thank the students, teachers, parents, staff, and administrators at Bay City High School, who trusted me enough to let me enter their lives during a period in the school's history when such trust did not come easily. Sue Ervin-Tripp, Leanne Hinton, Robin Tolmach Lakoff, John Rickford, and Barrie Thorne provided invaluable help at the earliest stages of this book's development. I am especially appreciative of the support and encouragement that Robin has given me throughout my career. For comments on various parts of the manuscript and suggestions at different stages I thank Asif Agha, H. Samy Alim, Penny Eckert, Kira Hall, Marcyliena Morgan, and an anonymous reviewer, as well as countless audience members and interlocutors at conferences and colloquia over the years. Since 2002 my colleagues and students at the University of California, Santa Barbara, particularly Pat Clancy, Jack Du Bois, Sandy Thompson, and the members of the Language, Interaction, and Social Organization Research Focus Group, have inspired me with their unflagging encouragement, interest, and insight. Special thanks are due to Pat for her crucial support as my writing partner, sounding board, and mentor in the final months of this project. I am also indebted to Stefan Gries for sharing his statistical expertise.

For financial support and research leave time, I gratefully acknowledge the Wenner-Gren Foundation for Anthropological Research; the Academic Senate, the College of Letters and Science, and the Department of Linguistics at the University of California, Santa Barbara; and the Center for Humanities Research, the College of Liberal Arts, and the Department of English at Texas A&M University. Indispensable assistance at various points with transcription, digitizing, references, coding, and data management was provided by Megan Barnard, Brendan Barnwell, Laura Carroll, Mackenzie Chapman, Jennifer Garland, Michael Godwin, Annette Harrison, Mara Henderson, Jonathan Himes, Andrea Milon, Kyung-Ae Oh, Rebecca Quiles, Katherine Rushton, and Stephanie Stanbro. I am indebted to Maura Jess and Rich Ayling for their help with the figures. I thank Sarah Green and Andrew Winnard at Cambridge University Press for their patience as this project took shape, Adrian Stenton for his care in copy-editing the manuscript, and Christina Sarigiannidou for shepherding it through production.

Finally, I am grateful to my family – my mother, Barbara Bucholtz, my siblings, Annie Tomecek, John Bucholtz, and Mike Bucholtz, and my nieces and nephews Sarah, Katie, Molly, Sammie, Cole, Seth, and Jackson – for their faith in me and for keeping me grounded in the real world. My greatest debt is to my partner, Jon McCammond, who has shared my life since before this project began and who made it possible in countless ways. This book is for him.

Transcription conventions

All names in transcripts are pseudonyms; some identifying details have been changed. Each line represents a single intonation unit (a chunk of discourse bracketed by brief pauses and marked by a single intonation contour), except when the purpose of the transcript is to illustrate content rather than interactional structure. Phonetic details are included when they are relevant to the analysis; otherwise spelling is normalized.

.	end of intonation unit; falling intonation
,	end of intonation unit; fall–rise intonation
?	end of intonation unit; rising intonation
!	raised pitch and volume throughout the intonation unit
↑	pitch accent
underline	emphatic stress; increased amplitude; careful articulation of a segment
:	length
=	latching; no pause between intonation units
–	self-interruption; break in the intonation unit
-	self-interruption; break in the word, sound abruptly cut off
(.)	pause of 0.5 seconds or less
(n.n)	measured pause of greater than 0.5 seconds
@	laughter; each token marks one pulse
n@	nasal laughter
h	outbreath (e.g., sigh); each token marks one pulse
.h	inbreath
[ ]	overlapping speech
[$_1$ $_1$]	overlapping speech in proximity to another overlap
( )	uncertain transcription
#	unintelligible; each token marks one syllable
< >	transcriber comment; nonvocal noise
{ }	stretch of talk to which transcriber comment applies
<[ ]>	phonetic transcription
" "	reported speech or thought
boldface	linguistic form of analytic interest
. . .	omitted material

Phonetic symbols

The following charts provide a rough approximation of the value of the International Phonetic Alphabet symbols used in the text, based on General American English pronunciation. The symbols are arranged roughly according to place of articulation.

Vowels and diphthongs

[i]	beat	[u]	boot
[ɪ]	bit	[ʊ]	book
[ej]	bait	[oʊ]	boat
[ɛ]	bet	[ɔ]	bought (Eastern US accent)
[æ]	bat	[ɔj]	boy
[a]	buy (Southern US accent)	[ə]	but (unstressed)
[aj]	buy (nonSouthern US accent)	[ʌ]	butt
[aʊ]	bout	[ɑ]	robot

Consonants

	bilabial	labiodental	interdental	alveolar	postalveolar	palatal	velar	glottal
voiceless stop	[p] pie			[t] tie			[k] kite	[ʔ] uh-oh
voiced stop	[b] buy			[d] die			[ɡ] guy	
nasal	[m] my			[n] nigh			[ŋ] king	
voiceless fricative		[f] file	[θ] thigh	[s] sigh	[ʃ] shy			[h] high
voiced fricative		[v] vile	[ð] thy	[z] zoo	[ʒ] vision			
voiceless affricate					[tʃ] chin			
voiced affricate					[dʒ] gin			
approximant	[w] wide			[ɹ] rye [l] lie		[j] you		
flap				[ɾ] city				

Diacritic symbols

ː	vowel lengthening
ʰ	aspiration
˜	nasalization
̪	dental

1 White styles: language, race, and youth identities

Introduction

At Bay City High School, a large, multiracial urban public school in the San Francisco Bay Area, race was a frequent topic in classrooms, hallways, and the schoolyard. But it was also an uncomfortable topic for many students, who preferred not to be racially labeled. One such student was Damien. A tall, thin sophomore with pale skin and wiry light brown hair, Damien was a talented artist and athlete who spent much of his time at school with a group of African American boys. His speech was influenced by African American Vernacular English, the linguistic variety used in his friendship group, and his clothing and hairstyle reflected current African American youth fashion. Damien attracted the curiosity of a number of his classmates of all ethnoracial backgrounds, because they could not figure out whether he was in fact black, and he himself refused to discuss his racial identity. By controlling this information and affiliating with African American youth language and culture, Damien was able to present an identity that aligned him with his friends without allowing others to categorize him racially.[1]

Damien's situation, which was unusual but by no means unique at Bay City High School, presents a number of challenges to commonly held views of identity as either a social category or a psychological state. First, individuals do not passively inhabit identity categories to which they have been assigned; rather, they negotiate and navigate these categories in a variety of ways within social interaction. As a result, the social classification of any given individual is not necessarily obvious to others, and one's assigned social category is not always the same as one's social identity. In the above case, for example, Damien's classmates were unable to classify him racially, and although some students believed he was European American, he did not embrace this category as his racial identity, at least at school.

Second, identities are not merely a matter of individual psychology. They are fundamentally the outcome of social practice and social interaction, because it is only within and by means of interaction with others in the course of daily activities that identities become evident and consequential, to oneself as well as to others. Damien's affiliation with African American youth culture, after all, was only evident because of the ways in which he displayed his involvement in that culture through his speech, his activities, and his choice of friends. Nor are identities entirely based in individual subjectivity, for how one presents one's own identity is shaped by how one interprets the identities of others, and an individual's self-presentation may be quite different from how she or he is interpreted by others.

Third, no single aspect of identity is independent of other aspects. Race and ethnicity are not separable from other components of identity such as gender, social class, sexuality, and so on, and an individual's identity cannot be arrived at simply by listing the social categories to which she or he is assigned. Identity instead operates as a repertoire of styles, or ways of doing things that are associated with culturally recognizable social types. Individuals position themselves stylistically and are stylistically interpreted by others as they present themselves within a given social context as specific kinds of people who engage in particular social practices. These styles go well beyond familiar demographic categories like race and gender to encompass entire ways of being in the social world – from talk to clothing to everyday activities – that involve more culturally specific sorts of identities. In this way styles create distinctions within as well as between broad social categories: Damien's style, for example, was influenced by African American youth culture, but other styles were available to students at Bay City High School, and each of these local styles was inflected by race, gender, social class, and other broad dimensions of identity.

This book is rooted in an understanding of identity as the social positioning of self and other. Social actors may take up various kinds of positions with respect to one another (Bucholtz and Hall 2005): similarity and difference, or *adequation* and *distinction*; realness and falseness, or *authentication* and *denaturalization*; and legitimacy and nonlegitimacy, or *authorization* and *illegitimation.* While these identity relations – and no doubt others besides – often work together, considering each of them and their component parts separately is analytically valuable, since it allows for a greater degree of specificity about the sorts of positions and relations involved in particular instances of identity construction.

Based on ethnographic fieldwork that I conducted in the mid-1990s at Bay City High School, in the following chapters I examine how white teenagers in the multiracial context of the school used language along with other social practices to position themselves both stylistically and racially within interaction. Scholars have recognized for decades that language is vital to the processes through which identities are created, mobilized, and transformed. The so-called "linguistic turn" or "discursive turn" throughout the humanities and social sciences has called attention to the ways that language brings the social world into being. But much of this scholarship, coming as it has from outside of linguistics and related fields, focuses on some aspects of language and not others, and often what is termed *language* or *discourse* in this research is quite different from the object of investigation in studies conducted by linguists. One central goal of this book is to demonstrate that the conceptual and analytical tools of sociocultural linguistics further enrich the study of identity all across the disciplines by revealing in delicate detail precisely how language is pressed into service as part of ongoing identity projects, as well as how the identity work of individuals is implicated in larger sociopolitical structures and processes.

My decision to focus primarily on European American students in my analysis emerges from the specific historical, cultural, and geographic context in which I did my research. At the time of my study, Bay City High had no racial majority; the two largest racialized groups were European Americans and African Americans. But these two groups encompassed a wide range of variability, and I became interested in the diverse ways that white youth positioned themselves stylistically in relation to one another as well as to students of color, and especially to black youth. I also noticed that even European American teenagers with different styles racially positioned themselves in strikingly similar ways. Due in part to widely publicized and highly sensationalized racial tensions between black and white students during the time of my research, many students, teachers, parents, and community members viewed the school as racially divided. In this context, my study became an examination of how European American youth linguistically constructed a range of identities for themselves and others within the ethnoracial landscape of Bay City High School at a time of significant racial turmoil.

The experience of white students at Bay City High in the mid-1990s was part of a much larger ethnoracial shift that is still taking place across the United States, a shift in which youth are at the very forefront. Even within the extremely diverse San Francisco Bay Area, the setting of this study, many adults live in largely white social worlds. Their children, however, often do not. Public schools are increasingly sites of ongoing cross-racial encounter, as school populations become "majority minority" – that is, predominantly composed of students of color – not only in California but all across the United States (e.g., Prescott 2008). As the relative numbers of European Americans decline in public schools, white students confront race and especially their own whiteness on a daily basis, sometimes for the first time in their lives.

But even those white youth whose schools remain more or less racially homogeneous may also encounter racial difference through their engagement in youth culture. For the past two decades, many European American teenagers have had to take some sort of stance toward the dominant form of African American youth culture, hip hop, which has emerged as the most influential form of youth culture both nationally and internationally in this time period.

Developing in primarily black communities in New York City in the 1970s, hip hop encompasses MCing (performing rap rhymes), DJing (musical improvisation using a mixer and turntables), breakdancing, and graffiti art, among other practices. Members of the Hip Hop Nation – an ingroup term for the culture – also share a distinctive linguistic style, which includes slang, genres of verbal performance, and typically at least some elements of African American Vernacular English (Alim 2006).

Not all European American youth embrace hip hop – on the contrary, as I demonstrate in this book, this style is only one choice among others – but many white teenagers must take a position toward hip hop culture's music, fashions, and other stylistic practices, whether that position is passionate involvement, passing interest, indifference, or active disdain. As the newest form of African American youth culture to claim this sort of stylistic authority among European American youth, hip hop is merely the latest iteration of a longstanding series of cross-racial appropriations of black cultural and musical forms, including jazz, blues, rock, reggae, and soul (e.g., Daley 2003; Hall 1997; Jones 1988; McMichael 1998). To be sure, in a number of local communities, Latino and Asian American forms of youth culture may also become stylistic resources for white teenagers, and conversely, cultural practices originating among European Americans may be taken up by youth of color. However, in the high school where I conducted the ethnographic fieldwork for this study, like many others around the country, African American youth culture shaped stylistic practice for young people of all races and ethnicities.

My analysis focuses in particular on how white youth identities at Bay City High School were constructed in significant part through language. In the following chapters, I examine the multiple styles of whiteness that were available to European American teenagers as they aligned themselves with local youth cultures, both black and white. In this process, language, from pronunciation to slang to grammar, was a crucial symbolic resource that allowed youth to locate themselves not just in relation to adults on the one hand and young children on the other but more importantly in relation to their peers. In addition to this symbolic dimension of language, I demonstrate the role of white youth's talk about race in reproducing larger American ideologies of racial difference. Such discourse generally promoted white interests by downplaying the structural power that European American students at the school enjoyed as well as the significance of race itself. Yet in this ethnographic setting whiteness was also unstable, as European American teenagers navigated competing discourses of race offered up by their parents, their peers, and the school. The instability of whiteness was evident in the complex ways in which white youth talked about – and often around or against – racial topics.

The present chapter discusses the importance of language in constituting racial identities as social realities and the need to examine such identities in the cultural and interactional contexts in which they emerge. I first discuss the centrality of language in maintaining and transforming race (and its related counterpart, ethnicity) in the United States in various ways. I then consider how recent sociocultural linguistic research on identity and style helps shed light on racial issues, especially in relation to youth. Finally, I examine the different ways in which whiteness is conceptualized as an ethnoracial category and argue for an understanding of whiteness as a racial identity that emerges through language and other forms of social action in specific cultural contexts. In this way, the present book adds to a growing field of research on the linguistic aspects of race and their critical role in constituting and altering the racial order.

Language and race

Language is often overlooked as an analytic concern in research on race, yet it is nonetheless central to how race is culturally understood. Language and race intersect in three main ways: in the use of racial terms, in discourse that takes race as its topic, and in the symbolic use of linguistic forms as ways of speaking associated with specific racialized groups. While these issues potentially overlap, each involves somewhat different aspects of meaning, both linguistic and social.

The racial lexicon: terms and labels

Systems of racial labels have been used to classify human beings for the past three centuries and more. These systems are based on ideologies – cultural beliefs that serve the interests of some social groups over those of other groups. Ideologies are so pervasive that it is often difficult for their proponents to view the world in any other way. Yet all ideologies are produced in specific social and historical contexts as resources for gaining or maintaining power, and they are therefore subject to contestation and change.

As a concept, race does not account for actual patterns of human genetic variation (Long 2003). Yet as a sociopolitical system for classifying human beings, it remains a powerful force. When I refer to *race* in this book, I mean this social construct, not a set of categories with a supposed biological basis. At other times I use terms such as *racialization* and *racialized* to highlight the fact that current ideas about race are the contingent and changeable result of specific historical, cultural, and political processes.

Racial classification is often contrasted with ethnic classification, but these two ways of categorizing human beings are closely linked. Whereas race is ideologically grounded in the notion of biological difference, ethnicity is rooted instead in the notion of cultural difference based on language of heritage, national background, and other factors. Nevertheless, race and ethnicity also share significant ideological foundations. Both forms of categorization rely on essentialism, an ideology that social groups are clearly delineated, internally homogeneous, and fundamentally different from other groups. Essentialism treats the characteristics of group members as inherent, fixed qualities that are either biologically or culturally determined (or both).

Race and ethnicity are deeply intertwined in both everyday and institutional forms of discourse. In principle, in institutional discourses such as government or medicine, *race* is reserved for categories that are based on observable physical qualities, and *ethnicity* for those based on language, culture, and national origin. In practice, however, the current classification system used within the United States combines both types of categories, and terms for ethnic and racial groups are often treated as synonymous: *African Americans* or *blacks*, *Asian Americans* or *Asians* (categories that sometimes also include groups of Pacific Islander descent), *European Americans* or *whites* (or sometimes *Caucasians*, a remnant of an earlier pseudoscientific system of racial classification). By contrast, within the US Census and similar institutions, Latinos (or Hispanics) are usually classified as an ethnic rather than a racial group, and Native Americans (or American Indians) are usually classified as a racial group, although individual tribal affiliation may sometimes also be specified. Ethnicity is further complicated by the fact that according to the most common definition, even the supposedly ethnic classifications in the above list are strictly speaking panethnic, since they incorporate multiple cultural, national, and linguistic backgrounds within a single overarching category (Lopez and Espiritu 1990).

The notion of ethnicity is applied asymmetrically across racialized groups. Ethnicity is often treated as obligatory for people of color but optional for whites: terms such as *ethnic food* in the grocery store or *ethnic models* in the fashion industry typically refer to cultures and people that are not classified as white. For many second-, third-, or later-generation European Americans, ethnic identity is an optional lifestyle choice displayed via such cultural trappings as ethnic food, costume, and holiday celebrations (Alba 1990; Waters 1990). Whites may alternatively choose to downplay their ethnic heritage and may even claim not to "have an ethnicity." It is more difficult for Americans of color to opt out of ethnicity, since they are ideologically positioned as racially and ethnically different from European Americans. Because American understandings of race are so closely interconnected with ethnicity, throughout this book I use the racial and (pan)ethnic terms for the above categories more or less interchangeably. The term *ethnoracial* is used where both race and ethnicity are relevant to the discussion; I also use *race/racial* as a cover term for both issues when the distinction is not crucial to the argument. I use the more specific term *ethnicity/ethnic* when I intend that particular meaning.

From the preceding discussion, it is clear that racial and ethnic labels, as well as the words *race* and *ethnicity* themselves, are by no means straightforward and therefore require analytic attention. The examination of racial terms typically involves some consideration of their semantics, or referential meaning. However, it is most useful to analyze lexical items not in isolation or in decontextualized lists but in discourse – connected stretches of language used in specific contexts.

The content and structure of racial discourse

Racial discourse includes all talk or writing about race or racialized issues, from everyday conversations to political speeches to discussions on the Internet. The linguistic analysis of racial discourse considers both content (what is said) and structure (how it is said), as well as the social context in which such discourse is produced, circulated, and interpreted by others. For many scholars outside of linguistics, however, the notion of discourse is often broader than it is for linguists, referring not simply to particular instances of speech or writing but more generally to the way in which a topic (such as race) is conceptually framed at a particular historical and cultural moment, especially within powerful institutional contexts like government, medicine, law, or education. Such cultural discourses are akin to ideologies in that they are culturally shared sets of beliefs that are often understood as simply "the truth" yet in fact bring social reality into being.

This understanding of discourse is also shared by a rather different approach to discourse, interactional analysis, which views spontaneous spoken language as the machinery that produces the social world moment by moment. In this approach, the structures of power authorized by institutional discourse are less central, and the agency of social actors instead takes center stage as speakers negotiate meaning within interaction. A fundamental principle of interactional analysis is that through talk, language users orient to the world as socially meaningful and thereby continuously and jointly create social reality, including their own and one another's identities (Antaki and Widdicombe 1998; Tracy 2002). For this reason, interactional researchers speak of social actors as actively "doing" race, gender, and other identities within interaction rather than simply "being" members of various social categories (Fenstermaker and West 2002). Thus in a very fundamental way, talk about race brings race into being by bringing it into discourse. At the same time, such talk also enables speakers to negotiate and challenge what race means in a given social context.

The relationship between race and language, however, is not always as overt as the use of racial labels or racial discourse. The final point of intersection between race and language, racialized linguistic practice, involves a different kind of meaning, one created not by the semantic reference of racial lexical items or the use of racial discourse but by symbolic associations between linguistic forms and racialized meanings.

The semiotics of racialized linguistic practice

Although interactional analysts typically focus their attention on the content and structure of discourse as it unfolds, speakers can "do" identity via other linguistic (and nonlinguistic) resources as well. Understanding this process requires attention to the social semiotics of language – that is, the use of linguistic forms such as words, pronunciations, and grammatical structures as symbols of social meaning. Racialized linguistic practices are ways of using language that are semiotically associated with racialized groups. Such practices can operate at the level of entire languages (such as Mandarin Chinese) or dialects (such as African American Vernacular English) or at the level of individual linguistic features (such as the inclusion or omission of the sound /r/ after a vowel in words like *brother*).

Language is a key resource for ethnoracial identity – and, indeed, for all identity work – because of the complexity and flexibility of linguistic systems in building the social world. Linguistic structure operates simultaneously on multiple, interconnected levels, from the production and organization of individual speech sounds (phonetics and phonology) to the smallest units of meaning like prefixes, suffixes, and word roots (morphology) to complete words (lexicon) to their combination into sentences or clauses (syntax). Although linguists conventionally divide their object of study into these discrete levels for purposes of analysis, all of these levels operate in unison as a system to produce discourse, or language in use.

Linguistic forms can gain symbolic associations, including racialized associations, through indexicality. Indexicality is the process of creating a link between a semiotic form, such as a linguistic structure, and a contextually specific meaning, such as an identity, via juxtaposition or co-occurrence in a particular context. In other words, the form indexes or "points to" the meaning (Silverstein 1976). One kind of indexical meaning that a linguistic form may acquire is an association with a specific stance or viewpoint. Within sociocultural linguistics, *stance* is defined as a social actor's public display of her or his orientation to ongoing interaction with respect both to the talk at hand and to the other participants (Du Bois 2007). Stances are indexes of speaker subjectivity that involve evaluation and displays of affect (or emotion) as well as claims of certainty or uncertainty. As particular linguistic forms are habitually used to take particular stances in ongoing linguistic practice, they may come to be associated with these stances (Ochs 1992). For example, as I discuss in Chapter 4, some European American teenagers at Bay City High School used the affiliative slang term *blood* (which is roughly similar in function to other affiliative address terms like *dude*, *man*, or *bro*) to index a casual, friendly stance toward a white peer. Through their use in staking out the speaker's positionality within an interaction, stances serve as building blocks of identity.

A second level of indexical meaning can be created when a linguistic form comes to be associated not only with a specific stance but also with a social category whose members are thought to habitually take such a stance (Ochs 1992). For example, the term *blood* was viewed by many white teenagers at Bay City High as belonging to black youth, because the term originated among African Americans and was used primarily by African American speakers. Consequently, a European American teenager who used the term *blood* could be seen not as using a generally available resource for doing casual friendliness but instead as illegitimately "talking black." This interpretation simplifies the indexical field – that is, the range of available semiotic meanings of a given linguistic form (Eckert 2008) – by erasing or backgrounding some meanings and highlighting others.

The process of moving from one indexical meaning to another is always ideological (Silverstein 2003). The associations created between linguistic forms and social categories are not simply based on observed linguistic practice – after all, given that some white students at Bay City High School used the term *blood*, it was clearly not an exclusively black form. Instead, indexicality relies on language ideologies, or cultural beliefs about language and its users. Language ideologies involve metalinguistics – language about language – and they may be either explicitly articulated or implicitly enacted (Agha 2007). Language ideologies are central to the construction of identity because they are not in fact primarily about language. Rather, they are in the service of other, more basic, ideologies about social groups, which they cloak in linguistic terms (Woolard 1998). Beliefs that certain linguistic forms are the property of specific racialized groups, for example, are used to reinforce social divisions by means of linguistic divisions.

In order to discover the social meanings of linguistic forms, it is necessary to know how these forms are interpreted by participants in the cultural and interactional context in which they are used. One method for arriving at this insider viewpoint is interactional analysis, which analyzes speakers' perspectives from the evidence of their talk, but the detailed analysis of discourse is greatly enriched when it is accompanied by attention to the often unspoken social and cultural knowledge that participants bring to interaction. Such information can be obtained through the use of ethnography, the study of a culture from the perspective of its members. In order to investigate the variously lexical, discursive, and semiotic resources that white teenagers use to construct their identities, then, it is not enough to draw on a single theory or method. Rather, this question requires an interdisciplinary, multilayered approach to language as a sociocultural phenomenon.

Language and identity

Sociocultural linguistics encompasses a wide variety of perspectives on the study of language, culture, and society. Despite its name, it does not belong to a single discipline but is a broad and loose coalition that includes sociolinguistics, linguistic anthropology, the sociology of language, language and social psychology, and various approaches to language within communication studies, education, and other fields. What unifies work in these areas is not a shared theory or method but a commitment to the systematic investigation of language in social life (Bucholtz and Hall 2008). In recent years, an especially important line of scholarship in many branches of sociocultural linguistics has been the study of identity (e.g., Bucholtz and Hall 2005; Joseph 2004; Llamas and Watt 2010; Mendoza-Denton 2002; Omoniyi and White 2007; Riley 2007). Numerous classic and recent studies within sociocultural linguistics take the sort of integrative approach to the question of identity that I advocate in this book, demonstrating how linguistic forms at multiple levels may be put to use in discourse to produce a wide range of identities and social relations (Agha 2007; Alim 2004a; Coupland 2007; Gumperz 1982; Kiesling 2005; Mendoza-Denton 2008; Rampton 1995, 2006; Reyes 2007; Schilling-Estes 2004).

In early sociolinguistic research, the concept of identity was primarily used as an explanation for observed linguistic differences across social groups. Such work did not view identity as a social phenomenon requiring study and explanation in its own right. By contrast, in much current scholarship, the workings of identity are unpacked and analyzed in detail; identity is no longer the answer but the question itself. In keeping with this reformulation, most recent sociocultural linguistic research views identity as a social and relational construct rather than an inherent, essential quality of individual psychology or demographic background.

Many contemporary scholars in sociocultural linguistics and other fields examine identity as outwardly directed social action, through which individuals interactionally negotiate their own and others' location within the social order. According to this approach, identity is jointly produced rather than individual, locally situated rather than universal, and agentively constructed rather than passively inhabited. In short, identities are inherently relational, so that acts of self-definition are also acts of other-definition and vice versa. Crucially, this social accomplishment is carried out primarily – but not exclusively – through language. Much of current sociocultural linguistics examines how linguistic resources, often in conjunction with other semiotic tools, are mobilized within social situations to perform such "acts of identity" (Le Page and Tabouret-Keller 1985). By viewing identities as originating in social action rather than in states of being, researchers have increasingly turned their attention to style, or socially meaningful ways of doing things, including ways of using language.

Style and identity

In early sociolinguistics, *style* was often defined as situation-based language use. For example, in a formal situation a speaker might use relatively standard English, whereas in a casual situation, she or he might use relatively vernacular English. More recent theories, however, view style as a property not of situations but of speakers. In this newer work, style is conceptualized as a bundle of semiotic resources indexically tied to a social type, category, or persona (Coupland 2007; Eckert 2003). Styles do not exist in isolation but acquire meaning only in relation to other styles within the same semiotic system – that is, styles are distinctive (Irvine 2001).

The elements of a style may be taken from any available semiotic material, an insight reflected in the concept of bricolage (Lévi-Strauss 1966) as borrowed by theorists of style (Eckert 2000: 214; Hebdige 1979: 102–106). In French, *bricolage* roughly means 'do-it-yourself' or 'improvisation'; according to theories of style, the bricoleur or improvising stylistic agent takes whatever resources are ready to hand to create new styles. All components of language may be used as stylistic resources, including languages and dialects; linguistic structures ranging from phonetics to discourse; and interactional resources such as pauses and turn taking. These linguistic components of styles are typically accompanied by other resources such as clothing and other aspects of bodily adornment; embodied actions like gesture, posture, and movement; the use of material culture and social space; sociocultural activities and the way in which they are carried out; and so on. Thus a style is an entire semiotic system, in which each element contributes to the production of social meaning.

The example of the slang term *blood* above demonstrates that the social meaning of any given stylistic form emerges within a local cultural context and cannot be arrived at without some level of insider understanding of the semiotic system. Yet stylistic forms are also open to interpretation, appropriation, and contestation by others. Indeed, what makes the semiotic markers of style flexible is their adaptability to new contexts. Sometimes a new context will entirely transform the semiotic value of an index, while at other times part or all of an index's social history will be retained in its new context. The same resources can thus be used by different social actors to do different kinds of identity work, and the same resources can sometimes be associated with one social category and sometimes with another. At the same time, stylistic practices are often conventionalized and easily recognizable due to their indexical association with specific social types (Agha 2007). From this perspective, styles make culturally available the sorts of identities that social actors can create.

Style has been an especially fruitful concept in the study of youth identities, for youth are often the source of stylistic innovations. The investigation of style has therefore fostered greater acknowledgment of youth as full-fledged cultural actors positioning themselves and others in the social order. Researchers who study children and teenagers have pointed out that the social agency of young people is often overlooked or underappreciated by scholars (Eckert 1989; Thorne 1993; Wulff 1995). Developmental research on adolescence, for example, often presents what might be called a conveyor-belt model of youth, focusing on adolescence as a life stage in which teenagers undergo the not-yet-complete process of becoming adults. According to this model, young people are acted upon by biological and psychological mandates that they do not control as they move inexorably toward adulthood (see discussion in Bucholtz 2002a).

Cultural research on youth identities, by contrast, is grounded in the age-based practices created by young people themselves. While preparation for adulthood is one aspect of youthful experience, the construction of youth identities and peer cultures is an equally pressing social task for teenagers. Young people organize themselves into a peer-based social order that is to some extent separate from, but also partly reliant on, adult-driven social structures. Contrary to the beliefs of many parents of teenagers, the social practices of youth are not designed or deployed primarily to rebel against adults but to identify with and distinguish themselves from their peers.

The process of identity construction among young people yields a proliferation of youth styles. Many ethnographic studies of social groups in US and UK schools, for example, have shown that students may divide into socially polarized clusters on the basis of gender (Eder, Evans, and Parker 1995; Goodwin 2006; Thorne 1993), but even within a single gender category, youth may form locally recognized contrastive groupings with different social practices. Thus burnouts and jocks in suburban Detroit (Eckert 1989, 2000), like their British counterparts, the disobedient lads and compliant ear'oles (i.e., "earholes") in Birmingham, England (Willis 1977), have different orientations toward school; some Latina girls in California define themselves based on their displayed allegiance to competing gangs, the Norteñas and the Sureñas (Mendoza-Denton 2008); and in northwest England, Popular and Townie girls engage in different levels of rebellious activity (E. Moore 2004). In these studies, binary social identities are consciously oppositional. Hence, members of polarized social categories do not merely "do their own thing" but purposefully create and carry out their defining stylistic practices while monitoring the practices of their social "opposites." For European American young people in particular, such styles may be constructed in relation to the practices both of other white teenagers and of youth of color.

Race and white youth styles

Although the relationship between race and youth has long been of interest to researchers, there is as yet only a small body of scholarship on the intertwined stylistic and racial dimensions of white youth identities. In his pioneering early study of style, Dick Hebdige (1979) traces the varied ways in which white working-class youth cultures in postwar Britain, such as punks, mods, teddy boys, glam rockers, and skinheads, orient to black cultural resources. These youth cultures instantiate a broader racial dynamic whereby blackness is crucial to the formation of whiteness. Hebdige argues that uncovering the symbolic significance of black youth cultures for white youth reveals what he refers to as "a phantom history of race relations": "It is on the plane of aesthetics: in dress, dance, music; in the whole rhetoric of style, that we find the dialogue between black and white most subtly and comprehensively recorded, albeit in code" (1979: 45).

In his analysis, Hebdige focuses on spectacular youth cultures – those with the most visually flamboyant insignia, from the punk's mohawk haircut to the glam rocker's androgynous beauty. But it is equally necessary to examine the less ostentatious styles that white youth take up as they position themselves in relation to their peers of color, for it is precisely through the perceived ordinariness of such styles, in contrast to the perceived conspicuousness of many nonwhite – and especially black – youth cultures, that whiteness is ideologically reinscribed as normative and unmarked. The investigation of both marked and unmarked white youth styles therefore requires the tools of ethnography in order to discover the local forms and meanings of stylistic practices, which may at times be hard to see from the outside.

In the US context, ethnographic research on white youth identities frequently focuses on educational settings. Schools are key institutions for the socialization of youth into racial identities and ideologies, as shown by a wealth of educational research on antiracist pedagogical practice as well as the reproduction of white privilege within classrooms and curricula (e.g., McIntyre 1997; Tochluk 2007; Warren 2003). In addition, schools also provide a physical site for the formation of peer cultures and for interaction across categories of social difference. Yet issues of race and style are rarely brought together in a single study.

One such study that addresses both questions is Pamela Perry's (2002) comparative ethnography of two California high schools, one in which European American students were in the majority and African American students in the minority and another with the converse demographic situation. In her analysis of white teenagers' situations at both schools, Perry examines stylistic and racial dimensions of identity alike. This focus allows her to consider the varying salience of whiteness (from invisible to hypervisible) between the two sites as well as to demonstrate that youth styles acquire different degrees of racialized meaning in these two different contexts. Her research, which focuses equally on structure and agency in the making of white identities, helps move youth to the center of the study of race and especially of whiteness (see also Nayak 2003). Another key step in achieving this goal, I argue, is to give close attention to the role of language in white youth identities.

Language and the study of whiteness

Many studies of race rely heavily on language as data, whether documented in ethnographic fieldnotes of social interaction or in audio- or video-recorded interviews. In most cases these materials are analyzed for their content alone and are used as more or less direct evidence of speakers' thoughts and experiences. A number of researchers, however, have begun to recognize that language is not simply a transparent reflection of speakers' inner states but a sociopolitical tool of ideological representation that merits investigation in its own right. For example, Michael Omi and Howard Winant's (1994) definition of *racial projects* as processes that unfold not only over the course of historical eras but also moment by moment in everyday interaction implies a central role for language in their theory of racial formation. John Hartigan (1999: 21–22), a leading figure in the study of whiteness, argues explicitly for the value of discourse analysis in such research. And qualitative researchers in US educational settings are becoming increasingly attuned to the specifically discursive elements of race (Lewis 2005; Pollock 2005; Staiger 2006). Such work is significant for shedding light on the importance of language in the constitution of the social world. However, the theories and methods developed in numerous areas of sociocultural linguistics have much more to contribute to the understanding of race in general and whiteness in particular.

The role of language in the social production of whiteness is evident in a growing body of sociocultural linguistic scholarship. A number of studies of the linguistic reproduction of white power reveal how racialized language ideologies allow European Americans to imagine whiteness as normative, superior, and contrastive to minority linguistic and cultural groups (Hill 2008), from English monolinguals' negative attitudes toward Spanish (Barrett 2006; Schwartz 2006) to white views of African American English as remote from and lesser than Standard English (Ronkin and Karn 1999; Walters 1996) to racially motivated changes in European Americans' pronunciation of English (Bonfiglio 2002). Other studies linguistically investigate how various sorts of white speakers talk about their racial fears, resentments, and desires, including college fraternity members (Kiesling 2001), police officers (McElhinny 2001), social elites (van Dijk 1993a), and researchers themselves (Gaudio 2001).

In addition to considering identity work by powerful white groups, researchers have examined how social actors at the outskirts of whiteness – those of mixed race and those with ethnically distinctive identities – discursively navigate rigid systems of ethnoracial classification (Bucholtz 1995; Modan 2001; Puckett 2001). Another productive line of investigation has been the issue of how language crossing – the use of a linguistic variety that is not one's "own" (Rampton 1995) – may function variously (and sometimes even simultaneously) as an appropriating act of power and as a gesture of social affiliation.

Such research documents how white speakers may reach across linguistic and racial barriers to take up other groups' linguistic varieties (Bucholtz 1999a; Cutler 1999, 2003a; Hewitt 1986; Sweetland 2002). Finally, sociocultural linguists attend to the critical views of whiteness circulating among people of color, from mock-white performances (Barrett 1999; Basso 1979; Preston 1992; Rahman 2007) to everyday critical commentaries (Chun 2001; Essed 1990; Trechter 2001) by African Americans, Asian Americans, and Native Americans, among others.

The range and richness of linguistic scholarship on whiteness demonstrates the value of a sustained focus on language in exposing the workings of whiteness and of race more generally. Sociocultural linguistics offers a largely untapped resource for nonlinguistic scholars concerned with racial power and racial identities to examine how race is built on the everyday ground of discourse and interaction. Conversely, sociocultural linguists have a great deal more to learn from researchers in other fields regarding the complex history and cultural variability of whiteness as a racial category.

What is whiteness?

Understanding whiteness requires attention to two different aspects of this racial category: its power to authorize the subordination of other racialized groups, and its variability and even instability in specific cultural contexts. These two general issues are not mutually exclusive, for due to its history whiteness is always endowed with structural or institutional power at some level, and as an embodied racial category it is always instantiated and negotiated by individual social actors in specific contexts.

What lends the white racial category much of its power is the fact that in many situations, *whiteness is hegemonic*. Hegemony is a form of power that operates via ideology rather than through physical coercion or force (although hegemony and violence often work in tandem). Through hegemony, social inequality is discursively framed as taken for granted, natural, and right (Gramsci 1971). Promoting the view that such asymmetries are "just the way things are" and therefore the way they ought to be is fundamental to maintaining white hegemony.

The hegemony of whiteness is typically exerted not by calling attention to white racial dominance but instead by treating whiteness as unremarkable – even unnoticeable. Indeed, in a variety of contexts, *whiteness is unmarked* – that is, it is ideologically positioned as racially normative and hence in some sense invisible compared to all other racial categories. The unmarked status of whiteness can be seen in cultural representations such as literature, film, and television, especially those that are created by white people. White characters tend to predominate in such representations, yet they are rarely positioned as specifically white; as Richard Dyer (1997: 3) remarks, "At the level of racial representation . . . whites are not of a certain race, they're just the human race." Unmarkedness thus reinforces hegemony by framing the dominant group as ordinary and subordinate groups as visibly "other."

A related ideology holds that *whiteness is cultural absence*. According to this formulation, whiteness is not simply one ethnoracial designation among others but constitutes, by its very nature, a lack of ethnicity. The ideology that whiteness is devoid of culture can reinforce its unmarked status and hence its structural power, but on the other hand, the perception of whiteness as absence may leave European Americans who lack a strong ethnic identity with the sense of not "having a culture" (Frankenberg 1993; Perry 2001). The view of whiteness as cultural lack is supported by a similar ideology in which whiteness is understood as cultural blandness, represented via such color-coded culinary signifiers as Wonder Bread, vanilla, and mayonnaise, which contrast with the literally and metaphorically "spicy," "colorful" cultural forms associated with other racialized groups.

These aspects of whiteness – the structural advantages it confers, its ideological invisibility, and its asymmetry vis-à-vis other racialized groups – are crucial to understanding this racial category, but there is a danger in focusing solely on whiteness as power. Such a perspective fosters a view of whiteness as an abstract force, monolithic and unchanging. Less deterministic and more complex ways of understanding whiteness allow for an appreciation of the category's variability without denying the continuing reality of white power. Such nuance is especially important in examining the lives of white youth at Bay City High School, who often did not experience themselves as racially hegemonic or unmarked even though they benefited from unacknowledged racial advantages. Moreover, the school's European American students did not all inhabit their whiteness in the same way.

Whiteness is not an abstraction, for it is manifested only in concrete contexts; in short, *whiteness is situated and situational*. It is situated in that it is located in specific times and places and embodied by specific persons, whose enactments of whiteness may variously include the reproduction, the revision, or the rejection of dominant ideologies. At the same time, whiteness is situational in that not every social interaction is equally racialized. While racial issues may be apparent to analysts taking a broad, critical view of a given social situation, the salience – or nonsalience – of race is most immediately determined by the varied perspectives of social actors themselves, both white and nonwhite. In some settings, race may be at the forefront, whereas in other contexts it recedes into the background as other parameters of identity emerge as more interactionally significant, or it may have different degrees of relevance for different participants.

Relatedly, *whiteness is multiple*. A growing body of ethnographic research as well as autobiographical accounts shows that there is no single way of being white. White identities take varied forms inflected by ethnicity, gender, sexuality, class, region, and many other factors (e.g., Berubé 2001; Frankenberg 1993; Hartigan 1999; Wray and Newitz 1997), yielding multiple forms and styles of whiteness. Moreover, whiteness accrues a range of different cultural meanings in these diverse contexts; there is thus no single meaning to which it can be reduced.

Finally, and most encouragingly for antiracist projects, *whiteness is unstable.* That is, whiteness is not a fixed and unchanging edifice, and what may appear to be a seamless ideological structure supporting racial inequities is in fact riddled with holes and fissures. This instability has become especially evident in the last fifty years and more, as the position of whiteness in the racial system of the United States has been altered by sweeping social and political trends that have transformed the country's racial landscape, from the civil rights movement to shifts in immigration patterns to the changing face of national political leadership.

Yet the status of whiteness has been uncertain throughout its history. In part the instability of whiteness is due to its very nature, which has led to self-contradictory racial logics: whiteness is claimed to be both everywhere and nowhere, both visible and invisible, both powerful and threatened, both fixed and fluid. But this instability is also due to the inevitable gap between ideologies of whiteness and the lived experience of being white. Sociologists France Winddance Twine and Charles Gallagher argue that it is precisely this gap – and the situated, multiple, and unstable forms of whiteness that it produces – that is central to the present moment in whiteness studies, or what they term the "third wave" of scholarship in the field:

> Third wave whiteness makes these contradictions [between different experiences of whiteness] explicit by acknowledging the relational, contextual and situational ways in which white privilege can be at the same time a taken-for-granted entitlement, a desired social status, a perceived source of victimization and a tenuous situational identity. It is these white inflections, the nuanced and locally specific ways in which whiteness as a form of power is defined, deployed, performed, policed and reinvented, that is the central focus of third wave whiteness. (Twine and Gallagher 2008: 7)

Combining attention to power and context, then, allows scholars to carefully unpack how whiteness works as the anchor of the racial system as well as how social actors work whiteness in local situations.

These issues emerge with particular vividness among white youth in multiracial settings. At Bay City High School, European American students adopted a variety of ways of being white, but they all profited from their structural position in the racial order, and many of them, despite considerable differences in their identities, were unified by a shared discourse of white racial marginalization, disadvantage, and danger. The unsettled situation of white youth therefore helps reveal the complexity of whiteness in the contemporary United States.

The present study brings together the diverse theories of sociocultural linguistics and research on race to examine in detail the various forms of race work that white youth perform through their talk. From linguistic anthropology I take the concepts of indexicality and language ideology, which account for how and why linguistic forms become socially meaningful. From variationist sociolinguistics I draw the notion of style, especially as it has been recently retheorized by scholars concerned with identity. I use the view of identity within interactional analysis as a discursive accomplishment, a matter of "doing" rather than simply "being." And from research on race I borrow ways of conceptualizing whiteness. The following chapters trace white teenagers' use of a variety of linguistic resources for accomplishing race, including lexical labels for ethnoracial categories and racialized styles; the linguistic resources of the lexicon, phonology, and grammar, through which such categories and styles are indexed; and discourse about race itself.

Overview of the book

This book focuses on European American youth language and culture; it does not examine in detail the equally rich range of linguistic and cultural practices available to African American, Asian American, Latino, and Native American teenagers, many of which have been recently examined by scholars (e.g., Alim 2004a; Mendoza-Denton 2008; Reyes 2007; Shankar 2008). My decision to focus on young people of European American descent is not meant to attribute lesser importance or vitality to other youth cultural styles – on the contrary, as I argue, other groups' styles are a crucial reference point for white youth identities – but rather to call attention to the often overlooked racial and stylistic projects of white youth. Many students of color participated in this study and offered a range of views of race, youth, and identity. Their experiences are different enough from those of their white peers to require separate discussion (e.g., Bucholtz 2009a); nevertheless, the perspectives of these young people greatly enriched my understanding of race and style at Bay City High.

The present chapter has outlined the theoretical underpinnings of this study. Chapter 2 lays out the local cultural context in which the research was conducted and describes my methodologies as an ethnographer and a sociocultural linguist. The chapter also addresses the ethical questions and practical challenges I faced as a white researcher working in a multiracial educational setting. The eight analytic chapters of the book focus on two different aspects of how European American youth constructed their identities through language: the semiotic practices constituting three emblematic local white styles – the preppy mainstream, white hip hop fans, and nerds – in the context of the larger social landscape of Bay City High School; and the discursive and referential practices that white young people of various stylistic orientations engaged in when talking about race and whiteness.

Chapters 3 and 4 examine how teenagers at the school created social categories of difference along lines of race, style, and other dimensions of identity through the use of socially meaningful lexical resources. Chapter 3 examines how youth cultural styles were lexically classified and discursively organized by students to create social boundaries during explicit discussions of social groups at the school. The chapter describes the school's key racial division, that between black and white students, and examines how European American teenagers formed a racialized system of style in this context.

Chapter 4 turns to another lexical domain, slang, and considers how slang was used by high school students as part of the shared enterprise of constructing coolness as well as for social differentiation on the basis of race and style. The chapter discusses the different ideologies and practices of slang associated with the three focal European American youth styles, demonstrating the ways in which race and style interacted in white teenagers' stances toward local youth slang of African American origin.

Chapters 5 through 7 survey the three key white identities that are the center of this study. Chapter 5 offers an in-depth examination of the preppy social category and analyzes the linguistic and other symbolic resources these teenagers deployed as part of their construction of a mainstream white identity. The primary focus of the analysis is the use of the innovative quotative markers *be like* and *be all*. I show that the symbolic association of the latter form with white preppy girls also provided an indexical resource for nonpreppy students' linguistic identity work.

Chapter 6 discusses another racialized and gendered white youth identity by investigating the use of African American English features among European American boys who affiliated with hip hop culture. I argue that African American linguistic forms were a key semiotic resource that white hip hop aficionados employed emblematically rather than fluently in order to distinguish themselves from mainstream whiteness without fully affiliating with African American youth at the school.

A third white youth style, that of nerdy teenagers, is the focus of Chapter 7, which demonstrates that for a number of students at Bay City High School nerdiness was an alternative to the dominant white youth cultural styles and values promoted by cool mainstream teenagers and hip hop fans alike. I demonstrate that nerds' rejection of trendy youth culture and its gendered pressures involved an avoidance of cool, colloquial linguistic forms in favor of superstandard English, a more learned register that was ideologically linked to an extreme version of whiteness.

Chapters 8 through 10 shift away from the earlier chapters' focus on individual youth styles to examine how white students of all stylistic orientations at Bay City High School talked about race in light of the racial tensions surrounding them daily at the high school and in the wider community. Chapter 8 considers the discourse of "colorblindness," an ideology that positions the speaker as nonracist by displaying a lack of awareness of racial categories. This ideology shaped European American teenagers' talk about race and especially about friendship across racial boundaries. Through discursive strategies of colorblindness, white youth were able to manage the delicate topic of race and friendship at the school while presenting themselves as racially well intentioned.

Where Chapter 8 considers talk about friendship across racialized divisions at the school, Chapter 9 examines discourse about an even more sensitive matter: racial conflict. The chapter analyzes how European American teenagers talked about their fears and resentments regarding racial others. Once again, such discourse, which reproduced ideologies of gender as well as race, exemplifies a widely shared racial ideology within US society, yet it also reflects the specific local situation of Bay City High School, where the community's moral panic regarding racial conflict shaped how white teenagers understood their relationships to their peers of color.

Chapter 10 demonstrates that whiteness itself was often an issue for European American youth. Examining students' ethnoracial self-classification in response to a formulaic question about their ethnicity at the beginning of each of the ethnographic interviews I conducted, the chapter shows that for many white teenagers at Bay City High School, defining themselves in ethnoracial terms in the context of an interview with a white researcher was a far from straightforward task.

Chapter 11 summarizes the key themes of the study and suggests the implications of this work for the study of race and language. The conclusion also sketches some of the ways in which race has shifted both at Bay City High School and across the United States since the research was conducted and points to the enduring issues of language and identity facing researchers, young people, and indeed all members of multiracial societies.

2 Listening to whiteness: researching language and race in a California high school

Introduction

In the first few weeks of my fieldwork at Bay City High, I had a conversation about my research with Ursula Chambers, a European American parent who served as a volunteer at the school. At the time, some students from neighboring cities, including youth of color from lower-income communities, were enrolled at Bay City High due to its relatively strong academic reputation. Eager to defend the school against these perceived interlopers, Ursula sought to document its enrollment of nonresident students. During our conversation, she tried to enlist me in her cause as a stealth agent who might be able to gain access to carefully guarded school demographic records, because, as she explained, "you're a researcher, not a rabble-rousing parent."

The ethnoracial profile of Bay City High's students was a central concern not only for Ursula but for many members of the school and the community. In its diversity, Bay City High School was a microcosm of California. As of the 2000 US Census, California officially became one of the nation's few "majority minority" states, with residents of color outnumbering white residents. At the time of my study in 1995–96, the San Francisco Bay Area and Bay City itself were both slightly more than 50 percent white; however, the high school had no racial majority. European Americans and African Americans constituted the school's two largest ethnoracial groups, although African Americans are only the fourth-largest ethnoracial category in California (after European Americans, Latinos, and Asian Americans) and were also a relatively small group in Bay City. This disproportionate black student population relative to the city's black population was partly due to the "white flight" of well-to-do families to private schools and partly due to the enrollment of African American students from neighboring communities in Bay City's schools, the phenomenon that was so troubling to Ursula. By contrast, Latinos, who are projected to surpass whites as the state's largest ethnoracial group and have displaced African Americans as the largest US ethnoracial minority, made up a small percentage of the Bay City population and the school's student body. The number of Asian Americans at Bay City High was likewise small, and there were very few Native American and Filipino students. In other California schools, however, racial anxieties like Ursula's have surfaced regarding large Latino or Asian populations.

California voters' worries over the state's changing ethnoracial landscape, especially regarding its educational institutions, led to a series of ballot initiatives in the 1980s and 1990s. The first, Proposition 63, which overwhelmingly passed in 1986, altered the state's Constitution to make English the official language of California. In 1994, the virulently xenophobic Proposition 187 deprived undocumented immigrants of all public services, including health care and education; the initiative was approved by the electorate but ruled unconstitutional by a federal judge. Two years later, Proposition 209 amended California's Constitution to ban affirmative action policies in public employment and education. Bay City High School students of all races and ethnicities publicly demonstrated against this initiative, which nevertheless passed and remains part of California law. In 1998, Proposition 227 sharply restricted bilingual education in public schools in favor of short-term English-only instruction for English language learners; it too is still in force. Besides these ballot initiatives, another racially charged educational controversy arose in late 1996 and early 1997 when the Oakland Unified School District Board of Education decided to use what it termed Ebonics, or African American Vernacular English, as a bridge to Standard English for the district's largely African American student population, resulting in a national outcry.

I began my fieldwork during this period of ethnoracial ferment. Bay City High School was also caught up in debates over race and rights. Ethnoracial issues were central to the curriculum and to the discourse of administrators, teachers, parents, and students; these issues also predominated in the community and in press coverage about the school. A much-discussed topic was the question of segregation, especially between black and white students. Concerns about segregation were of two types: institutionally segregated classrooms and student-driven "self-segregation" in the schoolyard. My original hope in selecting Bay City High as my research site was to challenge the perception of students as self-segregated by investigating hip hop language and culture. I anticipated that hip hop would bring white students together with teenagers of color to engage in a shared youth culture. As my research progressed, however, my optimism about the unifying effects of hip hop at Bay City High diminished. Meanwhile, the scope of my study expanded to include a wider range of ways in which European American teenagers managed their identities at a school that was perceived to be as ethnoracially divided as it was ethnoracially diverse.

In this chapter I discuss Bay City High as my fieldwork site, focusing on how cultural discourses of race as well as stylistic ideologies within the school's peer culture shaped local meanings of race and especially of whiteness. I then discuss the methods that I employed to make sense of Bay City

High School's racial and stylistic order. Finally, I reflect on my own identity as a white female ethnographer conducting research on the delicate topic of race in this context.

Discourses of race at Bay City High

The discussion of race among European American teenagers and adults during my fieldwork echoed the themes of national discourses of race in the same period: social class, violence, and segregation. In these ideologically saturated discourses, strategies of displacement – rhetorical techniques for shifting the terms of the discourse – set aside the concerns of people of color in favor of a white-centered viewpoint. Such privileging of whiteness is perhaps unsurprising given that it was primarily European Americans who wrote articles for the local newspaper, attended school board and Parent–Teacher Association meetings, and complained to school administrators. Against these racial discourses of class, violence, and segregation stood Bay City High's official discourse of multiculturalism, which did not elevate white issues above those of people of color. Consequently, it generated considerable resentment and anger among European American students and their parents. In the end, all four of these discourses of race united many white youth around a shared racial identity that was ideologically counterposed to nonwhiteness and especially to blackness.

The discourse of race and class

Concern with race permeated Bay City High's institutional structure; by contrast, social class was less overtly discussed, and when it was, it was generally linked to race. Students discovered the salience of race and ethnicity at the school the day they enrolled, when they and their parents completed forms reporting their ethnoracial category along with other demographic information. However, because students could select only one designation from a predetermined list, official categories did not necessarily reflect their own identities. This problem was particularly acute for the diverse groups that fell under the category *Asian*, for the many students of mixed race, and for teenagers of European descent with strongly held ethnic identities, especially Jewish students.

Tables 2.1 and 2.2 provide the school's official figures for its student population at the beginning of 1994–95, the year nearest to my fieldwork period for which such figures were available. The ethnoracial labels in the tables are those used by the school itself. As Table 2.1 shows, African Americans and European Americans each constituted roughly 40 percent of the student body, while Asian Americans and Latinos each made up around 10 percent. The small remaining percentages were Native Americans and Filipinos; a seventh

Table 2.1. *Ethnoracial breakdown for Bay City High School student population, total percentage*

Amer. Indian	Asian	Filipino	Hispanic	Black	White
0.3%	10%	0.7%	11%	38%	40%

Table 2.2. *Ethnoracial and gender breakdown for Bay City High School student population, by grade*

	MALE						FEMALE						
grade	AmI	As	Fil	His	Bl	Wh	AmI	As	Fil	His	Bl	Wh	TOT
9		44	4	45	130	145	1	32	1	37	149	132	720
10		37	2	38	130	125	1	40	2	37	126	133	671
11	1	15	2	17	86	108	1	31	2	33	103	114	513
12	1	21	3	18	67	122		25	2	30	82	106	475
other		1		3	36	5	1	1		1	11	6	65
TOT	2	118	11	121	449	505	4	129	7	138	491	496	2444

category included in the school's original document, *Pacific Islander*, is omitted because no students at Bay City High were counted in this category in 1994.

Table 2.2 tallies students by gender, ethnoracial category, and grade level (ninth, tenth, eleventh, and twelfth, corresponding to freshman, sophomore, junior, and senior). The figures show a striking pattern of attrition for African American students. Although black girls were the largest group in the ninth grade, by the twelfth grade their numbers had dropped below white boys (the second-largest group in the ninth grade) as well as white girls. Attrition rates of black boys were even more precipitous: it appears that barely over 50 percent graduated. One explanation for this gap is that black boys predominated in the "other" category, which included teenagers enrolled in a continuation high school program at a separate campus. The program enrolled students deemed unable to succeed in a regular school environment (often due to teachers' complaints about behavioral issues). However, many African American students left the school altogether for a variety of reasons (see also Foster 1996).

Race was such a sensitive issue at Bay City High School that it was extremely difficult for me to obtain this information, which was by law a matter of public record. Only after making repeated requests and obtaining increasing levels of authorization was I able to view the school's records for a few minutes in the main administrative office; I was not allowed to photocopy the records but had to hand-copy the information.[1]

Staff members' concerns to limit the circulation of this information were by no means unfounded. Students from outside the school district could petition to attend Bay City High, but the specific numbers of such students were not made public. Some upper-middle-class European American parents, like Ursula Chambers, suspected that many lower-income students, especially African Americans, lived not in Bay City but in economically depressed neighboring cities and were taking advantage of Bay City's superior school system. Such parents were eager to examine any records that would corroborate this impression, fearing that "our" tax dollars were being spent to educate "their" kids. As Ursula lamented to me, "[Bay City] kids are being driven out." She then added in a telling slip of the tongue, "The nature of the kids who are coming is changing the – not complexion, that's not the white [sic] word, but the composition and abilities of students." The ethnoracial subtext in Ursula's comments became more explicit, alongside a class-based discourse, in her complaints that black and Latino students from out of town were "free-lunch kids" who often needed "additional services."

Most of the school's African American, Latino, and Southeast Asian American students were indeed working class, while most European American and East Asian American students were middle class.[2] Identifying the socioeconomic status of any given student at Bay City High, however, could be problematic. To begin with, housing costs in the San Francisco Bay Area have long been among the highest in the nation; in 1995, the median price of a single-family home was $300,000, over twice the national median. Consequently, even middle-class families often rented their homes or lived in modest accommodations in less desirable areas. Moreover, many students divided their time between the homes of their divorced parents, who could have very different economic situations. Nor were students' clothing and other material possessions a direct indicator of social class, since fashionable clothing among working-class students (most of them African American) often involved designer labels and expensive athletic shoes, while many "preppy" upper-middle-class students (most of them European American) dressed in a deliberately sloppy style that displayed their calculated indifference to the niceties of fashion; one teacher called them "the studied poor" (Bucholtz 2007a: 389).

Class differences among students, if sometimes obscure to observers, were stark and almost always racialized. One African American boy was homeless throughout much of the academic year, although he managed to hide this fact from most people at the school; meanwhile, the families of the wealthiest European American students lived in the region's most exclusive ZIP codes and owned second homes in Tahoe or other resort areas. Likewise, only around 10 percent of the student population qualified for the federal free and reduced lunch program, but such students were overwhelmingly black. While many white youth ate lunch off campus at relatively upscale restaurants where a small meal could cost as much as ten dollars, black teenagers with lunch money generally bought meals from fast food establishments for a dollar or two.

The class-based discourse of race at Bay City High reinforced racial divisions even as it allowed European Americans to deflect charges of racism by using social class as a substitute for race. The problem of inadequate educational opportunities for many African American and Latino children in their local communities was reinterpreted as a threat to deprive European American children and their parents of scarce and coveted resources. Yet I saw no evidence that the presence of such students had any significant negative effects. Indeed, given that these teenagers had to make a special effort to attend the school, many traveling long distances by public transit each day, they were often more highly motivated than students who lived in Bay City. In short, the class-based discourse pitted middle-class European Americans against less-well-off African American students and other youth of color without foregrounding the centrality of race in this ideological struggle over resources.

The discourse of race and violence

A second discourse that made race a salient and sensitive issue at Bay City High focused on danger. The previous school year had seen a string of violent incidents on or near the school grounds, attributed by the administration and the local press to gang activity and to black aggression against white students. Partly because of these problems, the school had undergone multiple changes in administration, with numerous principals in the space of a few years, and a discourse emerged concerning the safety of (primarily white) students and teachers at Bay City High. Rumors of black-on-white violence were widespread among white students and their parents, and a common explanation for perceived self-segregation was that European Americans avoided African Americans out of concern for their own safety. Yet in fact black teenagers, and especially boys, have long been at greater risk of violence than other ethnoracial groups (Dyson [1996] 2004). To highlight the supposed danger facing European American students, then, was another instance of the discursive displacement of black concerns in favor of less warranted but more highly publicized white anxieties.

This discourse of fear and violence, which permeated media discussions of Bay City High and influenced community attitudes toward the school, bore little relation to the actual everyday life of the high school. In a year of fieldwork I witnessed only one episode of violence. In that incident, which occurred several blocks from the school, a European American girl viciously attacked an openly lesbian student (also white) because the other girl had supposedly flirted with her. I also observed the aftermath of a minor scuffle between two African American boys, in which school officials quickly intervened. This is not to say that violence or the threat of violence did not occur. But a single incident could become the source of widespread panic due to sensationalistic news coverage. For instance, a conflict between two boys over a girl, which ended with one boy setting off a firecracker, was widely reported in the media as a battle between rival black and Latino gangs that involved gunfire. Thus even minor acts of violence received unwarranted media attention (see also Lakoff 2000): during my fieldwork, fully a third of all news articles about the school in area newspapers focused on violence or racial conflict.

The discourse of violence created a caricature of Bay City High as a racially divided school in which underachieving black students from outside the city menaced white youth who were Bay City residents. This portrayal influenced students' own images of their school, and some European American teenagers described Bay City High to me in ways that did not match my own observations. To be sure, sometimes black students, particularly boys, whom white youth often found intimidating, played on this fear, for example, by yelling "Riot!" and rushing to the classroom door when there was noise in the hallway. But African American teenagers also expressed frustration and dismay regarding European Americans' perceptions of them.

The discourse of violence had powerful institutional effects. Beginning in the 1995–96 school year, the administration – led by a new principal with a strong law-and-order stance – instituted a number of strict measures recommended by a private security firm, including fencing in the campus and locking the entrances during school hours (though whether to keep strangers out or students in was never clear to me); assigning staff members to patrol school grounds and buildings with walkie-talkies; requiring staff and visitors to wear identification tags; and bringing a highly visible police presence onto the campus (cf. Devine 1995).

The school's martial atmosphere carried over to lunchtime, when the gates were unlocked and students were permitted to buy lunch at nearby shops and restaurants due to a lack of adequate food facilities on campus. During the lunch hour (reduced to 45 minutes as an additional security measure, allowing less time for students to "get into trouble"), students streamed to the retail area under the watchful eyes of police officers and private security guards hired by merchants. These uniformed figures were disproportionately in evidence in establishments frequented by black students; as many as three guards might be stationed in the cramped space of a fast food restaurant popular with African American teenagers, while several blocks away, at a much more expensive café whose student clientele was mainly white, no security guards were present. Individual shopkeepers sometimes took further steps, limiting the number of students allowed in their stores at one time and even physically barring the door to block teenagers' entry.

Given the large number of students and the short time and small space allotted to them, the lunch period was remarkably problem-free. Beyond occasionally blocking traffic or crossing the street against the stoplight, students did not generally disrupt the activities of the city around them. Indeed, after the first week or two of the school year, many precautions taken by city officials and shopkeepers were dropped as obviously unnecessary. The discourse of violence, however, remained a powerful ideology structuring European American students' talk about and understanding of race.

The discourse of racial segregation

Whereas the discourses of social class and violence problematized students of color and portrayed white youth as victims, segregration, the third racial discourse widely circulated in the community and the media, cast blame on the school and its students of all races for failure to overcome historically entrenched racial divisions. This discourse had two dimensions, one concerning the ethnoracial makeup of classes and the other regarding friendship groups.

The work of schools is to sort students into different life paths (Mehan 1991). Bay City High School had highly racially imbalanced classrooms due to the controversial practice of tracking, which placed students in courses according to perceived academic ability. The tracking system produced 90 percent white Advanced Placement and college-preparatory classes and mostly black, Latino, and Southeast Asian remedial and vocational classes (see also Staiger 2006), despite the high academic aspirations of many students of color, who aimed to earn at least a college degree. Bay City High, like many other schools, eventually began to phase out tracking in order to provide more challenging educational opportunities for students of color (e.g., Cooper 1996). Numerous European American parents vocally opposed this move, fearing a decline in standards that would endanger their children's academic performance and prospects for college admissions.

More often, however, *segregation* referred not to the school's official practices of routing students into different educational trajectories but to teenagers' informal practices of self-organization, based on young people's spatial arrangements on the school grounds at lunch and before and after school. The evidence for ethnoracial division seemed incontrovertible, the boundaries dramatically delineated by students' own bodies. Yet this easily available analysis overlooked the significant numbers of youth who crossed ethnoracial borders in their friendships and school activities. Admittedly, teenagers of different races and ethnicities were far from fully integrated, especially African Americans and European Americans, but this division was greatly exaggerated in the discourse of segregation. Meanwhile, social differentiation on the basis of youth styles was evident to students but often invisible to adult observers.

Figure 2.1 is the administration's map of Bay City High, indicating buildings and other spaces where the school's official work was conducted. Yet far more

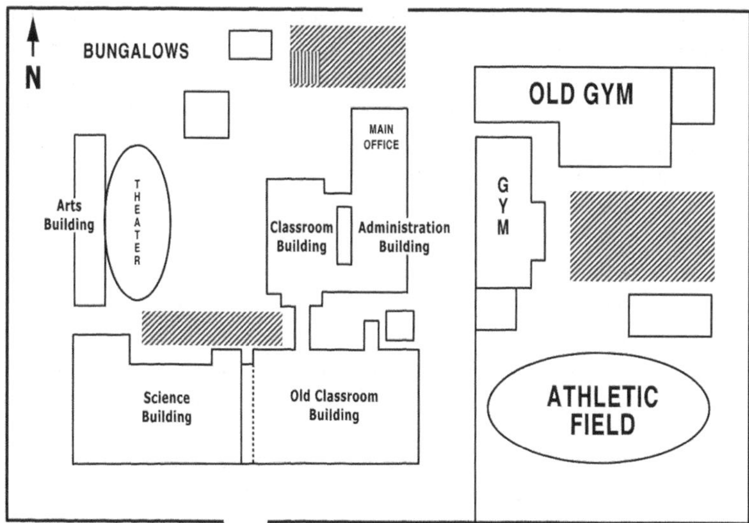

Figure 2.1: Official map of Bay City High School

important in most students' social lives were the unofficial interstices in which teenagers collectively constructed the semiotic practices that differentiated groups from one another on the basis of race and style. The school's main student hangouts centered on the courtyard, which was surrounded by school buildings. African Americans generally congregated in the area called the Hill, near the principal's office, while a large number of preppy European Americans sat on the steps of the arts building, facing the courtyard, an area often referred to simply as the Steps. Other groups were more dispersed: some Asian American students assembled at a low wall near the science building, called the Wall, and a few mostly low-status students sat on cement benches, called the Blocks, in the center of the courtyard. None of these areas is labeled on the official map.

Entirely absent from the official representation of Bay City High is the Park, a grassy lot across the street from the school that was a largely European American hangout. Both spatially and socially, the predominantly white Park, at the southwest end of campus, represented the farthest point from the predominantly black Hill at the northeast end. This arrangement replicated in microcosm the racialized arrangement of Bay City's neighborhoods, with primarily white, upper-middle-class families in the south and west parts of the city and primarily black, working-class families in the north and east.

Most adult observers attributed students' racial separation to free and autonomous choice, another ideological strategy of displacement. There were in fact racial asymmetries in where and how students could congregate. The white enclave of the Park was not school property, suggesting a kind of "white flight" away from the school grounds, where many black students hung out. But more importantly, the Park appealed to many students with rebellious, nonmainstream youth styles precisely because of its distance from the school, allowing them to smoke and at times to covertly use drugs. Such an activity would have been riskier for black youth, who drew attention from police and parapolice groups whenever they left the campus.

The discourse of segregation ignored the more complicated reality of students' social and physical arrangements. The racialization of particular areas shifted throughout the day, with groups assembling in established areas at lunch but leaving them available for other groups at other times. Moreover, although students typically did not make lasting incursions into the racialized space of other groups, it was extremely common for groups and individuals to move through others' space, or even to take up a spot for a short period, without incident or comment. In addition, interracial friendships were not uncommon, although for most European American youth, such friendships were limited to the presence of one or two teenagers of color within otherwise white groups. Groups of different races and styles mainly displayed not hostility to one another but disengagement, as youth operated in their own social domains with little attention to others' activities unless these infringed on them in some way.

Racial and stylistic divisions on the school grounds were less evident in required classes, which were far more ethnoracially diverse than classes within the tracking system. A student might look at a neighbor's paper, request help with classwork, compliment someone's clothing or doodled artwork, borrow a pen or a tissue, share music cassettes (in an era before CDs and MP3 players were widespread), ask the time, comment on classroom activities, or otherwise conduct brief but amicable interactions across social boundaries. Youth of different styles, races, and ethnicities, removed from their usual friendship groups, often formed friendly alliances in classroom settings. Such alliances primarily involved students of color, but some white youth, most notably European American hip hop fans, made efforts to align with students of color, especially African Americans.

The discourse of multiculturalism

The final discourse of race and ethnicity at Bay City High was the school's official discourse of multiculturalism, which celebrated ethnoracial diversity. This discourse was part of a national movement that swept schools, colleges, and universities beginning in the 1990s. At Bay City High School, a multicultural curriculum was introduced to provide an education relevant to students of color as well as to address the anxieties about racial conflict and segregation widely expressed by white students, parents, and community members. Yet this discourse did not have the intended effect. Many European Americans in fact blamed the school's multicultural educational philosophy for exacerbating its racial problems. These complaints were part of a wider national debate over what critics of multiculturalism termed *political correctness*, or hypersensitivity to minority concerns (Fairclough 2003).

Bay City High's multicultural curriculum was as focused on students' psychological well-being and interracial harmony as it was on their intellectual development. To foster what it called "self-esteem" and "respect for diversity" among all students, the school incorporated the history and culture of various ethnoracial groups into the curriculum and sponsored cultural celebrations and performances. Conventional courses like American literature and history added units on race and ethnicity, and several elective classes on ethnoracial topics were also offered. In addition, a controversial course entitled Multiculturalism was developed in order to educate students about issues of race and ethnicity in the United States. While students and parents of color generally welcomed the perspective that the multicultural curriculum provided, white students and parents argued that it promoted segregation both by guilt-tripping European Americans and by fostering separatist ideologies among youth of color. In this controversy, once again, white concerns took center stage at the expense of youth of color.

The racial discourses of social class, violence, segregation, and multiculturalism at Bay City High School were largely imposed on youth by adults, including teachers and administrators, parents and community members, and the media. By contrast, students had almost complete control over the local peer social order, which provided another way of organizing teenagers: on the basis of style. Yet youth styles too were deeply racialized.

Race and style

For white teenagers at Bay City High, stylistic positioning required taking a stance toward hip hop, the school's dominant form of youth culture. Although not all students participated actively in hip hop, many were influenced by its fashions, music, activities, and language, and even students who were disengaged from hip hop culture could not be entirely unaware of it. At Bay City High School in the 1990s, hip hop was strongly associated with African American youth. Hence black teenagers were the school's primary trendsetters, introducing stylistic innovations that were then adopted by other students (cf. Morris 2006; Perry 2002; Peshkin 1991).

In addition to their stylistic authority, African American teenagers held certain positions of prominence in the school's institutional structure as star athletes or cheerleaders in football and basketball, as homecoming queens and kings, and as members of the student council. While there was some racial overlap in these domains, especially the student council, many European American students separated themselves from such arenas, participating in other extracurricular activities, focusing on college-track academics, and developing their own stylistically distinctive groups. During my fieldwork I identified four general white youth styles – preppies, hip hop fans, nerds, and "alternative" teenagers – each of which oriented to black youth culture in a different way. In this book I focus in depth on the first three of these styles.

I did not begin this project knowing exactly what sorts of white identities I might find at Bay City High School, nor how they might be linguistically produced. In fact, early in my fieldwork I was initially – and naïvely – worried because I could not immediately find obvious examples of the stylistic categories familiar to me from my own high school experience. It was only through the ethnographic process that I eventually learned to interpret the semiotic meaning of students' stylistic practices, which were obvious to the youth I was studying. This meant learning to see and hear teenagers as their fellow students did, learning to recognize the social identities that they indexed through clothing and hairstyle as well as through what they talked about and how they talked about it. It also meant listening to how teenagers articulated their understanding of their own and others' identities. In most cases, the linguistic components of these identities emerged even later, as I reviewed my audio recordings of students' speech. Over the course of my fieldwork, I came to understand teenagers' identities by entering their social spaces and sharing, to the extent possible, some of their lived experiences.

Back to school

Despite its academic reputation, like most of California's urban high schools Bay City High was underfunded, rundown, and dingy, with a chronic shortage of basic supplies. Paper towels and toilet paper were rarely available, and restroom sinks and drinking fountains rarely worked; a number of teachers purchased their own supply of tissue, which they made available to students for bathroom use, and many students carried water bottles or other beverages to class. The halls and stairwells, shabby and in need of fresh paint, accumulated large amounts of trash throughout the day, some of which was never swept up. The hallway lockers were widely believed to be unsafe storage spaces, so most students carried all their belongings with them throughout the school day in large backpacks that sagged with the weight of their contents.

I spent about half of my time at Bay City High School in the classroom of Olivia Stein, an experienced and popular teacher who taught a health course required of all sophomores.[3] I ended up in her classroom more by accident than by design: as I was narrowing down possible fieldsites, at the suggestion of a mutual acquaintance I spoke with Ms. Stein about my research, and she immediately invited me to use her classroom as the launching point for my study. She allowed me to introduce myself to her students and ask them to participate in the study; I was also permitted to take fieldnotes during class. I quickly realized the extent of my good fortune. Not only did I have a comfortable space where I could hang out with students at lunchtime or conduct interviews, but in Ms. Stein I also had a sympathetic and generous ally, who assisted me in innumerable ways: paving the way for me to approach students and teachers about my study, giving me insight into students' lives, pointing out interesting peer interactions within the classroom. She asked very little of me in return, and I was free to come and go as my research schedule required. She even allowed me to conduct interviews with students in the hallway if their classwork was finished, for she viewed their participation in my study as a valuable educational opportunity for them. Ms. Stein's classes were ideal for my purposes, because they brought together students from different ethnoracial categories, stylistic orientations, and academic tracks. Moreover, the course focused on social issues, and class exercises often encouraged students to stake out their identities publicly, such as listing their favorite activities or their career goals.

Ms. Stein's passion for teaching and her commitment to her students' well-being created a welcoming and often exciting learning environment. Nearly every available wall surface of her classroom was covered with anti-tobacco posters, music album covers, and advertisements with inspirational slogans. Even teenagers with little interest in the academic side of school spoke up in her classroom, because the topics she addressed had immediate relevance for their lives. A middle-aged European American woman, Ms. Stein was slim and energetic; her loose-fitting pantsuits and brightly colored scarves projected a vibrant yet professional style. Her interactions with students maintained a similar balance: she was warm and encouraging, but she brooked no nonsense and strictly enforced classroom rules. Her unflappability in any situation made her the favorite teacher of many students, who confided their successes and struggles to her and sought out her advice on personal matters.

Each quarter Ms. Stein taught five sections of Life and Health, which addressed a range of sensitive topics frankly and unjudgmentally, including pregnancy and sexually transmitted diseases, the dangers of drugs and alcohol, rape prevention, lesbian and gay issues, racism, and family relationships. The emphasis was on providing young people with the information they needed to make wise decisions, and to that end Ms. Stein not only offered an abundance of facts and statistics but also brought in guest speakers to give firsthand accounts of difficult experiences like being HIV-positive or surviving a sexual assault. Although a few students, complaining that Ms. Stein used sensationalistic scare tactics, dismissed the class as "Tragedy 101," most found it extremely valuable.

Besides Life and Health, I was also a participant-observer in a year-long specially funded anti-drug course, Say No to Drugs, taught by Ms. Stein along with two other teachers and a teacher's aide. The course trained students as peer educators who visited other classes and schools and performed original skits about the dangers of drugs and tobacco. Say No to Drugs was an elective, which students took for reasons ranging from an interest in the topic to filling a gap in their schedule. The class was therefore unusually diverse, comprising all four grade levels, both genders, various ethnoracial categories and social classes, and numerous stylistic orientations. Because the course involved extensive peer-centered interaction, it allowed me to observe teenagers of different backgrounds working and talking together.

I attended all five sections of Ms. Stein's Life and Health course three days a week for its nine-week duration, and I attended Say No to Drugs an average of twice a week throughout the year. Additionally, I was a participant-observer, sometimes only once and in other cases for extended periods, in a number of other classes, including journalism, art, Latin, history, biology, photography, and computer skills, as well as the school's controversial Multiculturalism course. I also observed and participated in student life outside class, at lunch, and after school, including attending school-sponsored events and occasionally accompanying students to their homes or to other locations in and around Bay City.

As I gained insight into teenagers' perspectives through participant-observation, I was also compelled to confront my own subject position as a European American, a woman, and a former high school student at a school not unlike Bay City High. These reflections were sometimes uncomfortable, but they also helped me to understand how my own identity shaped the research process.

Race and the researcher

The salience and painful sensitivity of race at Bay City High inevitably affected my research. Early on I received numerous warnings from friends, colleagues, and even casual acquaintances that I was putting myself at risk by carrying out research at an urban public high school. Likewise, when I spoke to the school principal to request permission to conduct my study, he stipulated that I could meet with students only in public places. When I asked in surprise why he would impose this restriction – I wondered whether he perhaps feared that I would molest or harm the students – he told me that it was for my own safety: "You don't know who you're dealing with," he explained. This encounter later became a joke between me and the students who worked on the school newspaper, one of the activities that I became involved in through my participant-observation. I told them the story one day, and afterward, whenever I stayed late to help with the newspaper they would teasingly warn, "Mary, you're alone with students!" My usual response was the equally joking plea, "Don't hurt me!" In light of the racial politics of the school, however, it was presumably not these high-achieving, mostly European American youth whom the principal viewed as a threat to me.

Any initial apprehension I felt was shared, and with far greater justification, by the teenagers themselves. Most students at Bay City High felt betrayed by the media's representation of their school, and many were skeptical of adult outsiders who asked uncomfortable questions. Given the school's precarious racial situation I did not want to highlight my interest in black–white relations. On the other hand, I did not want to deceive students about the purpose of my project and leave them feeling betrayed once again by outside observers. I compromised by initially telling students that I was studying "the language of friendship," a topic that accurately characterized the original focus of my study but was sufficiently vague that those I talked to did not become extremely self-conscious either about their language use or about the topic of race. After teenagers got to know me better, I gradually introduced my more specific research interests. A related worry was that my own fieldwork might promote the discourse of segregation at the school. I tried to avoid this danger by not talking about race in interviews and other interactions until the students themselves had introduced the topic, as well as by focusing on friendship rather than the fraught issue of race relations. But given the intense scrutiny of the school's racial divisions, it was almost inevitable that students would view any researcher at Bay City High as primarily interested in racial differentiation, and teenagers frequently brought up the issue unprompted by me.

A second challenge of my research was that severe overcrowding at Bay City High made it impossible for me to be a full-fledged participant in many classrooms, simply because there was often nowhere for me to sit. I was frequently relegated to perching on a countertop, a situation that kept me an observer rather than a participant more often than I would have liked. However, I talked informally with students whenever I could, and sometimes I roamed the classroom while they worked on individual or group activities.

During my fieldwork I generally wore a casual uniform of jeans, sneakers, and unadorned T-shirts, which I hoped would be interpreted as sufficiently neutral not to align me with teachers or with any particular youth style (as it happened, however, my sartorial choices turned out to be most closely akin to those of nerdy teenagers). My assiduous efforts to appear innocuous were aided by my height – at four feet eleven inches I made even most freshmen seem tall by comparison. However, my age worked against me: I was twenty-eight when I began the fieldwork, a good ten years older than the oldest seniors. Although I was occasionally mistaken for a student by some teachers and administrators, students were well aware that I was not one of them, nor would I have wanted them to believe that I was. But they were also aware that I was not a teacher, and they did not perceive me as a typical adult. My undefined status inevitably raised the question of who – and what – I was. Hence, while teenagers referred to unfamiliar women in the school as *ladies*, they did not use that term for me, nor did I count as a *girl*, the usual term for a female student. Early in my fieldwork I was amused to hear myself referred to as *that person*; later I became known to some students as *our researcher*, while others simply explained my presence to friends and classmates by saying, "She's studying me."

As a peripheral participant at the school, I found my sympathies constantly shifting. My indignation at white teachers' and students' stereotyping of black youth was tempered by the recognition that these stereotypes shaped my own behavior as well. European Americans' fears – which were as genuine as they were baseless – fit in only too neatly with my personal collection of urban lore about race and danger. My secret criticisms of teachers' lesson plans and disciplinary decisions, my annoyance at administrators' abruptness or evasiveness when I sought information, softened when I realized the sheer number of students that teachers were responsible for every day, and when I realized the magnitude of the pressure being applied to school officials by parents like Ursula Chambers.

My first responsibility, however, was to the students. At times my commitment to them caused me to run afoul of a teacher whose goodwill I also needed. On my first day observing in one class I opened a locked classroom door for a late student and received a polite but firm reprimand from the teacher: "Didn't you see me lock that door a second ago? . . . Please don't do that again." I was fortunate that the teacher was good-natured enough to allow me to remain in the classroom despite my violation, but I knew that if called upon to open another locked door for a student, I would in all likelihood do so, given where my ethnographic loyalties lay.

This loyalty stemmed not just from my reliance on Bay City High School students for my research but also from my sense that they had been unfairly portrayed by the press and the community. When the public concluded that the high school was riven by racial tension, it blamed the students for spoiling the racially harmonious future that Bay City had hoped for. But these teenagers did not singlehandedly create the racial ideologies that circulated around them; the local community, the media, and the broader society were instrumental in producing the cultural discourses that dominated young people's experiences of race at their school. This book, then, attempts to allow the youth of Bay City High School to present their own perspectives on race and identity, even as I offer my own understanding of their situation. This process of co-construction of cultural meaning is central to the ethnographic approach.

Constructing data in ethnographic research

The goal of ethnography, to gain an insider's understanding of a local culture, is achieved by conducting fieldwork via participant-observation in a specific cultural context over an extended period. Fieldnotes are traditionally used to systematically document the details and meanings of everyday social practice. Audio and video recordings are often employed as well – methods of special importance for researchers interested in language. Ethnographers may additionally conduct ethnographic interviews, which unlike traditional social science interviews are relatively informal interactions oriented to the cultural concerns and norms of the interviewee rather than the interviewer (Briggs 1986).

Ethnography highlights an aspect of all socioculturally oriented research that often goes unacknowledged in other methodological traditions, namely, that data are not simply discovered by the researcher but are jointly produced in the encounter between researcher and researched and then recontextualized through analysis and writing. The data in the following chapters have been co-constructed and recontextualized in a number of ways.

My primary data source is a set of audio recordings of ethnographic interviews and informal interactions. Although I recorded students of different races and ethnicities, in this book I focus on the audio recordings of twenty-six European American students. I give special attention to ten teenagers with different stylistic orientations whom I came to know quite well through my fieldwork: the preppies Mark, Josie, and Zoe; the hip hop fans Al Capone, Brand One, and Jay; and the nerds Claire, Christine, Fred, and Erich. (All of these students and most of the others in this book chose their own pseudonyms.) My transcripts of these recordings recontextualize them and insert them into a new medium. A second type of data is a set of maps of the school that I asked students to draw during interviews, indicating their own and other social groups' hangout areas. A third source of data is ethnographic fieldnotes of student interactions in classrooms, on the schoolyard, in the corridors, and at school-sponsored activities such as talent shows, sporting events, and dances. I also collected a wealth of artifacts of high school life: transcripts of bathroom graffiti, small stickers bearing the tags of student graffiti artists, school newspapers and yearbooks, official bulletins, classroom worksheets, student notes to one another and to me. Only a small portion of the material I gathered in such ways is directly incorporated into these pages, but all of it informed my understanding of the school and its students.

In addition to ethnography, my methodology derives primarily from certain forms of interactional analysis, including conversation analysis, which likewise privileges the viewpoints of study participants over those of analysts. I also occasionally make use of quantitative methods similar to those adopted in variationist sociolinguistics in order to understand the social patterning of a specific linguistic form, and I share the broader variationist concern with linguistic innovation and variability. Finally, my work is informed by methodological discussions of the study of youth (Best 2007) and race (Bulmer and Solomos 2004; Twine and Warren 2000). In combining these different approaches, I have been less concerned with defining myself as a card-carrying member of one field or another – although I understand my work as speaking to all of these fields and others as well – than with discovering as much as possible about the language and identities of white teenagers at Bay City High School.

Much of the data in this book comes from audio-recorded ethnographic interviews that I conducted with Bay City High School students either individually or with one or more friends. In most cases students knew me before I interviewed them, although some I met for the first time when they accompanied their friends to participate in a group interview. Many students participated in several recording sessions with me, which often involved both interviews and more unstructured interaction with me and their peers. Yet in analyzing the data I have remained mindful that in both interviews and other sorts of interactions, students were aware that they were participants in a research study and conducted themselves accordingly.

A research interview is not simply an approximation of ordinary conversation but is itself a distinctive type of speech event (Briggs 1986; Mishler 1986; Wolfson 1976). In this situation, the interviewer is as important as the interviewee in what is said, how, and why. Interviews are not windows into the inner lives of research participants but sites for the discursive construction of identity (e.g., Johnstone 1995; Schiffrin 1993; Schilling-Estes 2004), allowing speakers to present versions of themselves to the researcher, which are neither more nor less "real" than any other social persona. Interviews are additionally useful for documenting explicit statements of ideology, including language ideology. While self-report data, particularly regarding language use, are rarely a reliable indicator of speakers' actual practices, such data can reveal the cultural beliefs that interviewees hold about language and the process whereby social meanings attach to linguistic forms.

As part of the interviews, I included two additional activities. The first was a request to draw a map on a blank sheet of paper that I provided, indicating where the interviewee's own group congregated at lunchtime and before and after school. In the second activity, students were asked to comment on a set of lexical items that I had collected from previous interviews and participant-observation, including current slang, terms for social activities, and labels (none explicitly racial or ethnic) for various stylistic groups at the school. Neither the maps nor the responses to the lexical activity should be taken as straightforwardly "true" reports of teenagers' spatial and linguistic practices; rather, like the interviews more generally, they are jointly crafted artifacts of a specific moment and interactional configuration, and they ideologically represent rather than reflect the local cultural context in which they are embedded.

Writing and representation

Another layer of representation in my data derives from the nature of linguistic analysis. This book relies heavily on transcripts of spoken language as evidence for many of its arguments. It is important to emphasize that all of the transcripts in this book are recontextualizations of audio-recorded interactions that I witnessed and participated in; they are not the interactions themselves. Because I am concerned with the structural and interactional dimensions of the data, I use a technical style of transcription that provides greater linguistic detail at the expense of readability by a general audience, and this too is a representation rather than a straightforward reflection of the original interaction. (The transcription conventions appear at the beginning of the book.) Moreover, in some cases the transcripts in these pages differ slightly from versions I have published previously; as a tool for representing a complex human activity, transcription is far from an exact science (Bucholtz 2000, 2007b).

Regardless of whether linguistic data were originally captured via a recording device and then transcribed, or jotted in a notebook and later fleshed out, the written representation of speech is always an incomplete record. Due to Human Subjects protections, I was frequently unable to audio-record in Bay City High School's classrooms, and hence a few of the data examples in the chapters that follow come from fieldnotes I took at the time; these examples are noted as such. (Vignettes based on fieldnotes at the beginning of each chapter are presented in narrative format.)

In sociocultural linguistics, audio- and video-recorded data are the norm, yet the use of fieldnote data is not uncommon (e.g., Basso 1979; Heath 1983; Irvine [1974] 1989; Labov 1972a, among others). Such data allow researchers to report interactions that are beyond the reach of recording devices, often for ethical reasons, although their uses are limited to linguistic phenomena that can be reliably documented in writing. Rudolf Gaudio (2001: 40) states that fieldnotes "are clearly inadequate for analyzing certain aspects of linguistic structure, such as phonology and oral-interactional strategies. However, they can provide important insights into the social use and significance of lexical, grammatical and rhetorical forms that are more pragmatically salient and therefore amenable to human memory and reflexive commentary." Other researchers have shown that even details of phonology and interaction can be investigated through fieldnotes if the utterances are sufficiently brief (Gumperz 1982; Labov 1972a).

The fieldnote data that I report in this book contain only as much linguistic and contextual information as I was able to document in real time with a reasonable degree of confidence, using a shorthand system of my own devising. Because I noted speakers' utterances in which interesting linguistic features were used but not those in which such features could have occurred but did not, I do not make any strong claims about the frequency or distribution of specific features based on fieldnote data. Despite this limitation, I found fieldnotes invaluable in identifying socially meaningful linguistic forms, associating these forms with particular social categories, and documenting interactions in which they were used. Additionally, in a few cases I was unable to audio-record especially interesting speakers, and thus my fieldnotes are my only research record of their linguistic practices. Without an audio recording, the researcher bears an additional responsibility to be conscious of the potential for mistranscription, and I have noted places where my fieldnote representations of speech are not definite.

In hindsight, there are things that I would have done differently during my time at Bay City High School, both as a researcher and as an often uncertain participant in a complex social milieu. In the years since I undertook this project, I have carried out several other ethnographic studies, both individually and collaboratively, and the mistakes and omissions in my initial foray into fieldwork have, I hope, strengthened the work that came later, even as the successes of this study laid the foundations for my subsequent research.

Conclusion

For the past two decades, anthropologists have made abundantly clear that every ethnographic study – indeed, every research study of social practice – is not a reflection of an absolute objective truth but a partial account in every sense of the phrase (e.g., Behar and Gordon 1995; Clifford and Marcus 1986). This book is no different, and for every story I have told that may resonate with the power of truth for those who were there, undoubtedly there are many more that I missed or misunderstood. The analysis in the following chapters, then, is not simply the story of Bay City High School, or even of the school's white students. Rather, it is the story of the all-too-brief time I spent sharing the lives of some European American teenagers at a very particular time and place, and the sense I made of those encounters both at the time and today.

California is both a bellwether of national ethnoracial trends and a harbinger of the tensions sparked by these shifting demographics. In this chapter I have sketched three of the dominant discourses of race circulating at Bay City High and its community: discourses of social class, violence, and segregation. In each, white concerns outweighed black concerns, thereby promoting continued white hegemony. In a fourth discourse, multiculturalism, whiteness held a less secure position. Likewise, the local peer social order destabilized the hegemony of whiteness due to the stylistic authority of African American youth culture and especially hip hop. The following chapter presents a first look at European American teenagers' stylistic choices by examining the local organization of racial and stylistic categories at the school as well as the ways that individual teenagers positioned themselves and others in relation to locally available identities.

3 Cliques, crowds, and crews: social labels in racial space

Introduction

During my research at Bay City High School, I got to know Sweet Pea, an outgoing African American girl, rather well, for she was in several of the classes I observed, sometimes as a student, at other times as a student aide to the teacher, and occasionally even as a guest speaker. Given her high profile in these contexts, Sweet Pea was well known and well liked by teenagers of all races and seemed comfortable in almost any situation. I was therefore surprised by her reply when I asked her whether she ever spent time in the Park, the open grassy area where many of the school's nonmainstream white youth – skaters, granolas, rastas, and punks, among others – hung out. She answered, "I went to the Park one time and everybody was getting arrested over there," and then added, "You know, people be stealing people's money off their backpacks, so I don't go there." Sweet Pea's apprehensiveness about the Park struck me because I had heard similar sentiments during my conversations with European American teenagers regarding the Hill, a primarily African American hangout area – including the same expression of anxiety about thefts from students' backpacks.

These comments confirmed what I had already observed from my first day of fieldwork: Bay City High School, like many multiracial American high schools, was a racially divided space. But at the same time, as I quickly learned from my work with European American teenagers, it was also a stylistically divided space, with the Park primarily associated with nonmainstream white styles and the school's courtyard primarily associated with mainstream white styles. To be sure, these symbolic boundaries were more ideological than real, for social groups and their geographies had porous borders, and students of both stylistic orientations (as well as those of other ethnoracial groups) hung out in both spaces. Yet teenagers were highly attuned to the rigid ideological divisions that organized the school's landscape.

As Penelope Eckert (1989, 2000) points out, by their very nature, schools foster the construction of oppositional youth styles. A number of cross-cutting parameters structured the social configuration of Bay City High School students, including class year, gender, educational track (college-preparatory versus vocational), participation in specific extracurricular activities, and so on. However, the powerful salience of race as a social boundary meant that it often influenced how other boundaries were drawn. Among the most significant of such racialized borders were those delineating teenagers' stylistic orientations. Other social categories were imposed or at least regulated by the school, from the division of students into class years according to age to the separation of girls and boys in team sports. Styles, by contrast, were created by young people themselves and operated almost entirely outside the school's institutional control. In fact, few teachers or administrators seemed aware of the complex semiotic work going on in Bay City High's classrooms, hallways, and school grounds. Teachers frequently invoked race and ethnicity, gender, and age in their efforts to make sense of students' behavior, but as far as I observed they never commented on the role of style in youth identities and practices.[1] Teenagers, meanwhile, regularly appealed to their peers' stylistic affiliations as central to who they were and what they did. Thus even as the school imposed an official classificatory system on its students, young people established a separate categorization scheme that only partly intersected with the school's concerns.

The categories constructed by teenagers were, like the school's classification system, deeply racialized. For example, most students were acutely aware of fine social differentiations within their own racial category but had little knowledge of even the broadest distinctions among other racialized groups, which tended to be viewed as monolithic and homogeneous. And stylistic categories were racially defined to such an extent that teenagers who adopted a style that did not conform to their own racial assignment ran the risk of being derided as "wannabes" or accused of "acting black" or "acting white."[2]

As noted in the previous chapter, for European American students, navigating these styles meant implicitly – and sometimes explicitly – positioning themselves in relation to hip hop, the form of African American youth culture that held the highest authority in the school's stylistic landscape. The three white styles that I examine in greatest detail in this chapter and throughout the book – the cool, nonmainstream hip hop style; the cool, mainstream preppy style; and the uncool, mainstream nerdy style – enacted three different orientations toward black cultural resources, from openly engaged to covertly engaged to disengaged. Other groups also figured in the stylistic spectrum of European American youth, particularly the nonmainstream "alternative" teenagers who frequented the Park and the self-described "normal" students, who did not have strong stylistic affiliations but emulated some of the stylistic practices of preppy students. The hip hop, preppy, and nerd styles, however, were maximally distinctive among white teenagers.

In day-to-day practice, European American students' semiotic displays stood most overtly in contrast to other white styles, the most immediately relevant points of comparison. These stylistic categories were enacted through clothing, language, and other semiotic resources. They were also the subject of discursive commentary as young people engaged in the ideological work of stylistic interpretation and evaluation. This chapter examines the semiotic system of white youth stylistic practice at Bay City High School as well as ideologies about local social categories. Both practices and ideologies were at times rigid and inflexible and at other times more fluid, demonstrating the complexity of teenagers' identity work.

Style and social division

European American youth styles at Bay City High School were distinguishable along three social parameters: mainstream or nonmainstream, oriented toward or away from local black youth culture, and cool or uncool. Although for clarity I present these parameters as binary, most students were located at various points between the polar extremes.

Mainstream versus nonmainstream styles

At Bay City High School, no single white style or set of styles was entirely hegemonic. This situation contrasts with Belten High, the mostly white suburban Detroit high school described by Eckert (1989, 2000), in which the predominant stylistic groups were the school-oriented jocks and the rebellious burnouts. The closest equivalents to Eckert's jocks at Bay City High were the high-achieving preppies and the sports-oriented jocks. These two categories were mainstream in that they were stylistically conservative and aligned with the school as an institution. The preppy and jock styles overlapped considerably, and henceforth I use *preppy* as a cover term for both, unless the distinction is relevant to the discussion. Preppies were the institutionally most powerful white students at the school; they were well known and highly visible, often holding prestigious roles within elite extracurricular activities such as the student newspaper and the student council. Preppy students typically limited their substance use to alcohol (albeit often in copious amounts) and occasional use of soft drugs like marijuana at parties.

By contrast, youth who participated in nonmainstream styles were similar to Eckert's burnouts in that they stood in opposition to the conformity and conservatism associated with mainstream students. Such teenagers often operated outside the institutional structure of the school and reveled in challenging its authority. They were typically involved in a narrower range of school activities, usually various forms of artistic production and occasionally sports, and their drug use tended to be heavier and more adventurous, in some cases extending to taking and sharing drugs at school. I call such styles *alternative* both to highlight their deliberate oppositionality to mainstream students' styles and to evoke the widespread use of this term in the 1990s (including by some Bay City High School students) as a label for a range of mostly independently produced and distributed popular musical genres, such as punk, goth, and grunge, that fell outside the commercial mainstream – and which, not coincidentally, were favored by many alternative teenagers. Unlike Eckert's jocks and burnouts, mainstream and nonmainstream students were not necessarily slated for dramatically different life trajectories: many members of both groups were high-achieving academically and aspired to attend college, and most came from middle-class families. What nonmainstream youth rejected was not academic success but the stylistic trappings of conventionality and conformity (Thornton 1995).

Whereas at Belten High the jocks were widely seen as pursuing popularity, or social prestige, much to the disgust of the burnouts, at Bay City High School the label *popular* was more contested. Even as alternative students withdrew from the institutional forms of power that preppies embraced, like student government, they themselves enjoyed peer-based prestige due to their engagement with edgy stylistic trends. Given the visibility of both kinds of teenagers within the school, each group viewed the other as obsessively concerned with popularity, a goal they both explicitly disavowed for themselves.

White-oriented versus black-oriented styles

Although alternative and preppy youth operated in different social spheres, they shared a largely white stylistic world. But at Bay City High, the relationship between white and nonwhite social categories was more complex than one of simple separation. African American youth culture in particular played a special role in the formation of the school's stylistic spectrum, for black teenagers introduced a wealth of semiotic resources into the local setting that came to be adopted by many students of all ethnoracial backgrounds. The dominant black youth style was hip hop, which set trends for musical tastes, fashion, and language, among other practices. While no single European American style held symbolic sway over others at Bay City High, hip hop predominated not just among African American students but among most students of color. Given the stylistic authority of black youth culture, African Americans at Bay City High were viewed as cool almost by definition; even relatively untrendy black teenagers could wield cultural authority among their nonblack peers.

Youth of color, especially those from the working class or lower middle class, could generally take up black stylistic trends openly and unproblematically. The situation for European American teenagers, however, was far less straightforward, with the process of cultural diffusion taking different paths and unfolding at different rates among white youth depending on their style.

European American hip hop fans were quick to adopt numerous black youth stylistic innovations, but preppy students drew on a more limited set of semiotic materials from African American sources and only after these had lost their associations with blackness and had become part of a local style available to teenagers of all races and ethnicities (Hewitt 1986). Many alternative teenagers fell somewhere in between, laying claim to elements of African American youth culture more rapidly and more extensively than their mainstream peers but less quickly and less completely than hip hop fans. Furthermore, some alternative styles (e.g., skaters) were more invested in these resources than others (e.g., punks).

Because of the relatively slow, off-record, and incomplete process whereby alternative and preppy students drew on aspects of black youth styles, such practices were generally not understood as a form of ethnoracial crossing (Rampton 1995). By contrast, in the racially divided context of Bay City High School, white hip hop fans' early, overt, and extensive use of semiotic resources from African American youth culture was seen by many European Americans and African Americans alike as an illegitimate appropriation of black stylistic practices. In claiming a style that was strongly associated with blackness, such teenagers positioned themselves against both the preppy mainstream and white-oriented alternative styles.

Cool versus uncool styles

In spite of their considerable stylistic differences, preppy students, alternative youth, and hip hop fans were unified by their pursuit of coolness. As I use the term in this book, coolness involves setting or participating in stylistic trends; I also use the term *trendiness* with more or less the same meaning.[3] Although what counted as cool or stylistically desirable varied greatly across styles, the quest for coolness was shared by most students at Bay City High.

Nerds, however, did not seek out the latest stylistic resources or strive for trendy coolness. Instead, they cultivated an eccentric intelligence and a quirky sense of humor that ran counter to all the cool youth styles. At the same time, nerdy youth shared with preppy students (as well as "normal" teenagers, who were similarly uncool) a mainstream orientation, including a generally conservative clothing style and acceptance of school values: following rules, recognizing teachers' authority, and striving for good grades.

Table 3.1 locates the most widely recognized European American styles at Bay City High with respect to these three parameters. The table also provides the defining practices of each style, including clothing and musical preferences. The category terms I use were generally in wide circulation at the school, although some categories had multiple or contested labels (e.g., *granolas* tended to be an outgroup term), and others (e.g., hip hop fans) had no agreed-upon label.[4]

Table 3.1. *European American youth styles at Bay City High School*

MAINSTREAM

Cool, white-oriented

preppies: clean-cut youth involved in high-profile extracurricular organizations who wore relatively conservative clothing styles and listened to commercial rock

jocks: a category restricted to athletes in predominantly white sports (e.g., soccer)

Uncool, white-oriented

nerds: students who rejected cool youth styles and valued quirky humor, intelligence, and eccentricity

normal: teenagers who had no highly distinctive style

NONMAINSTREAM

Cool, white-oriented

alternative: cool students who participated in white nonmainstream styles

punks: teenagers who listened to punk music and wore spiked leather jewelry and brightly dyed hair, often in a mohawk or similarly flamboyant style

goths: youth who listened to somber music and dressed in black, with dark makeup

skaters: mostly male students who favored an unkempt baggy style, performed skateboard tricks, and listened to loud, aggressive musical genres, including metal, grunge, and some punk and rap

granolas: teenagers who wore hippie-style clothing and listened to 1960s and 1970s rock and folk music

rastas: reggae fans who wore dreadlocks and Rastafari-style clothes

Cool, black-oriented

hip hop fans: mostly male teenagers who dressed in clean-cut baggy clothing and listened to rap music

Finer distinctions were made within the broad social categories listed in the table, such as *keggers*, or jock boys who were heavy beer drinkers and partyers, and *crusties*, a punk style that involved a rejection of personal hygiene, often as a pro-environmental political statement. Small numbers of students also adopted other, less well-defined and widely recognized styles. Many stylistic categories interacted to some extent, with the result that groups and individuals with different styles were often friendly with one another and a single individual could affiliate with more than one style. Likewise, social practices could be shared across different styles (e.g., smoking marijuana or wearing baggy clothing), although each group often differentiated these practices in some way. The table therefore provides brief characterizations of each style's key semiotic practices rather than the full range of individual and group variation.

The variability of stylistic practice and the fluidity of group boundaries formed the basis of a counterideology held by some students, which existed alongside the dominant ideology of social and especially racial division: namely, that Bay City High differed from other high schools in having a less rigid peer social structure. In example (1), Acme, a seventeen-year-old

European American senior, articulates this counterideology. Acme was a cool nonmainstream boy who hung out in the Park.

(1) Acme: If I went to a,
more segregated schoo:l?
↑Not like racially segregated,
but just like g:roup segregated?
and more shit was defined?=
=’Cause at ↑some schools there’s like,
.h::;, <inhaling from marijuana pipe>
<sing song> {the jo::cks:,}
you know,
the sports players,=
=and then there’s th(h)e::,
(0.6)
n-
you know like,
academics,=
=and then there’s the,
s::toners,
and the-=
=you know,=
=there’s just like—
.h::: <inhaling from marijuana pipe>
But ↑here it’s like,
you can be a j:ock,
a s:toner,
an aca↑demic,=
=all at the same ↑time.=
Mary: =[Right.]=
Acme: =[You know,]=
=and so how do you label yourself,
you know . . .

Though cast in the generic second person, Acme’s description captures his own varied stylistic practices. He was a heavy marijuana user who belonged to a group of taggers (teenagers who marked public property with their “tags” or graffiti names using a stylized form of writing). At the same time, he played on the school’s soccer team and aspired to attend college. His own style thus encapsulates his seemingly hypothetical example: *you can be a j:ock, a s:toner, an aca↑demic, all at the same ↑time* (lines 23–26). Acme was by no means unique in this regard; many other teenagers also moved across category boundaries in constructing their styles.

In his comment, Acme explicitly sets aside the issue of racial separation at the school, reinterpreting the term *segregation*, with its strong connotations of racial division, to refer instead to stylistic distinctions (lines 1–4). Yet styles like jocks and stoners were largely understood as white categories (although they had roughly analogous counterparts among students of color). In some instances this was because the original styles were pioneered – or were popularly represented as being pioneered – by white youth, such as punk, goth, skater, or hippie styles (e.g., Bannister 2006; Hebdige 1979). Even the rasta style, which derived from the Jamaican Rastafari religious movement espousing black liberation and thus could have been viewed as an African American form of youth culture, was locally understood as white and drew mostly European American participants (cf. Jones 1988), although the few black rastas were seen as far more authentic than their white counterparts (despite there being little difference in their practices). Regardless of race or ethnicity, rastas were usually not full adherents to Rastafari but participated in some of its practices: wearing the red, yellow, and green clothing and dreadlocked hairstyles popularized by the movement; listening to reggae music, a genre closely linked to Rastafari; and smoking marijuana, considered a spiritual practice within the religion. Such students hung out for the most part not with black youth but with largely white groups of teenagers in the Park.

The ideological association of these styles with whiteness did not preclude students of color from participating in them; all of the above styles included both white and nonwhite adherents. However, in all but the hip hop style, European American youth predominated. In addition, most of the individual friendship groups that embraced each style were overwhelmingly white, with only one or two teenagers of color, mainly middle-class East Asian Americans or African Americans.

The social divisions and connections between youth-cultural styles were apparent not only in the semiotic practices in which students engaged but also in Bay City High School's social geography, as teenagers formed stylistic alignments within the space of the school grounds. As with the symbolic boundaries between styles, the physical boundaries separating social groups were somewhat permeable and malleable in practice. Ideologically, however, these boundaries frequently hardened into sharp divisions. Such ideologies of distinction are inscribed in maps of the school's social geography that I asked students to draw.

White space: racialized geographies and youth styles

As discussed in Chapter 2, during ethnographic interviews I asked each student to draw a map of the school indicating where they and their friends hung out as well as "anything else you think is important." The maps were co-constructed by me and the interviewee (and in group interviews, by other students as well), for as the teenagers drew, they narrated their drawings, and I asked questions for clarification or additional information. The maps do not fully document the complex social reality of Bay City High School but rather provide partial ideological crystallizations of how local categories were organized. Apart from a few shared elements, they offer widely divergent portraits of the school's social landscape, with each map providing a visual representation of the borders and landmarks of the mapmaker's own social territory. These drawings therefore yield rich details both about individual teenagers' own situated identities as well as about which other groups they considered salient.

I did not explicitly suggest any particular social factor as a basis for labeling the maps, other than asking "what kinds of people" were at the school, but many students chose to emphasize two dimensions of social categorization, race and style. I have already described several key racialized regions in and around the school's central courtyard, including the Hill, the primarily African American space at the edge of the courtyard near the principal's office; the centrally located Steps at the entranceway to the arts building, where preppy European American teenagers clustered; and the Park, the grassy area across the street from the main school structure, where mostly white youth of various styles assembled, including alternative teenagers as well as some mainstream youth. This racial division of space is illustrated in many of the maps students drew. Figures 3.1 and 3.2 are two examples of such maps. Both represent more or less the same physical geography, yet they offer very different visions of the social world of Bay City High.

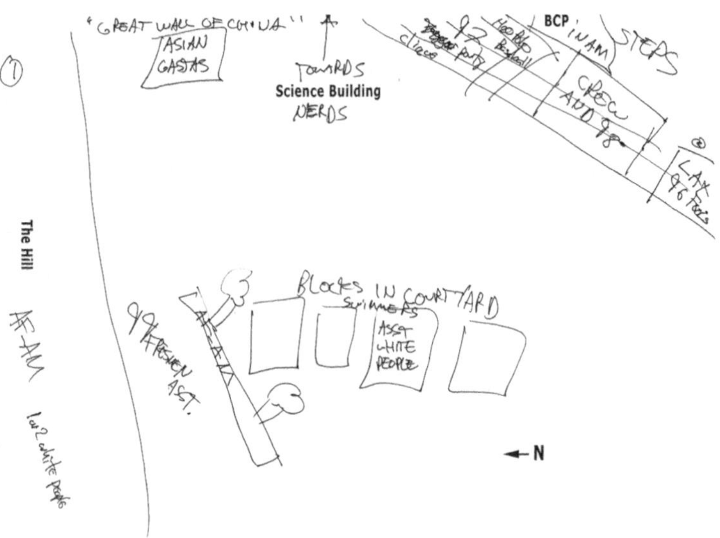

Figure 3.1a: Mark's map of the Bay City High School courtyard

Figure 3.1b: Mark's map of the Park

Figures 3.1a and 3.1b are maps drawn by Mark, a sixteen-year-old junior. Mark was a preppy white boy of Jewish ethnicity whose friendship group was almost entirely European American.[5] The gap between the school's institutional organization of space and the symbolic geography established by young people themselves is apparent in these drawings. The official school map presented in the previous chapter (Figure 2.1) represents the school's various buildings and other institutional spaces. By contrast, in his map of the schoolyard (Figure 3.1a), Mark focuses on the courtyard and excludes all campus buildings, other than indicating with an arrow the location of the science building, which he associates with nerds. However, in his representation of the Steps of the arts building, where many of his friends (and sometimes he himself) hung out, Mark exhaustively labels the nuanced social distinctions of particular areas, differentiating them by graduation year (*97 party clique, '98, 96 fools*) and by the sports they played, often in well-funded private leagues, including baseball, a sport played mostly by the school's white students, as well as elite preppy sports: crew, water polo (*H_2O Polo*), and lacrosse (*LAX*). He provides a similarly detailed map of the Park (Figure 3.1b); in fact, the Park is given more space than the school itself in his representation. Mark's map of the Park specifies the various groups of prestigious students who hang

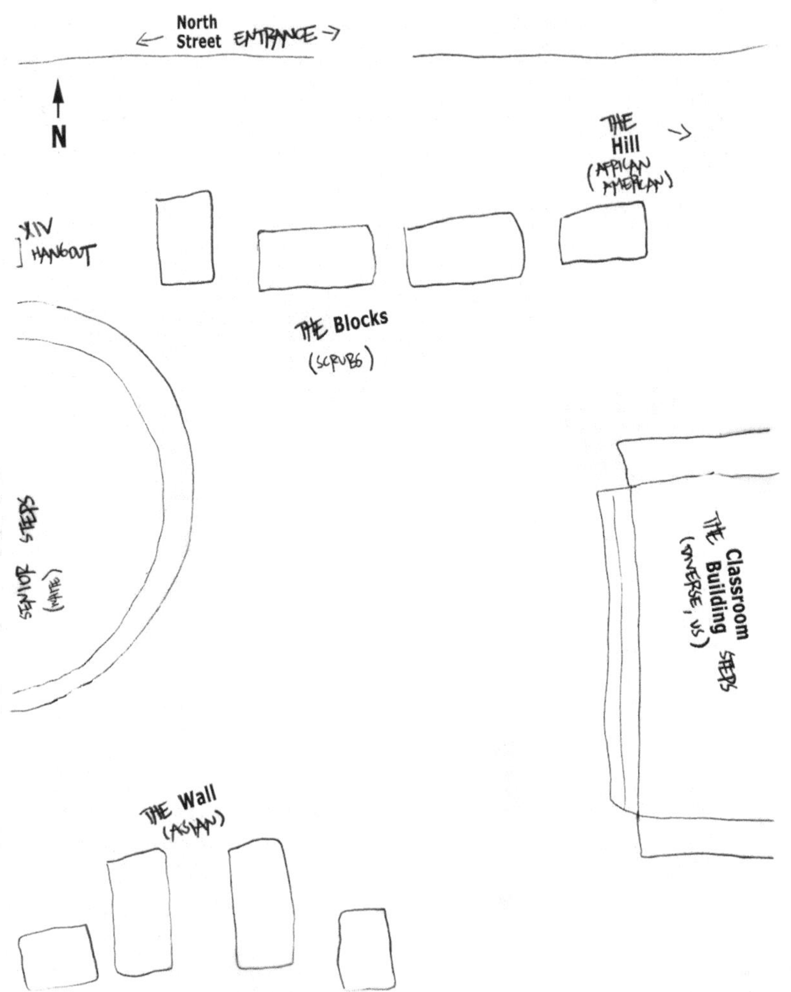

Figure 3.2: John Doe's map of Bay City High School

out there (*POPOLAR* [i.e., *popular*] *'97 GIRLS, 97 POWER CLIQUE*, and *97 WHITE NEO-POPOLAR GIRLS* – although he thought better of this last label and scribbled over the descriptors *white* and *neo-pop[u]lar*). He also includes a range of alternative styles: *STONERS, GRONLA* [i.e., *granolas*], *G's*,[6] and a group that Mark characterizes only as *WIERD* [i.e. *weird*] *PEOPLE*, a term that presumably refers to the more spectacular alternative youth styles, in contrast to his own relatively conservative style.

In both of Mark's maps, race is highly salient, a fact partly obscured by his tendency not to label white social groups. As he commented, "I can go *on* about like, the whole like, all the groups and everything that . . . that Bay City High has. But just for the white people though." The racially unmarked status of European American teenagers contrasts sharply with the racial markedness of students of color in his maps: "ASIAN GASTAS [gangstas or gangsters]" populate the "GREAT WALL OF CHINA" (a blatantly racist term that I never encountered from anyone else; the students in this area were in fact mainly working-class Southeast Asian American), and "Af[rican] Am[erican]" on the Hill, with "1 or 2 white people." It is only in contexts of racial integration or juxtaposition that white students become marked as such in Mark's map: the "ASST [assorted] WHITE PEOPLE" on the Blocks (cement benches in the courtyard) are presumably racially marked because they are near the "Af[rican] Am[erican]" hangout under the trees. Racial explicitness is unnecessary in his map of the Park, because this space was ideologically construed as white, both by Mark and by most other students. Mark's map supports his comment to me that he was intimately familiar with many of the white social groups at Bay City High but lacking in equivalent knowledge of other groups.[7]

Unlike Mark, John Doe, an African American junior who belonged to a multiracial group of hip hop fans including Asian American, Latino, black, and white members, does not include the Park in his map at all (Figure 3.2). And where Mark's map carefully documents the fine social distinctions among preppy students on the Steps, John Doe merely indicates that the area was a hangout for (white) seniors. But like Mark, he includes only those areas of the official campus grounds that have social significance for him. Hence the classroom building appears on his map because his own group gathered there. Additionally, John Doe shares with Mark an ideology of the school's social space as organized primarily around race. He labels the Hill *African American*, the Wall *Asian*, and the Steps *white*. The only nonracialized labels are *scrubs* (i.e., losers or low-status youth) and the designation of the group on the Steps by grade level (*senior*). In addition, John Doe notes the "XIV hangout," a meeting place for students who aligned with the Norteños, a Latino gang that uses the numeral 14 as a symbol, usually pronounced in Spanish as *catorce* 'fourteen' (see also Mendoza-Denton 2008).[8] Finally, while Mark leaves his own social group racially unlabeled, John Doe characterizes his as "diverse," a term borrowed from the school's multicultural discourse. This detail is significant, for the multiracial membership of John Doe's group was a point of pride for him and his friends. Thus although Bay City High students shared a generalized ideology that mapped racialized groups onto particular geographic locations at the school, teenagers from different social categories drew different levels of distinction within these broad groupings.

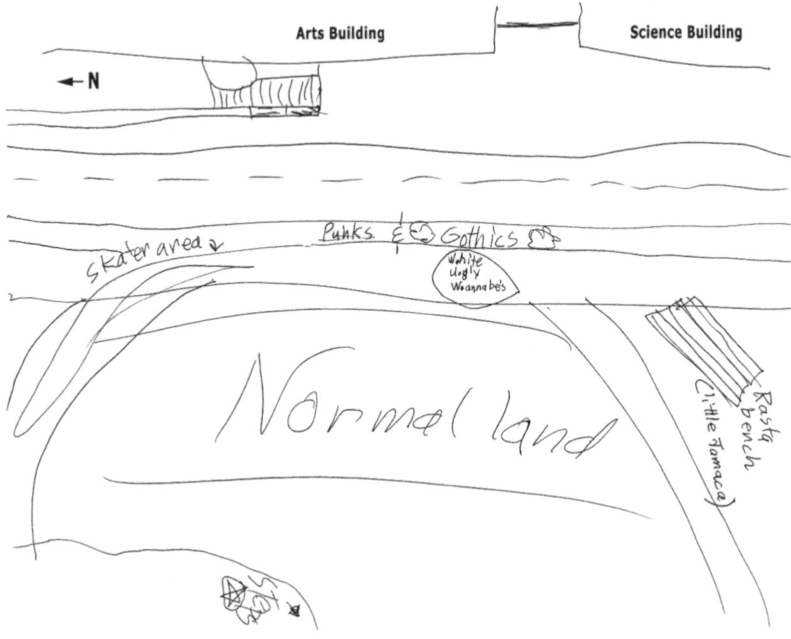

Figure 3.3a: Mr. Frisky's map of the Park

If students' maps construe social space in racialized terms, they also draw on ideologies of stylistic affiliation. The "XIV hangout" is the only activity- or style-based identity labeled in John Doe's map, but Mark's map enumerates a vast array of youth styles, nearly all of them ideologically classifiable as white. European American students with other styles offered very different representations. Figure 3.3a is a map of the Park drawn by Mr. Frisky, a fifteen-year-old European American sophomore who had an alternative style influenced by goth, punk, and grunge. As noted on his map, he spent most of his time in the Park, sitting with his friends on some steps at the far edge of this space, as physically removed from the courtyard (and the preppy students' Steps) as it was possible to be. Mr. Frisky's strong oppositionality to mainstream youth identities also manifests itself in other aspects of his map. Like Mark, in his map of the Park he labels numerous alternative styles, including skaters, rastas, punks, goths, and what he calls "White Ugly Wannabes" (European American hip hop fans, some of whom hung out in the Park). But where Mark noted the presence of mainstream groups as well, Mr. Frisky labels the rest of the map *Normal land* and provides no further details. It is unlikely that Mr. Frisky's use of *normal* here is the same as that of self-described "normal" teenagers, for

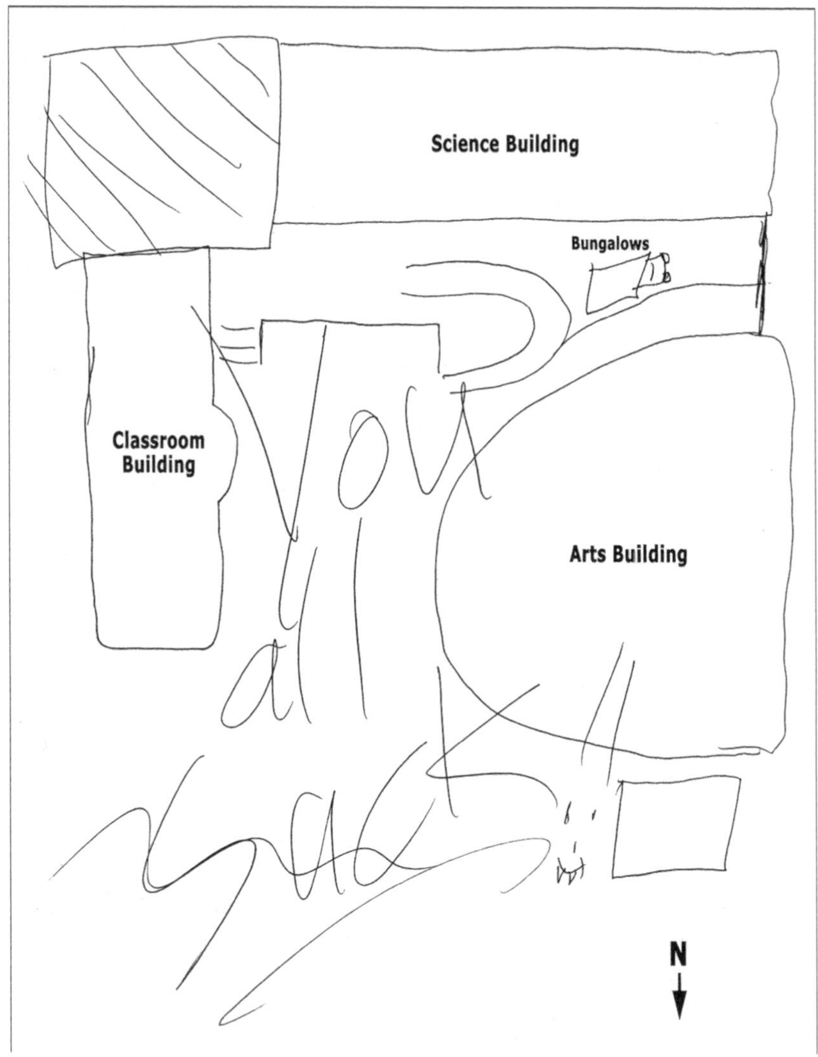

Figure 3.3b: Mr. Frisky's map of the Bay City High School courtyard

while some "normal" students did eat lunch in this area of the Park, so did some preppies and nerds. Thus *normal* in Mr. Frisky's map seems to mean 'mainstream'. Moreover, in his map of the courtyard (Figure 3.3b) he does not label any social spaces at all, instead summarily dismissing all the mainstream groups who hung out there by scrawling "You all suck!!" across the drawing (punctuated with two exclamation points and smiling fangs).

The differences among teenagers' maps demonstrate the ideological roles of race and style in the imagined social topography of Bay City High, yet the static nature of the maps represented social groupings as more clearly defined and sharply bounded than they were in practice. Indeed, the ideological separation of styles was so deeply etched that even the collective terms that teenagers used to refer generically to friendship groups were stylistically constrained. The friendship groups of European American students who were perceived as cool, for example, were often referred to either negatively or neutrally as *cliques* (see Figure 3.1 above). Meanwhile, the slang term *crew* 'friendship group', originally a hip hop term for a group engaged in activities such as rapping or graffiti, referred exclusively – and, in outgroup use, often mockingly – to hip hop fans. (This use was separate from the homophonous term *crew* for the preppy rowing sport, as seen in Figure 3.1a.) Many different stylistic groupings could be referred to through modification of a collective noun like *crowd* or *people*, as in *the preppy crowd* or *Park people*. Only nerdy groups tended not to be referred to with a collective term like *nerdy people* or *the nerd crowd*, perhaps due to cooler teenagers' erroneous belief that nerds were socially isolated individuals lacking a deliberate style.

Alongside these spatial and lexical reinforcements of stylistic separation, however, youth took up a wider range of discursive orientations to social categories, including at times a stance toward styles as problematic and artificially limiting. While no less ideological than their maps, students' talk about social categories allowed for a greater degree of nuance and flexibility that enabled them to acknowledge and at times to problematize the rigidity of social boundaries.

Making labels: styles of whiteness

Various sociocultural linguistic studies have shown that acts of social categorization are also acts of social evaluation (Evaldsson 2005; Garrett, Coupland, and Williams 2004; Goodwin 2002; Matthews 2005). Categories linking names for social types with their associated domains of practice may be evaluated by members of the category and outsiders alike (Sacks [1972] 1986; Schegloff 2007). Indeed, it is precisely by linking available categories of persons and their associated practices to cultural ideologies, values, and meanings that speakers arrange themselves and others within the locally defined social cosmos.

The examples below illustrate some of the ways in which European American teenagers at Bay City High School talked about the three white stylistic categories that are the main focus of this book. In each case interviewees are discussing categories with which they or their friends have some connection. Yet speakers manage their social identities not primarily by highlighting their similarities with others, as might be expected, but by highlighting social differences: rather than openly proclaiming their orientation to a particular established style, they instead negatively evaluate those styles with which they do not affiliate. That is, these speakers focus on distinction rather than adequation.

This strategy of differentiation may be seen as a way of "doing 'being ordinary'" (Sacks 1984) by foregrounding the stylistic markedness of others in contrast to the unmarked and hence unremarkable self. Indeed, several students resisted the very idea of "labeling" themselves (see example 1 above). In ethnographic interviews with me, some teenagers even explicitly disavowed or disaligned with a category with which they aligned in everyday life via their social practices. By distancing themselves from the stylistic system, speakers could position themselves as having unique, complex identities. This stance was not reserved for self-categorization. A number of students made hedging remarks like "I hate classifying people" or "I don't like generalizing" when talking about social categories. What these teenagers were rejecting was not style itself – the same speakers readily talked about their own and others' stylistic practices and activities – but labeling and categorizing, which many seemed to feel was too confining and judgmental (Widdicombe and Wooffitt 1995). Thus evaluations of social labels as well as the very act of categorization were often contested as teenagers negotiated their own and others' relationships to socially salient categories like preppies, hip hop fans, and nerds.

Preppies

As discussed above, preppies held positions of power within the institutional structure of Bay City High School as student government leaders, staff members of the school newspaper and yearbook, and participants in elite sports on and off campus. However, as mainstream teenagers they were not viewed as trendsetters by other cool youth, for their stylistic practices were relatively conservative. Like other cool teenagers, preppies oriented to popular youth trends, but the styles they embraced were commercialized and often modified versions of styles originally popularized by alternative white youth (e.g., girls' bellbottom pants) or by black teenagers (e.g., boys' chunky athletic shoes). Preppies' social dominance was instead primarily due to their academic and extracurricular accomplishments and hence was mostly restricted to institutional contexts. Despite their high status in these domains, they themselves recognized that other students rivaled them in peer-based forms of prestige.

In Example (2), Mark comments on this apparent paradox. Here he discusses one of the social groups he has labeled in his map of the Park (Figure 3.1b) as the *97 power clique*, a large group of preppy juniors with whom he is friendly:

(2) 1 Mark: In any other school.
2 These people would,
3 <sniff>
4 (0.5)
5 be,
6 totally good looking,
7 and totally popular,
8 just 'cause like,
9 the positions they have?=
10 Mary: =Mhm.=
11 Mark: =But in our school it's like,
12 n:ot like that at a:ll.
13 Mary: ↑Hm.
14 (0.5)
15 Mark: They're like,
16 they're kind of mo:re like,
17 more—
18 not—
19 not really ner:d,
20 but like,
21 (1.0)
22 not like,
23 (1.0)
24 not like,
25 (1.8)
26 they're—
27 like,
28 kind of,
29 keep into their ow:n.

Though a preppy, Mark did not have the same status as the "power clique" members, who collectively held many of the school's student leadership positions. He is thus able to comment on his preppy peers without implicating himself as a member of this social category. In doing so he invokes the "this school is different" ideology that Acme appeals to in example (1) above. This ideology appeared to stem from what students imagined to be a typical high school of the sort represented in popular culture, namely, a majority-white suburban school much like Eckert's Belten High, with a popular crowd that dominates both the school's institutional structure and its peer social order. Mark implies that unlike their counterparts at such schools, preppies at Bay City High are almost entirely lacking in peer prestige, being in his judgment neither popular nor good-looking (lines 1–7). Indeed, in lines 15 through 19 he hesitantly suggests (even as he withdraws the suggestion) that preppy students may be seen as similar to nerds, a category that is antithetical to popularity and one that he himself held in low regard. Despite his explicit rejection of this analogy, the very fact that it can be proposed indicates how far removed Mark considers preppies to be from the social heights of popularity.

Mark's comments also have implications for his own social identity. While lacking the often intense careerist ambition and drive of some preppy students, he participated in preppy style, preppy friendship groups, and preppy extracurricular activities. Yet he distinguishes such students from himself through the use of third-person pronouns and his focus on student leadership rather than other school activities. Hence Mark is able to position himself as an ordinary teenager, remote from the concerns of popularity (and perhaps from the risk of nerdiness).

Bay City High's peer hierarchy is represented rather differently in example (3). The speaker is Rebecca, a white Jewish seventeen-year-old junior. Rebecca was also preppy, but she had recently begun to develop a friendship with some punk teenagers at the school. In this example she first mentions her original preppy group (lines 1–3) and then her newer punk friends (lines 5–10).

(3) 1 Rebecca: They're ↑more of like a:,
2 (1.5)
3 considered more of a preppy crowd.
4 Mary: Oka:y.
5 Rebecca: And then the other people are considered more of like,
6 (1.6)
7 They aren't accepted as much:,
8 at Bay City High and they'r:e,
9 (1.6)
10 they're more punk,=
11 =and they <lower volume> {go to <a local punk club>,
12 and stuff like ↑that.}
13 And so,
14 (0.9)
15 There's a big separation:,
16 ↑a:nd,
17 (1.7)
18 The two groups,
19 they don't dislike each other?
20 But they don't accept each other, . . .

In contrast to Mark's assertion that preppies lack social prestige, Rebecca implies that these teenagers are more "accepted" (line 7) than alternative youth, specifically punks. Although she goes on to state that the lack of acceptance between preppies and punks is mutual (line 20), the scope of her original claim is broader: punks are not accepted at the school as a whole, not just by preppies.

Once again, this example is not only about others' styles but also about the speaker's own identity. As Rebecca moved into a more punk social circle, what was most salient to her was her preppy group's lack of openness to her new friends. The use of the third person to separate oneself from a social category, exemplified in (2) above, is seen here as well. In this case, however, the creation of social distinction is less about aligning or disaligning with a particular category than about critiquing the inflexibility of the stylistic system as a whole. These examples demonstrate that even relatively similar students – such as Mark and Rebecca, who shared the same class year, ethnic identity, and youth style – could view the school's stylistic divisions very differently. At the same time, both speakers signal the problematic nature of social labeling through repeated lengthy pauses, perhaps due to the evaluative stances that often accompany such labels.

Hip hop fans

If the status of preppies vis-à-vis other categories was open to debate, the place of European American hip hop fans within the school's social structure was much more clear. Such teenagers were derided by many white students and youth of color alike due to their perceived transgression of the racialized boundaries between white and black youth styles. Not only did white participants in hip hop listen almost exclusively to rap music and dress in baggy hip hop styles, but they also used African American youth slang that was deemed still too "black" to be available for white use, and they borrowed phonological and grammatical structures from African American Vernacular English.[9] The use of these semiotic forms, especially in combination, was seen by other European American students as an illegitimate claim to the cultural authority and coolness of black youth.

Example (4), featuring Mr. Frisky, illustrates the highly negative evaluation of white hip hop fans' style among other European American youth.

(4)
1 Mr. Frisky: ↑Those guys are r:eally irritating.
2 [$_1$.h $_1$]
3 Mary: [$_1$What$_1$] do you mea:n.
4 Mr. Frisky: I mean,
5 g-
6 ↑white guys?
7 who wa:lk alo:ng,
8 with the who:le,
9 you know,
10 African American style,
11 (of) pulling up one,
12 pant leg?
13 .h::
14 Mary: [$_2$Oh:. $_2$]
15 Mr. Frisky: [$_2$You know?$_2$]

Mary: What does that mea:n?
Mr. Frisky: A-
I d-
I do-
never under[$_3$stood $_3$]=
Mary: [$_3$Yea:h.$_3$]=
Mr. Frisky: =that.=
=I never understood that.
But it,
I:t,
It s:ee:ms to be:,
(0.5)
something that ↑actually l:ooks good,
on African American people,
and when white guys try and do it,
you're just sitting there going,
(0.5)
"Great.
We want to see even ↑more paleness on your <[joʊ]> a:ss.
Just,
w:a:lk o:n."

At the time of the study, the trend of wearing one leg of one's athletic pants pushed up to the knee was popular among African American boys but rare among youth of other races, even participants in hip hop. For a European American teenager to adopt this trend was therefore a strong statement of affiliation with black youth culture, and indeed, only a few white hip hop fans – and no other white youth – did so. Mr. Frisky foregrounds the racialized aspect of this practice, repeatedly emphasizing the incongruity of "white guys" (lines 6, 30) emulating an "African American" practice (lines 10, 29), not entirely successfully (as indicated by his use of *try* in line 30).

Strikingly, Mr. Frisky introduces his evaluation using quoted speech to ventriloquate a subject position that is presented as generic (line 31) but that is voiced using an African American English phonological feature, the pronunciation of *your* with a vocalized (i.e., vowel-like) /r/ (line 34). It is unclear whether his pronunciation is an alignment with black youth or an ironic imitation of white hip hop fans' African American English-influenced speech. In either case, his comments reinforce an ideology of essentialized racial division between black and white styles and a negative evaluation of white participants in African American youth culture.

While European American hip hop fans were sometimes subject to mockery, many were friends with other white teenagers who did not share their style. Even Mr. Frisky counted a white hip hop fan among his friends, despite his disdain for the other boy's stylistic choices. Likewise, in example (5) the speaker, Charlie, a sixteen-year-old European American boy with an alternative, stoner youth style, discusses why he sometimes finds his friend Jay annoying. Jay is also white but affiliates with hip hop (and is something of a jock as well). In this case, the negative evaluation of white hip hop fans is focused not on fashion but on language use.

(5) 1 Charlie: Sometimes he tri:es to act,
2 pretty ghetto.
3 Like,
4 Mary: Hm.
5 Charlie: Ta:lking like,
6 <chips bag rustling>
7 He played on:,
8 this,
9 @<baseball> tea:m,
10 which is like,
11 it's,
12 it's a:ll bla:ck ki:ds,
13 Mary: Hm:.
14 Charlie: a:nd,
15 and then he started like talking like them a:nd,
16 <chips bag rustling>
17 I don't know,
18 <[ʌʔ]>
19 we always,
20 we always clow:n him about it,
21 'cause,
22 it sounds pretty funny.

Charlie's comments invoke the same essentialist racial ideology that Mr. Frisky draws upon in example (4). Charlie suggests that Jay's black-influenced speech is inappropriate for a European American and a failed attempt to align with blackness. In this case, the hip hop fan is positioned as claiming an inner-city, and hence presumably cool and tough, identity (lines 1–2). Charlie underscores the ludicrousness of Jay's speech style: not only does he laugh as he explains the source of Jay's language use (line 9), but he also notes in line 20 that he and his friends "clown" Jay about his speech (*clown* 'tease' is a slang term of African American origin), and he explicitly evaluates Jay's speech style as "pretty funny" (line 22).

Charlie's mocking of Jay, though gentler than Mr. Frisky's ridicule of white hip hop fans, similarly frames the white hip hop style as marked, in implicit contrast to the speaker's own "ordinary" or unmarked self-presentation. Teenagers who adhere to this style are explicitly and negatively evaluated, being represented as striving for but failing to attain the coolness conferred by African American youth culture. Such denaturalization or foregrounding of others' perceived inauthenticity is central to speakers' work of doing "being ordinary" in these examples.

Unlike white hip hop fans, nerds were generally understood (both by themselves and by other students) as not even trying to achieve coolness. This decision located them squarely and undisputedly at the bottom of the school's social hierarchy. It was therefore socially risky to wholeheartedly embrace the label of *nerd*. At the same time, the nerd category also held some appeal for teenagers who valued nerdy practices or did not want to jockey for coolness. This situation required such teenagers to carefully manage their relationship to nerdiness.

Nerds

As I argue at greater length in Chapter 7, nerds are not – as they are popularly figured in cultural representations – socially dysfunctional oddities and outcasts. Instead, nerdiness, like coolness, is a deliberate identity choice, and teenagers at Bay City High who adopted a nerdy identity engaged in a wealth of social practices that allowed them to remove themselves from cool teenagers and the concerns of contemporary youth culture. Yet, like *popular*, the *nerd* label was problematic for many teenagers, even those who participated in nerdy practices.

The ambivalence of self-described nerds toward the *nerd* label is seen in example (6). The data are taken from an interview with Claire and Christine, both white sixteen-year-old juniors. The girls were high-achieving students who, while calling themselves nerdy, also drew on elements of cool styles. When I asked them to explain what they meant by the term *nerd*, their answer reflected a complicated perspective that emerged from their dual identification with nerdiness and coolness:

(6) 1 Christine: ↑Someone who's really smart and cares $[_1$about it$_1]$,=
2 Claire: $[_1$.h: $_1]$=
3 Christine: =and works on it,=
4 =and actually enjo:ys:,
5 learning,
6 and scho$[_2$o:l. $_2]$
7 Claire: $[_2$Yeah. $_2]$
8 (0.7)
9 Christine: I would sa:y.
10 Mary: ↑So it's a ↑positive thing.
11 (0.5)
12 Christine: No.
13 Claire: No.
14 Mary: @!

15 [$_3$@@@ It sou:nds $_3$] [$_4$positive. $_4$]
16 Christine: [$_3$I mean,
17 I: think it's a positive$_3$] [$_4$thi:ng. $_4$]
18 Claire: [$_4$Yeah. $_4$]
19 [$_5$@:: $_5$]
20 Christine: [$_5$Like,
21 like,$_5$]
22 the MIT nerd <creaky voice> {po:wer thing.=
23 =I think that's really [$_6$kind of $_6$] neat,}
24 Mary: [$_6$↑Mm. $_6$]

Christine's description in lines 1 through 6 suggests that nerdy qualities run counter to the norm (as indicated by the evidential marker *actually* in line 4). She frames these qualities in what I as the interviewer take to be a positive way (line 10), but both girls initially deny this positive evaluation of nerdiness (lines 12–13). Only then does Christine acknowledge that she does in fact value nerdiness; her lengthened pronunciation of the first-person pronoun in line 17 implies a contrast with the views of unspecified others. Finally, she mentions those who share her perspective, positively evaluating the Nerd Pride movement at the Massachusetts Institute of Technology (Hafner 1993) as "neat" (lines 20–23).

But the stigmatizing force of the *nerd* label was powerful, and even teenagers who enthusiastically participated in nerdy practices sometimes stopped short of embracing the term. Example (7) is taken from an interview with a group of sixteen- and seventeen-year-old white junior girls who ate lunch together either at the margin of the Park or in a math teacher's classroom. One girl, Fred, had eagerly recruited her group to participate in my study, telling me that she and her friends were especially interesting because they were nerds. However, in (7), when Fred raises the question of which of the available stylistic categories at the school they belong to, she quickly enters into a debate with another girl, Bob, who strongly resists labeling their group as *nerds*. (The two girls' choice of masculine pseudonyms is discussed further in Chapter 7.)

(7) 1 Fred: Like,
2 what would we be?
3 N:o:ne.
4 Bob: ↑Park people.
5 Loden: Yeah,
6 but [$_1$we're not really the$_1$]=
7 Fred: [$_1$Are we really? $_1$]=
8 Loden: = cla:ssic,
9 kind of people that—
10 Bob: [$_2$That's true.
11 (But #—)$_2$]

12 Fred: [$_2$Aren't we—
13 Aren't we usually$_2$]
14 <smiling quality> {i:n Mr. McDermott's room}?
15 Bob: <higher pitch> {Only when it ↑rains.}
16 Fred: Which is like— =
17 Bob: =Well then so are we preppy then?
18 Fred: No:.=
19 =Are we ner:ds?
20 <Bob shakes her head no>
21 Fred: Are you s:ure?
22 <Bob nods her head yes>
23 Fred: [$_3$How come$_3$]=
24 Kate: [$_3$@@ $_3$]=
25 Fred: =you ha@ve (a) four point o@h then?
26 Bob: ↑That doesn't mean I'm a ner:d.

Although Fred initially denies that the girls belong to any category and later appears not to have a particular category in mind, it emerges that she is moving the group toward a specific answer. Following Bob's proposal that they are "↑Park people" (line 4), Fred may already be laying the groundwork for her eventual argument by leading the other girl through a series of Socratic questions designed to challenge her suggestion (*Are we really?*, line 7; *Aren't we— Aren't we usually i:n Mr. McDermott's room?*, lines 12–14). After Bob briefly seizes the role of questioner (line 17: *Well then so are we preppy then?*), Fred quickly turns the tables, latching her own answer with a new question containing the answer she seems to have been aiming for (*No:.=Are we ner:ds?*; lines 18–19). When Bob twice rejects this proposal (lines 20, 22), Fred issues a final prosecutorial question, ensnaring her friend by pointing to Bob's consistently perfect grades, as evaluated on a four-point scale: *How come you ha@ve (a) four point o@h then?* (lines 23, 25). For her part, Bob rejects Fred's view, yielding little ground throughout the debate. This argumentative interactional style was common among these girls, who valued knowing the right answer in any domain and enjoyed matching wits with one another.

The debate rages for another several minutes, with the other girls weighing in. Although the tenor of the interaction is good-natured, it is clear that Bob's position is strongly held, and Fred ultimately yields to her. Fred may have had less difficulty than Bob in viewing herself as a nerd because, as I discuss further in Chapter 5, she was a formerly cool teenager who had deliberately chosen to move into Bob's nerdy group. Fred's relatively solid credentials as a cool teenager allowed her to embrace nerdiness without concern because her identity was so clearly her own choice. In most cases, however, as both examples (6) and (7) show, it was difficult to lay claim to the positive aspects of nerdiness without also seeming to embrace what could be considered the negative associations of a nerdy identity. Thus Bob's rejection of the *nerd* label enabled her to present herself as an ordinary teenager, not a member of a stigmatized category.

European American teenagers' identities were far more complex than the locally available category labels could capture. Through discursive practices of social distinction, they constructed themselves as variously too ordinary or too complicated to be captured within the stylistic system that governed the school's peer culture. Students' interpretations and evaluations of social categories were highly ideological, but they were less rigid than the representations of the school's social space inscribed in their maps, as their narration of the maps often explicitly acknowledged.

Conclusion

Social categories are more than labels; they are ideological bundles of labels, descriptors, activities, stances, and practices that allow for the classification of persons into social types that may then be discursively interpreted and evaluated. In this chapter I have suggested that at Bay City High, two of the most salient categories for organizing the social landscape were race and style. The stylistic categories of preppies, hip hop fans, nerds, and alternative youth occupied distinct positions along the dimensions of mainstream/nonmainstream, cool/uncool, and black-oriented/white-oriented. The symbolic dominance of style as an organizing principle for the peer social order was evident not only in social practice, but also in the ideologies that teenagers espoused about their own and others' social categories as they discussed stylistic labels.

In the next chapter, I examine another lexical resource for identity work: slang. Through white teenagers' use of and talk about slang, European American and African American youth again emerged as both racially and stylistically differentiated groups that were nevertheless closely interconnected.

4 Say word?: race and style in white teenage slang

Introduction

In Bay City High School's elective Say No to Drugs course, students were trained by a team of teachers to become peer educators, writing and performing anti-drug skits at local schools. Some students, however, who were taking the course not out of interest but because it seemed easy, were quite forthright about their own use of drugs, specifically marijuana. As the class prepared to perform before an audience for the first time, several students asked a white middle-aged female teacher, Priscilla, what they should say if audience members wanted to know whether they themselves smoked marijuana. Priscilla recommended that they say they did not, admonishing them, "Remember, you're role models."

This advice elicited a reproving response from Al Capone, a European American junior. "You want us to lie?"

Priscilla hastened to clarify her meaning. "Since you're not coming to school stoned –" she began, but she was interrupted by the students' laughter. "Stoned?" echoed Calvin, an African American sophomore, in a mocking tone.

"What do *you* say?" Priscilla asked.

"I say high," Calvin answered. "Bombed. Blitzed."

"Weeded," interjected Brand One, another white junior.

"Justified," offered Kerry, a white sophomore.

Brand One looked at her in admiring surprise. "That's kind of tight."

As the discussion continued, Brand One remarked that he did not want to lie about his use of marijuana. Priscilla, somewhat exasperated, argued that the students would not be lying: "You won't be doing it during the performance so say, 'I don't do it now,' because you're *not* doing it now."

"I'm not gonna go out of my way to say I get schwamped or something," Brand One replied testily.

It was not unusual for slang to become a discussion topic at Bay City High, as it does here. Prompted by Priscilla's use of the slang term *stoned*, students playfully vie with one another to supply more current words for marijuana intoxication. At the same time, class members evaluate Priscilla's slang use as laughably out of date. Besides proposing and evaluating slang terms, the teenagers use slang interactionally: for example, Brand One uses a positive evaluative term, *tight*, and later uses the innovative slang term *schwamped*. Through their displays of slang connoisseurship as users and observers, the students overtly position themselves as teenagers in contrast to their adult teacher. They also, less overtly, position themselves as teenagers of a particular kind: cool youth who are familiar with the lexicon of drug use. The students in this interaction were of different genders, races, ages, and styles – for instance, Al Capone and Brand One were both hip hop fans, and Kerry had a preppy style – but here they cooperated in a joint construction of youthful trendiness.[1]

This chapter considers how European American teenagers at Bay City High used slang to construct their identities. Slang at times forged a shared youth identity and at other times partitioned students into smaller groupings based on race and style; it was thus central to processes of both adequation and distinction. As a result, the use of particular slang terms by particular speakers could be contentious or socially risky. This situation was further complicated by the fact that much of the slang available to European American students originated among or was popularized by African American teenagers. A very fine line separated slang terms that were uncontroversially available as panracial youth resources from those that were considered racially specific, and young people with different stylistic orientations drew this line in different places. To use (or avoid) slang at Bay City High School was therefore an act fraught with racialized and stylistic as well as age-based semiotic meanings.

In most linguistic scholarship, *slang* is defined as a rapidly changing lexicon associated with casual social contexts and used primarily by youth (e.g., Eble 2004). Nonlinguists, by contrast, often use the term *slang* to refer to nonstandard linguistic varieties – that is, those that have not been institutionally legitimized, such as African American Vernacular English (AAVE). Linguists strongly object to this use because of its inaccuracy, for dialects include phonology and grammar as well as lexicon. To call nonstandard varieties *slang* often signals disregard for their structural complexity and systematicity. Such uses of the term reproduce a language ideology that positions nonstandard varieties of English as inferior to the standard. Thus in lay usage *slang* tends to be a trivializing and insulting label for the speech of less powerful social groups, even as it functions within linguistics as a neutral label for a particular component of language.

Although slang is widely viewed as signaling a generational identity for youth, the most salient social distinction produced through slang is based not on generation but on style. Certainly, slang may serve to construct age-based identities, as seen in the vignette above, but such situations are relatively rare, given that the vast majority of slang use is between peers. Slang is less important for creating a symbolic division between youth and adults (or between youth and younger children who do not yet use current slang) than for differentiating styles. Moreover, what unifies slang users is not necessarily their age but their orientation to coolness. While any use of slang allows speakers to position themselves as cool – a position that is in turn open to endorsement or challenge by others – the use of specific slang terms often creates distinctions based on competing definitions of coolness.

When I began my fieldwork, I had not yet fully realized the importance of slang in the constitution of youth identities, and it was not a focus of my research. In describing my study to Bay City High School students and teachers, however, I soon discovered that most of them assumed that slang would be a central part of my project. In response, I developed a method for investigating slang as part of my larger research goals. During ethnographic interviews, I asked students to discuss the slang terms they used or were familiar with. To facilitate this discussion, I presented them with slips of paper printed with lexical items that I had encountered during my research, including not only slang terms but also words for local social categories and practices. Teenagers' talk about slang was ultimately more than a methodological entrypoint into other issues; it became important in its own right. The elicitation of slang, like the map-making activity described in Chapter 3, was an invaluable source of ideologies – and especially language ideologies – relating to social identities. In addition, I examined slang use in my audio recordings and fieldnotes as well as in student-produced publications like the school's yearbook and weekly newspaper.

These different forms of data reveal the multifunctionality of slang in the discursive construction of identity among students at Bay City High. In the following analysis I examine how the school's racial and stylistic divide organized the use and understanding of slang, and how European American youth negotiated their relationship to lexical resources introduced into the local peer culture by African American students. Various terms popular at the time of my study were differentially racialized in teenagers' language ideologies and were thus available to white students to differing extents. White teenagers' stylistic orientations also shaped their relationship to black youth slang, with some embracing this resource openly and others adopting new terms more slowly or not at all. Slang was therefore a powerful semiotic tool for European American teenagers in forging identities along lines of race and style.

Slang and linguistic ownership

A governing language ideology at Bay City High was a racialized view of linguistic ownership. According to this ideology, which is found in many other settings as well, certain groups have a special claim to particular linguistic resources based on heritage, territoriality, or other criteria (Wee 2002).

Interactionally, linguistic ownership is foregrounded in the humorous imitation of languages, as with Mock Spanish (Hill 2008), and in the closely related phenomenon of language crossing, the outgroup use of ingroup linguistic resources, including slang (Hewitt 1986; Rampton 1995; Reyes 2005). In both of these practices, linguistic forms and even entire varieties are appropriated across social boundaries. Such an act can be either an authenticating move that stakes the speaker's claim to ingroup membership or a denaturalizing move that highlights the gap between the speaker's apparent alignment with the ingroup and her or his actual outgroup affiliation. Hence linguistic ownership is closely intertwined with identity.

European American students at Bay City High School confronted issues of linguistic ownership almost every time they adopted a new slang term, for most innovative slang came from African American youth culture. The wide dissemination of black cultural forms from jazz to hip hop, especially via the media, has led African American slang to have considerable national and global influence (Alim *et al.* 2008; Lee 1999). The cross-racial appropriation of black youth slang at Bay City High School therefore exemplified a much broader phenomenon.

Lexical items move with relative ease across linguistic borders and may not be perceived as the cultural property of a particular group after borrowing. In fact, at Bay City High European American teenagers were often unaware of the linguistic origins of a given slang term even a short time after it had been borrowed from their African American peers. Before and during the borrowing process, however, issues of linguistic ownership were paramount, as young people negotiated the boundaries between ingroup and outgroup language use.

The question of linguistic ownership at Bay City High is illustrated by the status of three different slang terms of African American origin – *hella*, *patna*, and *nigga* – documented in my fieldnotes and audio recordings as well as in published personal messages in the Bay City High School yearbook. The yearbook is a rich source of slang data, for it was produced by students with very little adult oversight; the only restriction on lexical choice was that profanity not be used.[2] All yearbook examples below were composed by graduating seniors as part of paid personal messages to friends, family, and (occasionally) enemies. The messages often address particular individuals by name and contain ingroup linguistic features such as initials and nicknames as well as numerous markers of youth language. In addition to slang, these markers include expletives (slightly bowdlerized due to the prohibition against them: e.g., *sht* for *shit* in example (2a) below) and feature deliberate nonstandard spelling and writing conventions reminiscent of graffiti, rap lyrics, and other vernacular and youth-centered forms of literacy (cf. Androutsopoulos 2000; Morgan 2001; Olivo 2001; Sebba 2003). Among such innovations are the use of *2* for *to* and *4* for *for* (e.g., *4get* for *forget* in example (3f) below) and the spelling of *-er* forms with *-a* to signal an African American English pronunciation (e.g., *sista* for *sister* in example (2g)).

Hella *as a panracial resource*

Widespread slang terms unite those who use them around a shared identity based not simply on age or style but more crucially on coolness. In the San Francisco Bay Area, one such word is *hella*, a quantifier and intensifier that has been grammaticalized from *hell of*, with which it occasionally alternates (example 1a). In its intensifer function, it is parallel to similar adverbial slang terms used elsewhere in the United States such as *wicked* and *mad*. *Hella*, together with its G-rated counterpart *hecka* (example 1b), is widely used by Bay Area youth. The examples in (1) and (2) illustrate the term's use by a variety of students in spoken and written discourse, respectively.

(1) *Hella* and variants in fieldnotes and ethnographic interviews
- (a) If we're gonna get back *hell of* late, then I'm just going home. (Al Capone, European American boy, fieldnotes)
- (b) It's *hecka* kids though. (Kendra, African American girl, fieldnotes)
- (c) I went to *hella* meetings. (Josie, European American girl, interview)
- (d) <Those are> *Hella* good drawings. (G.C., African American boy, fieldnotes)
- (e) I'd be *hella* trippin'. (Nikki, Asian American girl, fieldnotes)
- (f) And she goes, "Damn! You're h<u>e</u>lla smart." (Claire, European American girl, interview)

(2) *Hella* in yearbook messages
- (a) Yeah webn through *hella* sht 2getha. (Asian American girl)
- (b) Keep on drawing cause you can do it *hella* good. (Asian American boy)
- (c) IF I FORGOT YOUR NAME, ITS BECAUSE IM *HELLA* KEYED. (Asian American/European American boy)
- (d) I love ya'll *hella* tite. (African American girl)
- (e) I wont to say I had a *hella* fun time Playing with every one from the football team. (African American boy)
- (f) this year was *hella* fun! (Latina girl)
- (g) my big sista, known you for *hella* years, you were always there for me. (European American girl)
- (h) haven't seen ya for *hella* long (European American boy)

These examples indicate that teenagers of various ethnoracial categories and both genders use *hella*.[3] But the term is more than a generational marker; as slang it also signals an orientation to coolness, which is strengthened through the word's co-occurrence with other slang terms (e.g., *trippin*' 'extremely upset' in example (1e); *keyed* 'drunk' in example (2c)). *Hella* also occurs with non-standard grammar. In spoken discourse, such grammatical forms may be part of the speaker's ordinary vernacular (e.g., the AAVE existential construction *It's hecka kids though* in example (1b) versus colloquial Standard English *There's/There are hecka kids though*). Nonstandard grammar is also found in the yearbook messages (e.g., *webn* or *we been*, example (2a); *you can do it hella good*, example (2b)). Here nonstandard features appear to be used deliberately as part of a projected casual stance, given that by their senior year even nonstandard English speakers at the school were functionally bidialectal in the written standard (in fact, the authors of the messages in examples (2a) and (2b) grew up in Standard English-speaking homes). The association of *hella* with coolness meant that nerdy teenagers tended not to use it, instead favoring *really*, currently the most common intensifier among youth, or *very*, a form found primarily among adults (Tagliamonte 2008). In the speech of teenagers, *very* is often associated with a more formal or educated – hence nerdy – register. The only example of a nerdy student using *hella* in my data is example (1f), in which Claire scornfully quotes another student in her biology class who was impressed by Claire's academic abilities. Here the use of *hella*, which is given emphatic stress and is coupled with a "dopey" voice quality throughout the quotation, seems to underscore the stupidity of Claire's classmate rather than indexing Claire's own coolness.

Hella is a very stable regional lexical marker, apparently having been in use in the Bay Area for the past thirty years, although it has been little documented in the scholarly literature and in most print slang dictionaries (see, e.g., Waksler 2000). Despite its longevity, the term has not moved far from its locus of origin in the San Francisco Bay Area, with only isolated use outside of the region. At the time of the study, *hella* was largely restricted to Northern California, especially the Bay Area; more recently it has enjoyed a wider circulation, thanks to its occasional use in popular music, television shows, and films aimed at a youth audience. Beyond California it is generally a faddish, trendy term that peaks in use and then quickly disappears, in contrast to its enduring use as a feature of Northern California youth speech (see also Bucholtz *et al.* 2007). Within this region it has spread dramatically across social groups: from its probable origins among African American speakers, it has come to be used by cool young people of varied ethnoracial backgrounds and styles.

Patna *and* nigga *as racialized affiliative terms*

Other slang items served to differentiate rather than unify youth at Bay City High, particularly along the ideological black–white dichotomy. At the time of my study one such term was *patna*, derived from the African American English pronunciation of *partner*, in which postvocalic /r/ is vocalized – that is, after a vowel /r/ is also pronounced in a vowel-like way. As slang, *patna* is an affiliative term meaning 'close friend,' as illustrated by example (3):

(3) *Patna* in yearbook messages[4]

(a) PEACE to my *patnas* from the South. (African American boy)
(b) I only had a few true *patnas* through the High and they know who they are (African American girl)
(c) I just wanted to tell my *pantna'* MEL R.I.P. and we will always love you (African American boy)
(d) and thanx 2 my *patnas* that just never went janky <a negative evaluative adjective> on me (African American girl)
(e) all my *patnas* in 97 . . . I'll miss ya. (African American girl)
(f) neva 4get my *patna* RIP Mel (African American girl)

While students of all races and ethnicities could use this term in some contexts to refer to their friends, it was primarily used by African Americans. Of the twenty-five tokens of *patna* (and its variants) that I was able to identify in the school yearbook, seventeen or 68 percent were produced by African American students. But European American students – who by senior year constituted a larger percentage of their cohort than African Americans (see Table 2.2 in Chapter 2) – produced only five of the twenty-five tokens. Thus the term was not entirely off limits to European American students, but it was relatively uncommon in their speech. *Patna* was strongly associated with African American teenagers because of its frequent use by black speakers as well as its African American English phonology. White teenagers who had begun to adopt the word did so fully aware of these associations.

The case of *patna* shows that in some instances phonology may be crucially important in slang. Among European American youth in California and elsewhere, a vocalized pronunciation or spelling of a form that is rhotic (i.e., /r/-colored) in the standard language often indicates that the word is being treated as slang. With regard to *patna*, the consistent spelling of the final nucleus as *a* rather than *er* in the examples in (3) above suggests that this pronunciation is an obligatory element of the term. By comparison, the spelling of less semiotically potent lexical items, such as *never*, alternates between standard and nonstandard spellings (e.g., *never* in example (3d) versus *neva* in example (3f); see also Childs and Mallinson 2006).

This link between lexicon and phonology occurs with numerous African American slang terms. The most notorious such word, *nigga*, likewise has a frequently affiliative function. The difference between this form and the highly offensive word *nigger* is far more than a matter of pronunciation (Kennedy 2002; Spears 1998; Williams 2004). Hence one black girl at Bay City High could ask another in outraged incredulity, "She called you a nigger?" using the rhotic pronunciation to indicate the seriousness of the offense as a racist insult. With the vocalized pronunciation, however, as reflected in the spelling *nigga*, among some African Americans the term is largely devoid of racist force and functions instead as a more or less neutral term for a male referent with no necessary racial associations (Alim 2004b; Spears 1998); in this use, it is roughly equivalent to *guy* or *dude*. Like the latter word, *nigga* may serve not only as a reference term but also as an affiliative address term, particularly between males (cf. Kiesling 2004). *Nigga* was widely used in both ways by black boys at Bay City High School. However, the long history of European Americans' use of *nigger*, regardless of pronunciation, as a racist insult against African Americans meant that it was extremely risky for white youth to use even the nonrhotic form to refer to or address African Americans – or, for that matter, European Americans. Conversely, given the strongly ingroup, affiliative associations of *nigga* as an address term, it was extremely rare for African Americans to use it in this way toward European American teenagers. However, black youth occasionally used the word race-neutrally for a white referent, particularly in the plural (e.g., *those niggas*, referring to a group of white businessmen in a class video).

At least in public settings such as classrooms, some European American hip hop fans used *blood*, another affiliative African American address term primarily used between males, rather than *nigga*. In its original use, *blood* positions the speaker and addressee as sharing a physically essentialized link such as familial or ethnoracial background (i.e., the two "share the same blood" or are biologically related; the African American-origin affiliative address terms *brother* and *sister* draw on a similar metaphor). Given these associations, *blood* is a strongly ingroup term, but unlike *nigga/nigger*, it lacks a history of racist use, and its adoption by white youth is therefore less problematic. Nevertheless, at Bay City High School *blood* was strongly racialized as black, and so barriers remained to its use by European American speakers. Although some white hip hop fans addressed both black and white boys as *blood*, black students did not generally address their European American peers in this way, instead using the more racially neutral affiliative term *man*.

In light of its history and potential offensiveness, few students of any race used *nigga* in their yearbook messages. It is noteworthy, then, that two European American students, both with alternative styles, did so (example 4):

(4) European American students' use of *nigga* in yearbook messages
  (a) Let's not stop puffin fat chronic tgthr *nigas*. (European American boy)
  (b) 9th <grade> was high season 10th <grade> was cut class and f**ked with that dope feen azz *nigga* Santo! (European American girl)

In both examples, the term is used to address or refer to other white youth, and in each case it operates in a neutral or affiliative way rather than with apparent racist intent. Yet any outgroup use of *nigga* by European Americans was highly taboo. It may be significant in this regard that both teenagers had alternative styles; hip hop fans, who might be expected to use the word more than other white youth, were keenly aware of the problems associated with its cross-racial appropriation and hence did not use the term publicly.

The teenagers in example (4) seem to associate *nigga* not with a specific racial category but with a specific stance: a laid-back attitude that is indifferent to mainstream concerns. In doing so, however, they run the risk of perpetuating racial stereotypes. The above examples focus on drug use (*fat chronic* 'excellent marijuana'; *dope feen azz* [*dope fiend ass*, i.e., 'drug addict' + intensifier *-ass*]) and the violation of school rules. The use of a strongly racialized term in such contexts suggests an ideological link between blackness and rebellious or illegal practices. Thus even as these alternative white teenagers challenge the ideology of linguistic ownership by laying claim to *nigga*, their use of the word reproduces entrenched racial ideologies. To be sure, the examples project the use of *nigga* as part of a persona that these teenagers clearly value and seek to emulate. Yet the projection of even a positively valued persona by such means unwittingly draws on negative racial stereotypes.

African American Vernacular English as European American youth slang

The preceding examples suggest that slang, especially for European American youth, is not located entirely in the lexical realm but can also extend to phonology. Similarly, AAVE grammar was sometimes reinterpreted as slang by white students at Bay City High:

(5) Look yall, school maybe wacandtedious but there be ways 2 us <i.e., use> it 2 your Advantage! (European American boy)

This boy, who had social ties to some African American students at Bay City High, uses several apparent elements of AAVE, most notably the highly recognizable invariant *be* form, a verbal aspect marker of habitual actions or states. Given the earnestness of his message, the author does not appear to be using AAVE mockingly (cf. Ronkin and Karn 1999), and his use of *yall* (i.e., 'you all'), a second-person plural pronoun that is rare among white speakers in the Bay Area but common in African American English in California and elsewhere, may be designed for an audience that is at least partly black. However, the use of *be* in a nonhabitual context to express existence is not a possible grammatical function of the form in AAVE. This use, especially in conjunction with the author's use of slang (the negative evaluative adjective *wac*, usually spelled *wack*) and innovative orthography (*2* for *to*), suggests that *be* was selected for stylistic rather than syntactic reasons. That is, it is used as slang, not grammar. Notwithstanding the author's apparently well-meaning use of an AAVE form in this instance, it contributes to the widespread language ideology of AAVE as no more than "slang."

Even European American students who had little affiliation with African American youth culture and relatively little interaction with their black peers adopted some elements of AAVE that they treated as slang. When Vince, a preppy white boy who was the editor of the school newspaper, asked Brenda, a European

American girl whose primary friendship group was with African Americans, for her assigned newspaper article, she replied (in her usual AAVE-influenced speech style), "I'll get it out the car." Vince mocked her in response: "Out the car? Out *of* the car." Yet a month later, he used the same structure, apparently unironically, to clear a space in a crowd of students: "Get out the way."

European American teenagers' appropriation of slang terms of African American origin was ideologically saturated. Sometimes the terms were used in contexts that invoked racially stereotypical scenarios, while in other cases structural elements of AAVE were reinterpreted as slang, thus unintentionally perpetuating negative language ideologies regarding the variety. White teenagers of different stylistic affiliations staked out different positions regarding the question of linguistic ownership in their talk about and use of black youth slang.

White styles and black slang

The various stances that European American youth took toward slang of African American origin positioned them within the stylistic matrix of Bay City High School. Through both metalinguistic commentary and linguistic practice, white teenagers' orientations toward African American slang aligned them with particular youth styles. Hip hop fans openly adopted slang terms that had currency among African American youth and strong indexical associations with blackness, while preppies took up such terms relatively later and more covertly, once these associations had become deracialized. For their part, nerds professed little or no knowledge of or interest in slang, including slang of African American origin, although they often knew more than they claimed. These styles thus represented three disparate positions toward African American linguistic resources.

White hip hop fans and the appropriation of black youth slang

One of the primary factors mediating transmission of slang across racialized boundaries was stylistic affiliation. Preppy white teenagers encountered black linguistic forms mainly indirectly, through interaction with European American students who had African American social ties, as well as directly through interaction with a handful of African Americans in their classes or extracurricular activities. Meanwhile, those who had a strong affiliation with hip hop, and to a lesser extent some alternative teenagers, constructed their stylistic identities by learning black youth slang from African American friends and acquaintances and from popular culture and then incorporating it into their everyday speech (cf. Hewitt 1986). To examine the relationship of style to slang, it is useful to look at the definitions of slang terms that students provided, not as a guide to the meaning of the word being defined but for the use of other slang terms in the definition. Through such definitions, speakers laid claim to particular forms as part of their ordinary vocabulary.

For example, European American hip hop fans more than other white teenagers drew heavily on the racialized term *patna* as part of their production of a cool urban youth identity. The data in (6) are taken from one such student, Jay, and his friend Charlie; both boys were white sophomores, aged fifteen and sixteen respectively. Charlie was not a hip hop fan and did not use African American slang terms to the same extent that Jay did, although as a teenager with a stoner style he did use some such forms. The example takes place as the boys discuss slang terms printed on slips of paper.

The association of *patna* with African American English is suggested in (6a), where Jay, seeing the word written in Standard English spelling as *partner*, uses marked pronunciation and prosody to emphasize the oddity of the orthography.

(6a) 1 Jay: <high-pitched, nasal, rapid> {Partner:! <['pʰɑɹʔnəɹː]>
2 What's up,
3 partner:? <['pɑɹnəɹː]>}
4 @
5 (1.3)
6 <nasal> {Hello:.}
7 ↑@

Jay repeatedly uses prosodic lengthening of the final [ɹ] of *partner* to call attention to the nonslang spelling on the slip of paper on which the word is printed; in fact, he went on to correct the form to *patna* with a pen. That Jay considers the standard spelling and hence pronunciation of this term not simply wrong but uncool is indicated by his use of a nasal voice quality, a popular linguistic stereotype of nerdiness. The emphasized final [ɹ] creates an implicit indexical link between nerdiness and an exaggerated version of whiteness, in contrast to the African American English-influenced cool pronunciation ['pʰɑːʔnə].

Many white teenagers knew the meaning of *patna*, but it was primarily participants in hip hop who used this term in their own speech. In (6b) and (6c), Jay uses the word to define two other slang terms of African American origin: *kick it* 'spend time, hang out' and *blood*. In both cases he uses the requisite vocalized pronunciation along with other linguistic forms that authenticate his language use and thus signal his stylistic affiliation with African American youth culture. (Example (6a) occurs after (6b) and before (6c).)

(6b) 1 Jay: Kick it,
2 that just means to (like),
3 chi:ll,
4 with your patna,
5 you know?
6 (0.6)
7 Just do nothing,
8 watch some TV:,

(6c) 1 Jay: Bloo:d.
2 I don't know,
3 sometimes it slips out.
4 (0.9)
5 For me:,
6 I say it $[_1$a lo:t. $_1]$
7 Charlie: $[_1$Yea:h,
8 me too. $_1]$
9 (0.6)
10 Jay: <creaky voice> {Just like,
11 "Shut the fuck ↑up,
12 bloo:d."}
13 (0.5)
14 Charlie: $[_2$Yeah,
15 "Bloo:d,
16 what the fuck$_2]$ (have you: been)?"
17 Mary: $[_2$How d-
18 What's it mea:n? $_2]$
19 (0.5)
20 Jay: We:ll,
21 just—
22 Mary: Like,
23 per:son?=
24 Charlie: =Ma:n,
25 du:de,
26 (0.5)
27 <creaky voice, lower volume> {A:ll tha:t shi:t.}
28 Jay: <creaky voice> {Yea:h.
29 Just like,
30 patna.}

In (6c) Jay's characterization of his own use of the word *blood* makes clear that it is ideologically off limits to him: his assertion that the term "slips out" in his speech (line 3) suggests that to use it is some sort of faux pas, even as it implies that the word is so much a part of his authentic speech style that he uses it without thinking. In this ethnographic context, it is obvious to all the participants (including me) that the barrier to Jay's free use of the word is a racial one. Despite the language ideology that sanctions such cross-racial linguistic appropriations, both he and Charlie go on to state that they often use *blood*.

The two boys define the slang term *blood* rather differently. Charlie, who unlike Jay did not listen to rap music or dress in black-pioneered styles, uses the racially neutral terms *man* and *dude* (lines 24–25) while Jay proposes the synonym *patna* (line 30), which, like *blood* itself, is strongly associated with African American speakers. Thus Jay makes an identity claim through his choice of synonym that Charlie does not. In not only talking knowledgeably about African American linguistic resources but also competently using them, Jay constructs his stylistic identity as a hip hop fan. This stylistic positioning is coupled with more general elements of coolness like creaky voice (Bucholtz 2009b: 158; Mendoza-Denton 1997) in Jay's turns beginning in lines 10 and 28, a resource that Charlie uses as well (line 27).

As with *nigga* in example (4) above, these white teenagers' use of *blood* reproduces racialized language ideologies. Their illustrative utterances collocate *blood* with the intensifier *the fuck* (lines 11, 16) and take confrontational stances toward an unspecified addressee. Given that *blood* was a recognizably black term at Bay City High, such aggressive stances become indexically linked not only to the term itself but also to its prototypical users, African Americans. Through such representations, slang terms of black origin may become ideologically associated with a deeply problematic racially stereotypical persona: the violent or dangerous African American youth.

This same recognition of racialized boundaries and similar representations of stereotypical blackness were also found in white preppy teenagers' talk about slang of African American origin. As with the previous examples, such representations focused on qualities like aggression and criminality. But where European American youth with alternative and hip hop styles aligned themselves with these qualities and used black youth slang to display similar stances and personas, preppy teenagers distanced themselves from their imagined version of black youth culture, even as they adopted some of its linguistic resources.

Redefining and deracializing slang among preppy youth

The racialized and stylistic divisions at Bay City High School were evident in the definitions of slang terms that teenagers provided during ethnographic interviews. Mainstream and especially preppy European American students often offered definitions for slang terms of African American origin that revealed their lack of engagement with black youth culture. In some cases, these white teenagers reported using a term but provided a definition that did not correspond to black students' use of the word. In other cases, rather than acknowledge that they did not know the meaning of a particular word, mainstream white teenagers attempted to explicate unfamiliar slang terms associated with black youth by inventing their own definitions. This phenomenon may be partly attributable to the context in which these interactions occurred. As an adult researcher inquiring about slang, I positioned myself as a naïve outsider and my study participants as experts in youth language. Under such circumstances, it would have been difficult for them to display a lack of knowledge of individual slang terms, and due to my own presumed ignorance, they might have felt free to claim more knowledge than they in fact had. Yet, as I discuss later in this chapter, some white interviewees, specifically nerdy teenagers, readily acknowledged their ignorance of current slang as a way of separating themselves from the trendy coolness that other youth pursued.

In attempting to define slang terms, white mainstream teenagers relied on two resources, homophony and folk etymologies, that allowed them to position themselves as knowledgeable about current slang even when they were not. When presented with a slang term that had one or more homophones (i.e., words that are pronounced identically but have different meanings and sometimes different spellings), students could display knowledge of one of its meanings while overlooking alternative senses. For example, *punk*, which a number of African American students used to refer to a weak or cowardly person, or (rarely) as a derogatory term for a gay male, was understood by many mainstream European Americans as referring to the overwhelmingly white youth culture of punk rock. Likewise, *folk(s)*, a collective term for one's friends among African Americans, was defined as a type of music by mainstream European Americans or, in the plural, as an outdated term for one's parents. Similarly, *crew*, another African American term for a friendship group, was taken by a number of mainstream European American youth to refer to the preppy rowing sport; and *jock*, which numerous black speakers used as a verb meaning 'hit on' or 'flirt,' was taken as a noun meaning 'preppy athlete' by most mainstream white students.

The second strategy that mainstream teenagers used to define slang terms, folk etymology, enabled them to propose a more or less plausible but incorrect account of the origin of an unfamiliar word based on its perceived similarity to more familiar words. For example, *notch*, a term used by many African American students to refer to an attractive person of either gender, deriving from *top-notch*, was thought by a number of mainstream European American students to be a term for a sexual conquest, based on a folk etymology from *a notch on one's belt*. Example (7) illustrates this definition as provided by Josie in an interview with her friend Zoe. Both girls were white seventeen-year-old juniors with preppy styles.

(7) 1 Josie: No:tch:?
2 I suppose it has sexual connotations,
3 but I:,
4 <creaky voice> {don't,
5 really use it,
6 so.}
7 Do you use it?=
8 Zoe: =I've n:ever heard of it,
9 at a:ll.=
10 Josie: =(Well I only/Probably on a) like,
11 a n:otch,

12 on your b:elt,
13 is like,
14 .h
15 <smiling quality> {like,=
16 =how many people you've ki:lled,
17 or how many people you've sle:pt with,
18 or,}
19 Zoe: ↑Wh(h)oa!
20 O↑kay!
21 Josie: Isn't that ↑true?
22 Mary: Well the w-
23 <higher pitch> {That's what I: thought?}
24 it first meant?=
25 =But,
26 it—
27 the peop-
28 w:ay people describe it is like,
29 top notch,
30 like somebody who's really good loo:king?
31 Zoe: [O:h,
32 I see:.]
33 Josie: [O::h!]

Josie initially evinces some uncertainty about the meaning of *notch* (*I suppose*, line 2), and Zoe disavows any knowledge of the term (lines 8–9). Yet in spite of her doubt about the word's meaning, Josie forges ahead with an explanation encompassing both sexual promiscuity and murder. It is only after Zoe's shocked response to her friend's proposed definition (line 19) that Josie defers to me in line 21 as having greater expertise regarding this word. I align with her original definition (lines 23–24) before going on to explain how "people describe it" (line 28).

A number of white teenagers besides Josie associated *notch* with unsavory activities. Given that this term was used almost exclusively by African Americans, by proposing such interpretations while distancing themselves from the word, mainstream European American youth implicitly separated themselves from their black peers who supposedly engaged in these activities. At the same time, these students were able to display their knowledge of slang and thus maintain their claim to coolness.

Notch was one of numerous slang terms originating among African American youth that was subjected to folk etymologizing. For example, *Watch your back*, which could serve either as a warning to an antagonist or as a characterization of how friends look out for one another, was taken to mean *Watch your backpack* by Josie and Zoe, who went on to tell me a series of stories about actual or potential thefts from backpacks (Chapter 9). A similar phenomenon occurred when I asked various teenagers about the meaning of the slang expression *Break yourself* as part of a legal case for which I was a pro bono consultant. The public defender with whom I was working hoped to find possible meanings for the phrase other than as the initiating speech act of a mugging, the crime of which her client was accused. I therefore surveyed a number of students for their definitions of the expression. Three European American hip hop fans defined it variously as “Give me all your money” (Al Capone), “Give me all your valuables” (Billy), and “Give me your wallet. Or anything valuable” (Brand One). The phrase was similarly defined by George, an African American boy, and by Brandy, an African American girl. But Erin, a European American girl with a “normal” style, offered the definition “Don’t stress,” perhaps on the model of phrases like *Pace yourself* and *Take a break*. By offering this folk etymology, Erin may have sought to obscure her unfamiliarity with the expression, but in fact she underscored her lack of knowledge.[5]

Although mainstream youth did not necessarily know the meaning of new African American slang terms, they eventually adopted many of them. Crucially, they did so in earnest only after such terms had lost their associations with black teenagers through deracialization. In the deracialization process, slang of black origin initially circulated among white teenagers via stylized mock language performances in which speakers denaturalized their claims to the language they used (Coupland 2001). As with *patna* and *nigga*, these lexical items often came bundled in semiotic packages with phonological or grammatical features of African American English. Such features were tied to individual lexical items and were not treated as productive processes that applied to nonslang linguistic forms as well.

The examples in (8) come from a discussion of slang during my ethnographic interview with Mark, a preppy white Jewish boy. In example (8a) he discusses two lexical items of African American origin, *instigate* ‘initiate a conflict, especially through gossip’ (Goodwin 1990) and *represent* ‘display pride in one’s group’:

```
(8a)  1 Mark:  Instiga:te.
      2        (1.0)
      3        All right.
      4        I—
      5        U:m:.=
      6             =I: use that.
      7        (0.5)
      8        P-
      9        Only when I'm,
     10        (0.8)
     11        m-
     12        m:o:cking.
```

13 (1.7)
14 Mary: In what sense?=
15 Mark: =Only when I'm mocking,
16 um:,
17 like,
18 ghetto s::peak,
19 I guess.
20 Mary: ↑Hm:.
21 Like=
22 Mark: =Like,
23 "Why you trying to instigate this?"
24 or something like that.
25 Mary: [$_1$Oh. $_1$]
26 Mark: [$_1$It's main$_1$]ly used in like f:ighting,
27 and like,
28 (0.8)
29 Mary: So you would just do that,
30 as a joke?
31 Mark: <coughs>
32 Yeah.=
33 Mary: =Okay.=
34 Mark: =Represe:nt, <[ɹɛpɹə'zɛ̃ːnʔt]>
35 same thi:ng.
36 "We gotta represent. <[ɹɛpɹə'zĩnʔ]>=
37 =Fu-"
38 like,=
39 =l:ike,
40 (1.0)
41 Like if I'm like at—
42 (0.6)
43 <lip smack> at something with like a bunch of white people,=
44 =I'll be like,
45 <higher pitch, lower volume> "Represent! <[ɹɛpɹə'zĩːnʔ]>
46 <deeper pitch, exaggerated "shout-out" prosody> {Sou:th↑si::de!"}
47 or something like [$_2$that.=
48 =Just$_2$] to like,
49 Mary: [$_2$Mhm:. $_2$]
50 Mark: just to like <smiling quality> {mess arou::nd.}
51 (1.3)
52 But this are—
53 these are bo:th,
54 (2.3)
55 words I use,
56 in,
57 (0.5)
58 je:s:t.

As Mark notes, his use of such terms is "mocking" (lines 12, 15) and "in jest" (lines 56–58). In response to my question for clarification, he specifies that the target of his mockery is "ghetto s::peak" (line 18) – a negative term for AAVE. He goes on to note that he engages in this practice only among "white people" (line 43), when he jokingly "represents" the largely white region of south Bay City. Certainly, for a European American teenager to use mock AAVE in the presence of African American students would be extremely risky. His report thus also creates a racialized affiliation with me, as the white interviewer.

Mark's performances of African American language involve not only lexicon but also grammar, segmental phonology, and prosody. In line 23, for example, he illustrates his use of *instigate* with a zero copula form (i.e., the omission of all forms of *to be*). In addition, in lines 36 and 45 he raises the [ɛ̃] next to the nasal [n] in *represent* to an [ĩ], a characteristic of African American English phonology (by contrast, he uses an [ɛ̃] in his ordinary pronunciation in line 34). Finally, in line 46 he lowers his pitch and increases his volume, in an apparent imitation of a rallying cry used by many African American boys at Bay City High in contexts like sporting events. Mark's understanding of the grammar of these terms, however, is imperfect. In AAVE, both words are intransitive verbs rather than transitive verbs as in most other varieties of English. Mark correctly uses *represent* intransitively in line 36, but his example sentence using *instigate* in line 23 incorrectly includes an object, *this*. His stylized linguistic performances highlight racial divisions by highlighting linguistic divisions, both intentionally and unintentionally.

Only after words of African American origin become racially unmarked through repeated use do they cease to be resources for mockery. In (8b), which occurs about five minutes later, Mark discusses a widespread slang term, *tight*, a positive evaluative adjective that is somewhat similar to *cool* in meaning but is restricted to modifying only inanimate nouns.

(8b) 1 Mark: Tight.
2 I use this:.
3 (1.2)
4 D-
5 I just u:se it.
6 (0.5)
7 But like,
8 it's a-
9 a remnant,
10 of making fun of,
11 Mary: Mm.
12 Mark: [$_1$thi:ngs. $_1$]
13 Mary: [$_1$But you $_1$] just started,
14 (0.7)

15 using it,
16 for:,=
17 Mark: =Yeah,
18 "A:w,
19 Mary: [$_2$(serious)?$_2$]
20 Mark: [$_2$this is $_2$] ↑tight."=
21 =Just like use it.
22 But like it is:,
23 .h::
24 more of a,
25 (0.9)
26 <blows out softly>
27 African Ame:rican word.
28 Mary: (O[$_3$kay.)$_3$]
29 Mark: [$_3$Phe$_3$]nomenon.

Here Mark shows a striking degree of awareness of the cross-racial borrowing process, acknowledging both the African American origins of *tight* and his own changed stance toward the term. He observes that he "just u:se[s] it" (line 5), a formulation that seems to imply that it is part of his ordinary speech style, but he also notes that *tight* is "a remnant, of making fun of, thi:ngs" (lines 9–12). The precise nature of the "things" that are the object of Mark's former mockery are not specified until quite late in his remarks, when he adds, "it is:, . . . more of a, . . . African Ame:rican word" (lines 22–27). (This discursive practice of delaying the naming of blackness was common in white teenagers' talk about race; see Chapter 8.)

While Mark was remarkably aware of the origins of many of the slang terms in his vocabulary, which he had appropriated only recently or was still in the process of adopting, preppy white teenagers often did not recognize the African American source of much of their slang. The deracialization process that Mark acknowledges above faded into the background as cool mainstream white youth claimed black slang as their own.

White nerds and the rejection of slang

Unlike preppies, white nerds tended to shun current slang primarily because of its associations with coolness and trendiness, not because it originated among African American teenagers. When I asked nerdy youth to discuss specific slang terms, a task that other students usually found the most enjoyable part of our interview, most expressed dismay and professed unfamiliarity with the words; this was one of the rare instances when nerds, who greatly prized intelligence and knowledge, were willing to admit ignorance. As Fred, a nerdy junior girl, confessed as she and her friends struggled to define the slang terms I presented to them, “We’re not very good at this.”

Nerdy youth distanced themselves from slang in various ways, such as providing literal, nonslang definitions (example 9) or offering nonslang terms that conveyed the same meaning as the words under discussion (example 10). Through such practices students simultaneously positioned themselves as knowledgeable yet disinterested in coolness, thus balancing two potentially competing values of nerdiness. In (9), Bob announces to her friends the slang term, *blood*, printed on the slip of paper she has selected:

(9) 1 Bob: Bloo::d. <[blʊ::d]>
2 Kate: @@@[$_1$@ $_1$]
3 Bob: [$_1$↑B $_1$] L:,
4 Fred: [$_2$@:@ $_2$]
5 Bob: [$_2$O O,
6 D.$_2$]
7 Kate: @[$_3$@@$_3$]
8 Mary: [$_3$@: $_3$] [$_4$@@ $_4$]
9 Loden: [$_4$Hurr ↑a::y.$_4$]
10 Bob: [$_4$The word is$_4$] bloo:d. <[blʌ:d]>
11 Kate: @@@@
<7 lines omitted>
19 Mary: What does it,
20 [$_5$mea:n,
21 do you— $_5$]
22 Bob: [$_5$That’s the stuff: which$_5$] [$_6$is inside of your$_6$] vei:ns,
23 Fred: [$_6$Just b:loo:d. $_6$]
24 It doesn’t me[$_7$an,
25 li$_7$]][$_8$ke, $_8$]
26 Bob: [$_7$or some$_7$][$_8$thing.$_8$]
27 Kate: [$_8$@ $_8$]@@[$_9$@ $_9$]
28 Fred: [$_9$like,$_9$]
29 Loden: [$_9$@@$_9$]
30 Bob: I don’t know.
31 [$_{10}$I haven’t gotten to that cha$_{10}$]pter yet.
32 Fred: [$_{10}$brother or whatever,
33 you know.$_{10}$]

Bob turns the task of defining slang terms into a quasi-academic and hence prized nerdy activity by humorously invoking the discourse format of a spelling bee: state the word, spell it, restate it. This academic orientation continues in her literal definition of the term, which she casts in a more formal register through the use of the relative pronoun *which* (line 22), in contrast to cool teenagers who couched their use of slang in highly colloquial language, including nonstandard forms and profanity. Bob's allusion to one of her textbooks where the answer can be found likewise conjures up an academic domain. Through such strategies Bob repeatedly distances herself from slang. But she also distances herself from the origins of the term among African American youth. She first utters the word *blood* with stylized African American English phonology and exaggerated prosody (line 1). Bob's denaturalized linguistic performance expresses the ideological distance between her own identity and that of African American youth. Her return to her normal pronunciation in the second production of this word (line 10) coincides with her attempt to provide a nonslang definition. Thus Bob displays her unfamiliarity with this slang term, even as she reveals her awareness of it through her stylized, "black," pronunciation. Similarly, Fred provides a slang definition of the term in the course of denying that such a definition exists (lines 24–25, 32). With this switch, the coolness of slang and its ideological associations with blackness are linked to each other and separated from the world of white nerds.

By contrast, Erich, a fifteen-year-old nerdy white Jewish boy, asserts that the absence of slang in his lexicon is a matter of preference. When I ask Erich to comment on which of the printed slang terms he uses, he responds by rejecting slang as a whole while making clear that some of the activities to which the terms refer are nevertheless relevant to his life:

(10) 1 Erich: ↑Some of them,
2 the,
3 idea,
4 behi:nd,
5 the te:rm,
6 fits,
7 but the term itse:lf doesn't,
8 isn't the way I: prefer it to be:.
9 .h::
10 So like,
11 "kick back."
12 I just,
13 prefer something,
14 some normal term.
15 [$_1$.h @$_1$]
16 Mary: [$_1$Mm.$_1$]
17 [$_2$What would you$_2$] sa:y?
18 Erich: [$_2$@ h .h $_2$]
19 Like,
20 "to rela:[$_3$x,"
21 t-$_3$]
22 Mary: [$_3$Re$_3$]la:x?

23 [$_4$Rela:x,$_4$]
24 Erich: [$_4$@@@$_4$]
25 Something li@ke [$_5$tha@t.$_5$]
26 Mary: [$_5$Oka:y.$_5$]

In lines 10 through 14, Erich accepts the semantics of *kick back* but not its semiotic associations with coolness. (Unlike cooler students, Erich did not correct the form from *kick back* to *kick it*, the term then in vogue.) Referentially, the term denotes the activity of relaxing, something that "fits" (line 6) his own life. Indexically, however, the term is problematic for him. Thus, entirely apart from the semantics of individual slang terms, for Erich slang in general carries an undesirable association with youthful trendiness.

To be sure, nerdy students used some slang, particularly older terms, like *neat*, a positive evaluative term roughly synonymous with *tight*. But more recent slang items were often marked in some way in their speech, as when Claire, a nerdy sixteen-year-old junior, explains why she doesn't like her peers who behave immaturely (or, as she puts it in line 1, "people [who] are really young"):

(11) 1 Claire: When it seems to me that people are really you:ng?
2 (0.5)
3 It's like,
4 (0.5)
5 their emo:tional respo:nse to different things.
6 Mary: Hm.
7 Claire: just,
8 see:ms,
9 really w-
10 (0.6)
11 wa:cked.

Claire's utterance of the slang term *wack(ed)* in line 11 is preceded by a false start and a pause, both possible signals of some kind of difficulty. Whether her hesitance is due to uncertainty about the form of the term or simply its appropriateness in front of me, it suggests that the word may be unusual for Claire, at least in this context. Supporting this interpretation is Claire's formal language elsewhere in her turn (e.g., *emo:tional respo:nse*, line 5; the careful articulation of *just seems* in lines 7–8) and the standardized form of the slang term itself, which was usually pronounced as *wack* at the school at the time of the study, as seen in example (5) above. The form *wacked* is the past participle of a verb, but in African American English the term *wack* functions as an adjective. The addition of the inflection is therefore an example of hypercorrection.[6] In adding a Standard English past tense marker to a word popularized by African American students, Claire – a nerdy teenager who was gravitating toward coolness – reveals that she is not quite as cool as her use of the term might imply.

Moreover, Claire's standardization of the term is not racially neutral: the hypercorrect form *wacked* is more standard-sounding and hence ideologically whiter than the original term (Chapter 7). This complex dynamic of nerdy and nonnerdy, white and nonwhite, in Claire's speech is partly a result of her ongoing negotiation of her identity and its representation to me. But the use of careful, formal, highly standard English and the avoidance of much current slang were characteristic of many nerdy students at Bay City High School and were among the constitutive practices of nerd style.

Conclusion

Slang is a crucial linguistic element in the creation and display of coolness, a central value of trendy youth styles of all kinds. Hence slang fulfills a unifying function for speakers who strive for coolness, insofar as displaying familiarity with a rapidly changing lexicon allows them to bolster their credentials as individuals who are on top of current trends. But slang divides as well as unites its users. At Bay City High, practices and ideologies of slang established identity divisions of various kinds. Semiotically, slang signaled coolness and engagement in youth culture but also marked off racial boundaries and constructed participation in particular youth styles. Semantically, specific slang terms could be assigned different referential meanings by members of different social groups.

The next three chapters explore in greater detail the varied semiotic resources associated with preppiness, hip hop, and nerdiness as European American youth styles. In the following chapter, I consider the ideologies and practices of the preppy style and its role in the white stylistic order.

5 I'm like yeah but she's all no: innovative quotative markers and preppy whiteness

Introduction

Early in my fieldwork, I spent the lunch period wandering the school grounds, getting a sense of who hung out where. I was immediately recognizable as an outsider to many students, but given the number of student teachers, classroom observers, guest speakers, and other campus visitors, my presence was never questioned. Yet I could feel curious eyes upon me as I moved through the school's social space. Over time, I formed connections with various groups that I could hang out with and talk to at lunch, but I never completely lost my discomfort walking alone through the school grounds at lunchtime, and particularly past two large, predominantly European American groups of students: one in the school's central courtyard and the other in the Park. It was only later that I learned that these groups were as salient to other students as they were to me, and that they comprised some of the most elite white teenagers at Bay City High School.

As a large, multiracial urban high school, Bay City High differed from many smaller suburban schools in lacking a hegemonic popular crowd that forged trends, tastes, and social alliances. But the two groups I noticed at lunchtime were highly visible among the school's European American youth, based on the spaces they claimed on the school grounds. These students were sometimes called *preppies* (or *jocks* if they were involved in athletics); at other times they were simply referred to as *popular*, a term that was usually not complimentary, for it was associated with social exclusion and negative evaluation of others. Such students were ambitious, high-achieving, and deeply involved in the school's institutional structure via prestigious extracurricular activities such as the student council, the school newspaper and the yearbook, and white-dominated sports like soccer and lacrosse. Although these teenagers were genuinely interested in enriching their high school experience through challenging classes and time-consuming after-school activities, they also knew that excelling in such domains would strengthen their applications to the selective colleges and universities to which they aspired.

In the previous chapter I discussed how preppies and other white youth used slang to construct their identities both stylistically and racially. This chapter examines other elements of the preppy style, including the indexical use of clothing, geographic space, and innovative linguistic structures. I focus in depth on a particular innovation used primarily by European American students in my data: the quotative marker *be all*, which introduces reported or imagined speech, thought, or action. *Be all* predominated among preppies, and especially girls, who used the form mainly as a general quotative marker. Nonpreppy students, meanwhile, often used *be all* in a more specialized way to take stances about those whom they quoted. Thus the ideological association of white preppy femininity with social evaluation carried over into how the form was used by other teenagers.

Preppy as a local category

In American culture, the *preppy* label has been used at least since the 1950s to refer to a particular social type. Originating in elite East Coast college-preparatory boarding schools (or "prep schools"), *preppy* traditionally designates a clean-cut conservative style ideologically associated with those who attend such schools and more generally with inherited wealth and privilege. The preppy clothing style gained cultural prominence in the 1980s with the publication of the satirical *Official Preppy Handbook* (Birnbach 1980) and an accompanying national craze for preppy fashions such as oxford cloth shirts, Izod Lacoste polo shirts, khaki pants, and penny loafers.

At Bay City High, preppiness was linked to some extent with class privilege, although youth with other styles also often came from well-to-do families. In general, however, race and style were far more foregrounded than class as categories of social organization at the school. The clothing styles of students categorized as preppy did not generally reflect the fashions of prep schools and country clubs, which at the time of the study had been appropriated and semiotically reinterpreted by participants in hip hop culture (Chapter 6). Indeed, the self-presentation of many preppy youth was not as clean-cut as the category's origin might suggest. Preppy teenagers' clothing had expensive labels but were often unironed, torn, or threadbare: ripped blue jeans purchased from vintage clothing stores and wrinkled, frayed button-down shirts borrowed from parents or older siblings. The ragtag style that these students adopted seemed to signal their unconcern with markers of wealth (Bucholtz 2007a), although they frequently combined their well-worn clothing with new, trendy fashion items.

Preppy fashions were also highly gendered. This was true of the clothing styles of cool nonmainstream teenagers as well, but among white youth, preppy fashions were the most sharply differentiated by gender. Preppy boys wore their shirts and pants loose but not as baggy as in hip hop fashion, and many wore baseball caps and jackets with sports insignia. Heavily padded, thick-soled athletic shoes were the standard footwear for most boys at Bay City High School regardless of race or style, including preppies, but whereas boys of color and nonmainstream European American youth favored black shoes, preppy boys typically wore white shoes, continuing an enduring stylistic distinction in American high schools (Riggle 1965).

By contrast with the oversized styles of preppy boys, preppy girls often wore close-fitting, revealing clothing, such as tight baby-doll T-shirts that provided glimpses of their torsos, short shorts and miniskirts, low-slung bellbottom jeans, and low-cut tank tops and camisoles that left their satin bra straps in view. These fashions were often simultaneously sexual and infantilizing (cf. Miller 2004), an effect reinforced by the trend among many girls of pulling back their hair with children's pastel plastic barrettes shaped like animals or flowers. Pastel colors were also common in preppy girls' clothing, and their makeup (fingernail polish, lip gloss, and occasionally eyeshadow) was soft-colored and lightly applied, in contrast to the dark clothing and bold makeup of punk and goth girls.

Due to their adherence to commercialized styles, preppies were not trendsetters like nonmainstream youth, whose flamboyantly nonconformist clothing, hair, and makeup were designed to be noticed. Yet preppies' conservative style was distinctive enough to be emulated by "normal" teenagers, who adopted a more nondescript version of the fashions worn by preppy students. Preppies were nevertheless socially powerful thanks to their symbolic authority in the school's institutional structure and in the orchestration of social connections and conflicts – or "drama" (Eckert 2004). At Bay City High, this power was manifest in preppy teenagers' control of social space and in their practices of social exclusion and evaluation.

The geography of popularity

A number of students told me that because of Bay City High School's size and diversity, the notion of popularity was not relevant to the local peer social order. This widely circulating ideology was bitterly disputed, however, by teenagers in elite social circles. Example (1) is taken from an interview with the preppy girls Zoe and Josie (although Zoe also oriented, somewhat ambivalently, to an alternative, granola style):

(1) 1 Zoe: U:m:.
2 I guess everyone says at Bay City High there's no:,
3 popular crowd,
4 [There's no not pop]ular,
5 Josie: [Bu:ll shit.]

In line 2, Zoe articulates the ideology of the school as free of concerns with popularity, but she does not claim this ideology as her own stance, instead qualifying it as what "everyone says." Before she finishes her turn, Josie overlaps with a vehement and mildly profane disagreement marker (line 5). Josie's disagreement is not with Zoe's assertion but with the reported ideology. For Josie, herself a very popular girl, the reality of popularity was self-evident. Yet Zoe and Josie did not classify themselves as popular, and here Josie is not defending her identity but challenging what she considers a naïvely idealistic view of the school's social structure. In fact, not a single teenager in my study admitted to being popular, although many were readily able to classify others in this way.

While some alternative youth were considered popular by preppies, preppies were most widely viewed as popular at Bay City High because of their high visibility in school activities and in the schoolyard. In the school's racially divided space, preppy European American students claimed some of the most physically central and most desirable real estate. One such immediately noticeable space was the steps of the arts building, referred to by preppies simply as *the Steps*, even though other buildings facing the school's central courtyard had similar concrete steps on which other groups of students congregated. The arts building, however, had the most prominent and spacious stairway, which radiated into the courtyard in a wide semicircle rather than receding into the shadows of the building entrance. The Steps could therefore accommodate large numbers of students, loosely clustered into groups by class year, while elevating them above the pavement, a vantage point from which they could monitor ongoing activities as well as attract the notice of others sitting or standing elsewhere in the courtyard. This space was overwhelmingly but not exclusively white, with preppy students of color participating as scattered individuals in groups numerically dominated by European Americans.

The other social space reserved for preppy white students was a grassy area underneath an oak tree in the Park. Although there were other trees in the Park, only this one was socially meaningful for most European American students, and it was the only one marked on most students' maps of the school. In his map of the Park in Chapter 3 (Figure 3.1b), the preppy boy Mark labels the area under the oak tree as the *97 Power Clique* (i.e., the graduating class of 1997, or juniors during my study) and estimates the group's numbers at "20–30." Whereas many of the students on the Steps were athletes and heavy partyers, the preppy teenagers in the Park were primarily leaders in student government and similar extracurricular activities.

The significance of this spot for white teenagers of different stylistic orientations is illustrated in maps drawn by Josie and by the nerdy girl Bob (Figures 5.1 and 5.2).

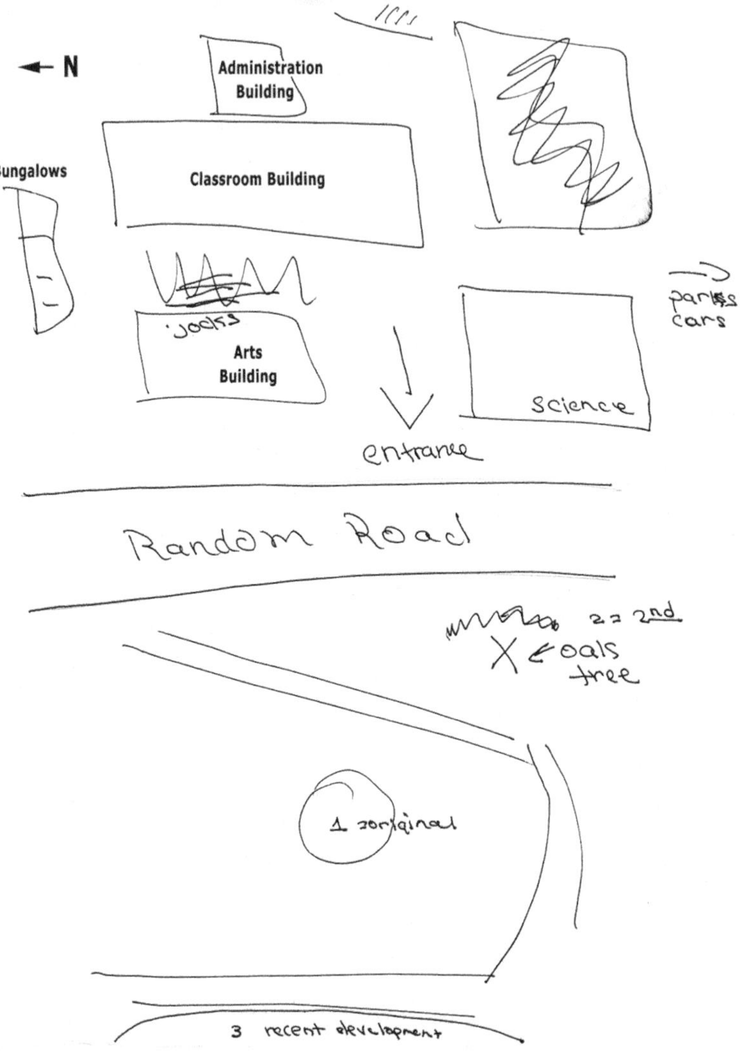

Figure 5.1: Josie's map of Bay City High School

In these maps the Park, where both girls usually ate lunch, is allotted the same amount of space as the school grounds, and within the Park both girls highlight the location of the tree. Josie marks it with a large X, an arrow, and the label *oak tree*. Until recently, she spent her lunch hour beneath the tree as part of the "97 Power Clique." Her previous lunch spot, in the very center of the crowded

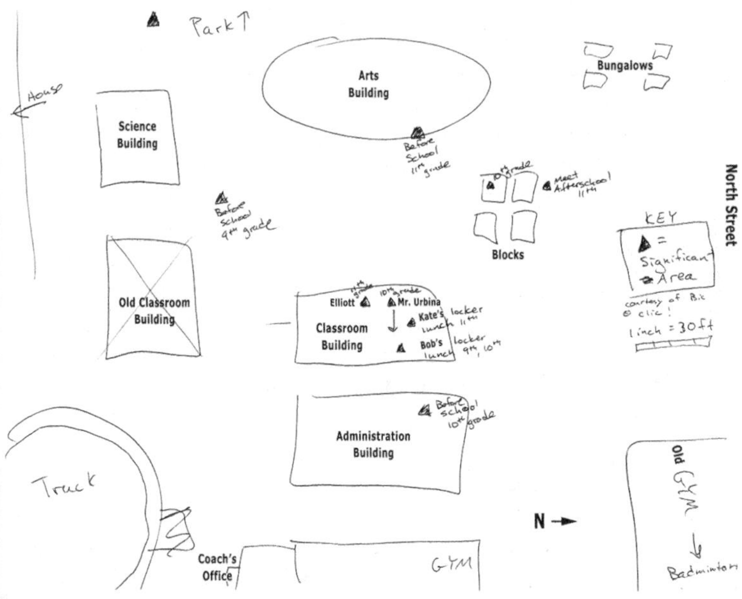

Figure 5.2a: Bob's map of the Bay City High School courtyard

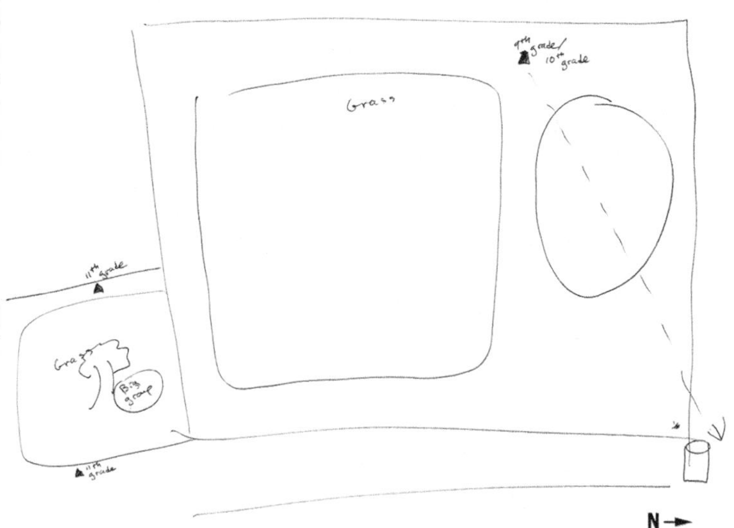

Figure 5.2b: Bob's map of the Park

Park, was likewise highly visible. However, in what she labels a "recent development," she moved to the far side of the Park as part of a smaller but still prominent clique. Josie's mobility within the Park is indicative of the dynamic social arrangements of popular youth, which were witnessed with interest by other students as well.

Bob's representation of the same lunch spot is rather different. She notes the presence of Josie's group (the "Big group") under the tree, but she draws a border around this area and indicates that her own various locations in the Park at lunchtime fall outside that boundary. This division was not impermeable, however: at times, especially when most of their own group members were absent, Bob and her friends joined the periphery of the larger group for lunch. Despite – or perhaps because of – this proximity to Josie's group, Bob was well aware that she and her friends remained largely separate from it; as her friend Fred vividly – and nerdily – characterized the situation, "They're the chromosome and we're the plasma."

In short, the social geography of popularity was familiar even to many students who were not part of the popular crowd. This was the case with Erin and Iris, two sixteen-year-old juniors who self-identified as "normal" and who closely attended to preppy goings-on. In their jointly constructed map of the school (Figure 5.3), these girls provide detailed distinctions among the various

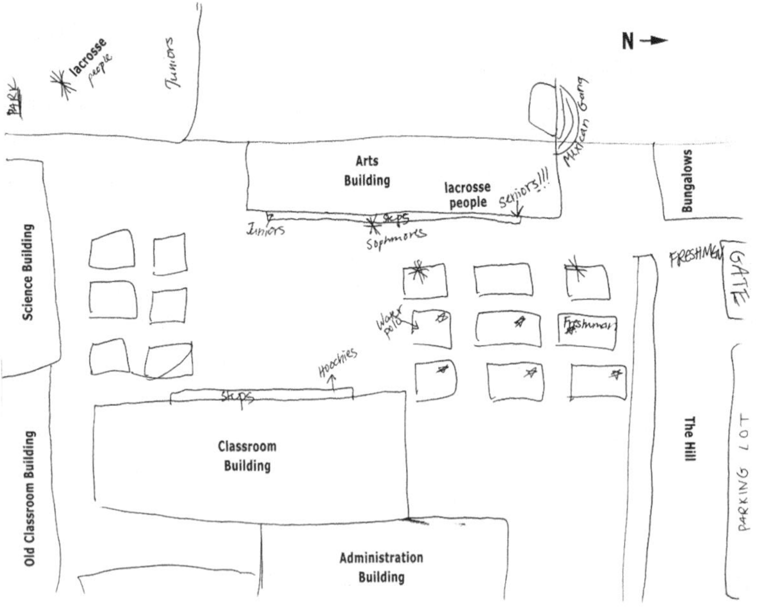

Figure 5.3: Erin and Iris's map of Bay City High School

preppy groups in the Park and on the Steps based on either class year or extracurricular activities: *Juniors*, *soph[o]mores*, *lacrosse people*, *seniors!!!*.

While nonpreppy youth took note of the activities of their more popular peers, preppy teenagers oversaw Bay City High's entire white social order. The centrality of both preppy lunchtime spots meant that students moving to more peripheral areas of the school's space did so in clear view of them and became available for evaluation and commentary. Thus preppy students' hangouts were akin to panopticons, or structures designed to enable maximal observation for purposes of power and control (Foucault 1977). I soon learned that I was not alone in feeling discomfited by the gaze and murmurs of popular teenagers when I walked through their space. Indeed, even Josie confessed the vulnerability she felt in walking across the courtyard in front of the Steps at lunchtime.

(2) 1 Josie: When I: walk by the courtyard?
2 Oka:y,
3 when—
4 I: feel really self-conscious?
5 .h
6 <smiling quality> {And whenever I'm wearing a skir:t,
7 I like spend the whole time [$_1$pulling my$_1$] [$_2$skirt do:wn,$_2$]}
8 Zoe: [$_1$m@: $_1$]
9 Mary: [$_2$@: $_2$]
10 Zoe: [$_3$@$_3$]
11 Josie: [$_3$@$_3$]@Like I get all <creaky voice> {n:ervous,
12 And I just hate walking by the courtyard?}
13 Because,
14 .h
15 it's like.
16 (Um:/I'm:,)
17 (0.5)
18 I don't know really why:,
19 I mean maybe 'cause,
20 (0.7)
21 It's ↑like,
22 the jo:cks,
23 and like,
24 everything like tha:t.
25 And like,
26 kind of like the quote unquote,
27 coo:l people?=
28 Mary: =Mhm.=
29 Josie: =And they just make me feel really like,
30 self-conscious about myself?

Although Josie was very popular, her wholesome persona and particularly her marginal involvement in the heavy partying scene favored by many preppies kept her from close friendships with most of the Steps crowd. Josie's and others' insecurity when walking past the popular cliques was partly due to the sheer number of preppy teenagers that converged on the Steps and under the oak tree, often two dozen or more, forming much larger groups than most other student clusters scattered around the school grounds. But the self-consciousness of passers-by was also due to their knowledge that they might easily be the subject of gossip or ridicule among the students who observed them. Indeed, one of the most dreaded moments of social humiliation at the school was tripping and falling, or "scrubbing," in the middle of the courtyard (not coincidentally, Bay City High's lowest-status students were termed *scrubs*). Such an act was viewed as tantamount to social suicide because it took place in full view of the entire schoolyard. The students on the Steps, from their higher vantage point, were often quick to initiate and sustain the inevitable mocking laughter that followed such mishaps.

The panoptical gaze of preppy youth was tied to their power within the school's social order. The social practice of noticing and commenting on others was crucial to popularity, a fact recognized by popular and nonpopular teenagers alike. Social evaluation reinforced the selectiveness of preppy circles by marking the borders of inclusion and exclusion and was therefore widely viewed as "mean" or unkind by students of all stylistic orientations. Yet far from being unique to preppy youth, social evaluation was a practice in which all teenagers at Bay City High engaged.

The social meaning of being "mean"

As other scholars have noted (e.g., Eckert 1989; Eder *et al.* 1995), to be popular in an American public school is not necessarily to be universally beloved but rather to wield the power to shape the school's social market, to determine who is "in" and "out." At Bay City High, popular teenagers – and especially girls – were frequently characterized as "not nice" or even "mean" (cf. Matthews 2005): they excluded others from their social group, they mocked peers to their faces and gossiped about them behind their backs, and they generally showed insufficient consideration for others' feelings. Indeed, a growing literature argues that girls' creation of social hierarchy can be a rather ruthless business (Goodwin 2006; Simmons 2002; Wiseman 2002), and the term *mean girls* has even entered public discourse, thanks to the commercially and critically successful 2004 Hollywood teen comedy *Mean Girls* (itself based on Wiseman's 2002 self-help book about girls' cliques).

Although the expression *mean girls* was not in circulation in Bay City High during my study, the evaluation of popular girls as "mean" certainly was. In example (3), for instance, Iris explains to me why she and Erin stopped eating lunch with a group of girls who took up lacrosse, a sport associated with the most elite preppy students at the school:

(3) Iris: Our groups just sort of split?
Because,
you know,
they—
they always talked about lacro::sse,
and so,
we were kind of like,
"Okay,
We'll just eat."
And ↑then they just started being like,
really,
u:m,
(1.3)
mea:n.
And,
I mean,
they just like—
they totally—
(0.5)
they jus:t,
like,
thought they were so great.
And like,
n:othing could ever touch the:m,
and we were just so n:er:dy,
and,
.h
so we just started to like—
Our whole group just started to really ha:te them.
@

Negative evaluation of another is a risky interactional move, and Iris delays her assessment of her former friends with the discourse marker *u:m* and a lengthy pause (lines 12–13) before producing the characterization *mea:n* in line 14. She goes on to report the popular girls' view of herself, Erin, and their "normal" friends: *we were just so n:er:dy* (line 25). Here Iris makes clear the social category that stands in starkest contrast to preppy popularity – nerdiness – and suggests that to position oneself as "great" (line 22) and others as "nerdy" is grounds not just for strong negative assessment but also for strong affect: hatred (line 29). In this way, she is able to frame her evaluation of the popular girls as justifiable anger rather than meanness.

Iris's attitudes toward her popular peers and even her word choice are echoed in remarks on popularity made by the popular girls Josie and Zoe:

(4) 1 Josie: I-
2 I h-
3 I hate popularity.
4 I think it's really,
5 awful.
6 'Cause I: think pop-
7 like a lot of what makes people po:pular is,
8 <slow rate> {ho:w mea:n you a:re?}
9 Mary: [$_1$Hm. $_1$]
10 Zoe: [$_1$Yea::h.$_1$]
11 Josie: [$_1$To $_1$] oth[$_2$er people? $_2$]
12 Zoe: [$_2$Social climb$_2$]ing.

Like Iris, Josie assesses popular people as "mean" (line 8) and takes a strongly negative affective stance (line 3). Thus even popular girls distanced themselves from popularity.

In fact, the problematic nature of popularity led one girl, Fred, to go so far as to abandon her formerly prestigious social status in favor of a nicer – and nerdier – group of friends. Fred was a member of Bob's friendship group, which also included Kate and several other girls. Earlier in her high school career, Fred associated primarily with a group of popular, preppy girls. As she explained to me, she decided to move out of that group and into a nerdier group:

(5) 1 Fred: I mean,
2 last year I,
3 (0.9)
4 I was like,
5 good friends with Ka:te?
6 But I never s:aw her on weekdays for some reason?
7 Mary: [$_1$Hm:. $_1$]
8 Fred: [$_1$I was w-$_1$]
9 sitting with this other group of people at lunch,
10 who like,
11 (1.0)
12 were coo:l,
13 but they like,
14 liked to talk about everyone who pa:ssed,
15 and make,
16 negative comments [$_2$about everyone who$_2$] passed,
17 Mary: [$_2$Mm:. $_2$]
18 Fred:
19 and I: just kind of sat there.
<20 lines omitted>
40 Fred: And then,
41 (0.5)

at the end of the semester I said,
"What am I do:ing?
Why: am I not hanging out with her:."
And so [$_3$I, $_3$]
Mary: [$_3$Ri:ght.$_3$]
Fred: moved in with the@m.

The interactional challenge of attesting to the "meanness" of popular teenagers' evaluations of others was that to do so speakers themselves had to engage in social evaluation. Fred does not explicitly label her former friends *mean*, but she notes that they made "negative comments about everyone who passed" (line 16), a characterization that further highlights the role of social geography as well as social evaluation in popularity.

The geographic visibility of preppy white students was matched by their linguistic audibility. Although their conservative and commercialized style of dress did not attract wide imitation, preppy youth nevertheless held some sway in trend setting, and over time nonpreppy youth adopted some preppy linguistic practices for their own purposes. In particular, the quotative marker *be all*, a linguistic resource heavily used by preppy girls, spread to other groups at Bay City High while retaining traces of its social and interactional history as a stance marker and an index of preppy popularity.

Quotative markers and social differentiation

Quotative markers, or forms for marking upcoming speech as attributed rather than uttered in the current speaker's own voice, were an important linguistic resource for identity work at Bay City High. Large-scale changes in the quotative system had been under way since before these teenagers were born, and consequently some innovations were so well established in the speech of European American youth in California that they had lost much of their semiotic power to create local stylistic distinctions. Others of more recent vintage had not yet been widely adopted outside of preppy youth and were therefore available as potential indexical markers of that style.

For the past several decades, the quotative system has been undergoing a dramatic change throughout the United States as well as in many other countries in the English-speaking world.[1] Before this shift, the primary verb for introducing direct quotations was *say*, which has now been joined by at least three other forms: *go*, *be like*, and *be all*. All three forms have been in use at least since the 1980s and in some cases probably much earlier. *Go*, the oldest of the "new" quotative markers, was first attested in the *Oxford English Dictionary* in the eighteenth century but became more widespread in the latter part of the twentieth century (Buchstaller 2006a; Butters 1980; Schourup 1982). *Be like* – which combines any form of the copula *to be* with *like* – was first observed by linguists in the early 1980s (Butters 1982) and has now become the primary quotative marker of many American English speakers (Rickford *et al.* 2007; Singler 2001). This form is distinct from the discourse marker *like*, which is used for emphasis, mitigation, and other functions (e.g., Underhill 1988). The most recent form to appear in American English, *be all*, seems to be a newer and perhaps regionally and temporally restricted development, given that most attestations come from the speech of Californians in the 1990s (Gilman *et al.* 1999; Rickford *et al.* 2007; Waksler 2001).

A number of language ideologies have developed regarding innovative quotative markers. In particular, a certain trendy style of youthful femininity is ideologically associated with at least one such form, *be like*. Although *be like* is used by speakers of various ages, ethnoracial backgrounds, and regions, the ideology does not reflect this widespread use. One early study based on an attitude survey of *be like* reports, "Typical epithets . . . for [users of] *be like* were 'vacuous,' 'silly,' 'airheaded,' 'California.' In fact, the connotations for *be like* can be summed up by the most frequent epithet of all in our survey, 'Valley Girl,' an American stereotype with social and regional connotations" (Blyth *et al.* 1990: 224; cf. Buchstaller 2006b; Dailey-O'Cain 2000). Another study links the indexicality of *be like* not only to California but specifically to "the 'preppie' movement of the 1980s" (Tagliamonte and D'Arcy 2007: 212). Similar language ideologies have been reported for the discourse marker *like* (Dailey-O'Cain 2000; D'Arcy 2007). These studies reveal the ideological meaning of *be like* in other geographic regions, but because the research was not conducted in California it is difficult to know whether Californians themselves – and especially youth – share such ideologies.[2] Indeed, given how thoroughly *be like* has been adopted by younger speakers, it may no longer be a salient social marker for many of them; the apparently more recent form *be all* may therefore be a more viable candidate for indexing social meaning (but cf. Bakht (2010) for a different situation among high school students in New York).

At Bay City High School in the mid-1990s, *be all* was primarily used by preppy students, especially preppy girls, who were often considered by their less popular peers to epitomize the same sort of vapid trendiness that has been ideologically associated with *be like* by non-Californians. Such characterizations were in fact quite unfair: the preppy girls I spent time with were fully conscious of the problematic nature of popularity and offered thoughtful and critical commentaries on it. What set them apart from other students I spoke to was certainly not their level of intelligence or self-awareness, which were quite high, but rather the complexity of their social lives. Preppy teenagers, much more than other students, often did not either like or trust many of their friends, and some even formed friendships outside their primary social group in order to have someone to discuss their problems with. This complexity, along with the

Table 5.1. *Quotative marker use by white Bay City High School students, by gender*

	be all	*go*	*be like*	*say*	Total
Female	44 (10.0%)	42 (9.6%)	247 (56.4%)	105 (24.0%)	438 (100%)
Male	10 (5.2%)	14 (7.2%)	123 (63.7%)	46 (23.8%)	193 (100%)
Total	54 (8.6%)	56 (8.9%)	370 (58.6%)	151 (23.9%)	631 (100%)

χ-square = 5.515, df = 3, $p = 0.14$

social demands of popularity, made for a great deal of narration and evaluation of peer interaction in preppies' talk, a task for which quoted speech was well suited.

To quantitatively analyze the use of quotative markers at Bay City High, data were extracted from digitized audio recordings of twenty-six European American teenagers who produced at least one token of *say*, *go*, *be like*, or *be all*.[3] African American speakers did not produce any tokens of *be all* in my data set, although it is probable that some black teenagers at Bay City High School used it. *Be all* thus potentially carried some indexicality as a local linguistic resource of nonblackness, and especially of whiteness. Every quotative token produced by a European American speaker was extracted and coded for linguistic, interactional, and social factors; the latter two types of factors are considered here. The number and length of recordings varied by speaker, and different speakers used quotative markers to different degrees. The smallest number of quotatives produced by a single speaker is 1; the largest number of quotatives produced by a single speaker is 115 (in both cases the speakers were nerds). The following variables are examined below: quotative form (*say*, *go*, *be like*, and *be all*); speaker gender (female, male); speaker style (alternative, hip hop, nerd, normal, preppy); and speaker stance toward the speech being quoted (negative, neutral; positive stances are excluded because they were extremely rare).[4]

In the audio recordings, most speakers used quotation – some quite heavily – and the majority used at least some innovative quotative markers. The distribution of the four quotative markers is similar for both genders, and there are no significant differences between girls and boys in the use of all four forms (Table 5.1).

The finding that *be like* was strongly favored over *be all* among my study participants differs from the results of a previous study of California adolescent speech, based on sociolinguistic interviews and online data collected in the early 1990s and in 2005 (Rickford *et al.* 2007). The authors found that in the earlier period, *be all* was the most frequently used quotative form, with *be like*

Table 5.2. *Quotative marker use by white Bay City High School students, by style*

	be all	*go*	*be like*	*say*	Total
Alternative	8 (6.8%)	14 (11.9%)	69 (58.5%)	27 (22.9%)	118 (100%)
Hip hop	2 (2.2%)	1 (1.1%)	68 (73.9%)	21 (22.8%)	92 (100%)
Nerd	14 (5.7%)	34 (13.8%)	135 (54.9%)	63 (25.6%)	246 (100%)
Normal	0 (0.0%)	3 (6.3%)	30 (62.5%)	15 (31.3%)	48 (100%)
Preppy	30 (23.6%)	4 (3.1%)	68 (53.5%)	25 (19.7%)	127 (100%)
Total	54 (100%)	56 (100%)	370 (100%)	127 (100%)	631 (100%)

χ-square = 50.91, df = 3, $p < 0.001$

a distant second; this pattern was reversed in the later period, leading the authors to argue for the decline of *be all* in the past decade or so.

The strong preference for *be like* shown in the Bay City High School data from the mid-1990s indicates that even in the peak period for the use of *be all* in the San Francisco Bay Area, not all youth used the form heavily. The speaker's stylistic orientation is an important variable in the use of this quotative marker (Table 5.2).

As shown in Table 5.2, *be like* was the preferred quotative marker for students of various styles. However, not every student used this form, and the two study participants with the nerdiest styles, Bob (a girl) and Erich (a boy), used neither *be like* nor the older quotative marker *go*; instead they generally favored *say*. These speakers also produced very few instances of quoted speech overall, perhaps viewing this practice as indexical of a cool or trendy youth style, which they did not embrace.

The distribution of *be all* indicates that preppies were significantly more likely to use this form than other teenagers, with preppy girls the heaviest users.[5] This differential use of *be all* by style is illustrated in the following examples, the first involving Josie and the second involving two relatively nerdy girls. In example (6), Josie uses *be all* repeatedly in describing her nonserious attempts to convince members of the student Macintosh computer society, who were widely considered to be archetypically nerdy, to let her join their club.

(6) 1 Josie: And then there's like people like,
2 the Mac Group?
3 (0.5)
4 Who ar:e,
5 .h
6 a b-
7 <lower pitch> {group of f:re:shmen?
8 who m:eet every um,
9 .h

10 F:ri[$_1$days to play on the Mac computers?$_1$]}
11 Zoe: [$_1$<tongue click> Ri:ght.
12 Right. $_1$]
13 Josie: ↑They would n:ot let me join their club,
14 <creaky voice> {by the wa:y.}
15 Mary: You tri:ed,
16 and they woul[$_2$dn't let ↑yo:u? $_2$]
17 Josie: [$_2$Oh,
18 **I was all,**
19 "Can$_2$] I join your club?"=
20 =Of course I'd been sitting in the corner,
21 laughing at them for like the last twenty minutes.=
22 =And **they're a:ll,**
23 <lower pitch> {"No::."}
24 <creaky voice> {And **I was all,**}
25 "Well,
26 I don't like you either."

Example (7) involves Claire and Christine, both self-described nerds, although their identities were actually more complex than this label would suggest. At the time of the study, they were ambivalent about their nerdiness and were making forays into cooler social crowds. Yet they recognized that their intelligence was an obstacle to coolness, and here they lament that they must hide the fact that schoolwork comes easily to them by pretending that they have private tutors.

(7) 1 Claire: It's not,
2 very,
3 popular to be smart.
4 Like **everyone goes**, <breathy>
5 {"Oh man,}
6 that test was so hard,
7 what'd you get on it?"=
8 =<deeper pitch> {"Oh I got a C: on it."}
9 .h
10 <breathy> {"Well I got a B minus,
11 I was so excited,
12 I thought I was going to ↑f:ail it.}
13 .h
14 What'd you get?"=
15 =<lower volume> {"O:h,
16 I-
17 I-
18 I-
19 I got an A:."}
20 Christine: And everyone [$_1$kind of $_1$] falls silent.
21 Claire: [$_1$"O:h." $_1$]
22 Christine: "O:h."

23		You know like,
24		"Nnn."=
25	Mary:	=Mm.
26	Claire:	And then you feel compelled to say,
27		.h
28		<higher pitch> {"But it was so ha:rd,
29		ma:n!"}
30		[$_2$ I mean, $_2$]
31	Christine:	[$_2$ "I studied $_2$] s:o [$_3$ ha:rd!"$_3$]
32	Claire:	<higher pitch> {[$_3$ "I stud$_3$]ied so hard!"
33	Mary:	[$_4$ Mm. $_4$]
34	Claire:	[$_4$ "O:h! $_4$]
35		I al-
36		I-
37		I stayed up [$_5$ till like o:ne!"} $_5$]
38	Christine:	<lower pitch> {[$_5$ "My tutor helped $_5$] me:."}
39		[$_6$ @@@ $_6$]
40	Claire:	[$_6$ I know. $_6$]
41		I know,=
42		=and then you say,
43		the magic word,
44		"I have a tu:tor."
45		@=
46	Mary:	=Mm:.
47	Christine:	And **everyone goes**,
48		"O::::h,"
49		<lower volume> {and they're all jealous,}
50		<creaky voice> {and **they're like**,
51		"O:h,
52		wo:w,
53		I wish I had a tutor."}

These two excerpts provide neatly polarized ideological positions regarding the relationship between nerdiness and coolness. Josie's disdain for the nerds in the computer club finds its counterpart in Claire and Christine's disgust toward their cooler classmates' stupidity and the subterfuge required to interact with such students. (The identity issues in example (7) are analyzed in greater detail in Chapter 7.) This ideological divide is matched by a linguistic divide. Although all three girls use innovative quotative markers, in (6) Josie uses *be all* exclusively (lines 18, 22, 24), while in (7) Claire and Christine use *be like* (line 50) as well as *go* (lines 4, 47). The latter two girls also use a number of null quotatives, as in lines 31–38.

However, the general pattern of preppy teenagers' using *be all* more than nonpreppy teenagers does not tell the whole story of how quotative markers served to construct distinctive styles at Bay City High. In particular, it does not reveal when and why some nonpreppy teenagers used *be all* instead of the unmarked form *be like*. To address this issue, it is necessary to combine quantitative and qualitative analysis.

Quotation and social evaluation

One consequence of the elaboration of the quotative system of American English is an expansion of the expressive range of quotation. The representation of the speech of another (including a past or hypothetical self) always involves stance, for such discourse is "double-voiced" – that is, the other's voice is ventriloquated by a speaker who aligns or disaligns with the original voice (Bakhtin 1981, 1984). Quotation enhances the expressive dimension of speech by providing an enacted performance of what was said rather than an indirect report (Besnier 1992; Buchstaller 2003). Such performances depict not only a (purported) past or imagined event but also the present speaker's stance toward represented others and their speech. Moreover, although the material introduced by a quotative marker is often represented as having actually been uttered, so-called "reported speech" may not be based in any actual prior utterance but may instead be constructed for dramatic narrative effect or other purposes (Tannen 1989). Represented discourse potentially becomes more affectively laden with the emergence of new quotative markers, which can convey subjective stances. While quotative *say* introduces represented speech, the innovative forms *go*, *be like*, and *be all* introduce not only speech but also (depending on the specific form) thoughts, attitudes, nonlinguistic sounds, gestures, and facial expressions. Quotation is thus a powerful resource for stance taking in discourse. At Bay City High it was used by youth to position themselves in relation to others in the social order.

Be like, though probably originally associated with strongly affective stance taking (e.g., Romaine and Lange 1991), has broadened its semantic and pragmatic range and is now an unmarked quotative form for many speakers. The affective dimension of *be all*, however, remains salient in many cases; as Rachelle Waksler notes, "*all* often appears in emotionally charged stories in which the speaker's particular interpretation of characters and events is crucial" (2001: 137).[6] Such a use of *be all* is illustrated in the high-affect story in example (6).

Among popular teenagers at Bay City High, however, quotative *be all* did not always index a strong affective stance toward ongoing talk. In example (8), Josie tells a story about a conversation that took place among staff members of the *Trojan*, the student newspaper (Josie and Zoe were also on the newspaper staff). The reported conversation involves the slang term *hoogie* or *hoochie*, an insult for European American girls who adopted an African American or Latina style (such girls were also scornfully dismissed as "wannabes"). In the story,

Vince, a white newspaper staff member, uses a variant of *hoogie* to playfully insult Josie, who is also white. A black staff member, Kelly, who witnesses Vince's remark, corrects his use of the term.

(8) 1 Josie: um, <chewing>
2 Kelly?
3 who's,
4 African American,
5 she's on Trojan, <the student newspaper>
6 And,
7 .h::
8 Vince called me a hoogified heifer,
9 <smiling quality> {which is like his take on the wor:d,}
10 [$_1$you know?$_1$]
11 Mary: [$_1$Mm. $_1$]
12 Josie: @
13 A:nd,
14 Zoe: [$_2$@ $_2$]
15 Josie: [$_2$like$_2$] he [$_3$ca@lls$_3$] e@veryone —
16 Zoe: [$_3$@ $_3$]
17 Josie: Like he—
18 Last y-
19 like,
20 o:h-
21 we got in this big like,
22 insulting thi:ng?
23 .h
24 And he came up with hoogified heifer?
25 And [$_4$like,$_4$]
26 Zoe: [$_4$@ $_4$]
27 Josie: [$_5$**Kelly's**$_5$] **all**,
28 Zoe: [$_5$@ $_5$]
29 Josie: "You [$_6$kno:w,$_6$]
30 Zoe: [$_6$@@ $_6$]
31 Josie: no: offense,
32 but I:'ve never heard a white person called a hoogie:."
33 (1.0)
34 Mary: [$_7$Really:. $_7$]
35 Zoe: [$_7$↑Really?$_7$]
36 Huh.
37 (0.8)
38 Josie: An:d,
39 an:d,
40 and,
41 and **we're all**,
42 <higher pitch> {"That's so wei:rd,"}

43 'cause like,
44 I'd never heard,
45 like I had heard,
46 (0.5)
47 like,
48 black people being called hoogie:s?
49 But,
50 it wasn't like,
51 I: just,
52 .h:
53 It's something so:,
54 .h
55 like,
56 something so: like,
57 (0.7)
58 I: associate with,
59 white,
60 wa:nnabe <smiling quality, creaky voice> {gir:ls,
61 you know?}

This story could have occasioned a number of strongly affective stances: Josie is called an insulting name by Vince (line 8), and according to the narrative, Kelly herself views her comment as possibly offensive to Vince and perhaps other European American students (lines 27–32). Yet the story is not emotionally charged. Although Josie uses *be all* to introduce quoted speech that is potentially emotional (an apology in line 31, an evaluation in line 42), both are at best mildly affective, with prosody that is, for her, relatively undramatic. For preppy students, then, *be all* could function as a relatively neutral quotative marker similar to *be like* or *say*. Meanwhile, among nonpreppy students, *be all* was more likely to involve stance taking compared to preppies' use of the form.

Table 5.3 presents preppy versus nonpreppy teenagers' use of *be all* as a stance marker. At issue is not the specific stance taken by the quoted speaker, but rather whether the quoting speaker takes an overtly nonneutral (and in this case, negative) stance toward the speech being quoted.

Table 5.3. *Use of* be all *by nonpreppy versus preppy students, by stance*

Stance	Nonpreppy	Preppy	Total
Negative	12 (67%)	6 (33%)	18 (100%)
Neutral	12 (33%)	24 (67%)	36 (100%)
Total	24 (100%)	30 (100%)	54 (100%)

χ-square = 5.4, df = 1, $p = .02$

Among preppy teenagers, *be all* was significantly more likely to be used with a neutral stance, as illustrated in example (8) above. Among nonpreppy teenagers, conversely, *be all* was significantly less likely to be used to take a neutral stance.[7] Looked at another way, nonpreppy teenagers were far more likely than preppy teenagers to use *be all* to take an overt stance toward the speech or speaker they were quoting. Moreover, such stances were overwhelmingly negative.

The following examples illustrate the use of *be all* by nonpreppy teenagers to take a stance (in each case, a negative stance) toward quoted speech. In example (9), Acme and two of his friends debate whether Acme is a "social butterfly," a negative social label that for this group of friends involves striking up conversations with strangers. Acme and Rachel belonged to a large, loose social group of stoners, or recreational drug users, and during this interaction the three participants were smoking a marijuana pipe in an alley across the street from the school. Billy was also a member of this group, but during the course of the academic year he became more affiliated with a hip hop style. At the time of this interaction early in the school year, Billy was still primarily affiliated with the stoner style. Thus all the speakers were cool but not preppy; their identities stood in opposition to the mainstream identity represented by Josie and Zoe. As example (9) opens, Rachel has just accused Acme of being a social butterfly.

(9) 1 Billy: I only talk with people I can relate with.
2 Acme: Mhm.
3 (1.0)
4 Yeah.
5 My friends.
6 I don't go—
7 Yeah,
8 but see,
9 I don't go around just talking to fools I don't know,
10 just **being all**,
11 "Blahblahlahlahblah,
12 [$_{1}$blahdah,
13 blahdah:."$_{1}$]
14 Rachel: [$_{1}$That is no:t $_{1}$] ↑tru:e.
15 Acme: Tha@t [$_{2}$is so: true.$_{2}$]
16 Rachel: [$_{2}$That is $_{2}$] no:t [$_{3}$↑tru::e!$_{3}$]
17 Acme: [$_{3}$@: $_{3}$]
18 @:
19 [$_{4}$See now I (ge@t/ca@n't)— $_{4}$]=
20 Rachel: [$_{4}$You and Andy, $_{4}$]=
21 Mary: @@
22 Rachel: =we:re,

23 [$_5$c:amping,$_5$]
24 Acme: [$_5$@@ $_5$]
25 Rachel: and **these fools are all**,
26 <sing song> "Let's go [$_6$ meet (him)."$_6$]
27 Acme: [$_6$ Well,
28 that's $_6$] messing with people,
29 there's a difference between trying to like,
30 strike up a frie:ndship,
31 [$_7$ and like messing with peop$_7$]le.
32 Rachel: [$_7$ It's sti:ll being ↑so:cial. $_7$]
33 Acme: [$_8$@@ $_8$]
34 Rachel: [$_8$ But it's so:cial, $_8$]
35 it's being social.

Both Acme and Rachel use the form *be all* (lines 10–13; lines 25–26); in both occurrences, the speaker takes up a negative stance toward the speech she or he quotes, which is represented as characteristic of the speech of a social butterfly. Affect is further signaled through prosodic cues such as vowel lengthening (line 13) and sing-song intonation (line 26) and – in the case of Acme – through the use of nonlexicalized sounds (lines 11–13).

Example (10) illustrates another instance in which *be all* is put to affective use in stance taking, this time involving another cool nonmainstream youth style. Here Brand One and Willie, both white Jewish sixteen-year-old junior boys who aligned with hip hop, discuss a recent conflict that arose between them related to their interest in clothing and shopping.

(10) 1 Brand One: Like today,
2 right?
3 I-
4 we-
5 we: like,
6 you know,
7 like,
8 Mary: [@]
9 Brand One: [clothes] and stuff.
10 And so,
11 he had a:,
12 a Polo:,
13 Polo sport,
14 deodorant,
15 right?
16 He liked it.
17 And I didn't—
18 I did-
19 I thought he finished it.
20 I could have sworn he told me that,

right.
So I was at the Polo outlet.
And I almost bought him it?
The Polo sport=
Willie: =[$_1$k@: $_1$]
Brand One: =[$_1$deodor$_1$]ant,
right?
And I—
I told him,
and **he's all**,
(0.7)
<lower pitch, denasalized> {"Well,
why?
Willie: @:
Mary: [$_2$ @@ $_2$]
Brand One: [$_2$ Well why did you— $_2$]
Willie: [$_3$ @@ .h $_3$]
Mary: [$_3$ @@ $_3$]
Brand One: Well,
why are you gonna do that?"}
you know?
I was like,
<smacks fist into palm> "I was trying to do something nice,"
'cause he's—
'cause sometimes he (usually) gets ma:d,
Willie: [$_4$@: $_4$]
Brand One: [$_4$he gets a at$_4$]titude about stu:ff.
(Little jerk.)=
Willie: =It's not even close to do:ne,
though,
it's (I)—
It's like,
a f:ive,
like,
sixth:s:,
(0.5)
Like I've used like one sixth of it.
@

In line 30 Brand One uses the *be all* quotative to introduce Willie's ungrateful response to his thoughtful gesture (lines 32–40); again, the quoted speech is also marked by special prosody (here, a deeper-pitched denasalized voice quality indexing stupidity or "goofiness") that serves to characterize the quoted speaker in a negative way. By contrast, Brand One's quotation of his own speech is demarcated by *be like* and is not prosodically marked (lines 42–43). This use of *be all* is quite rare in Brand One's speech; in other contexts, including an extensive emotionally charged narrative that I have analyzed elsewhere (Bucholtz 1999a), Brand One uses *be like* almost exclusively.

A further illustration of negative stance taking with *be all* is found in example (11), in which the nerds Christine and Claire tell a story about a classmate who bought a leather outfit during a school trip to Italy:

(11) 1 Christine: And she—
2 O:h my god,
3 it was horrible.
4 She walks into the room,
5 and a:ll the guys that we were—
6 that came along with us,
7 didn't like her either,
8 but we were all sitting in a ho↑tel room,
9 and she walks in,
10 in her,
11 leather jacket and her leather pants,
12 and **she goes**,
13 .h
14 <higher pitch, nasal> "Loo:k!"
15 And she models it arou:nd,
16 and she turns arou:nd,
17 and **they're just like**,
18 <lower pitch, monotone, quiet> {"Oh yeah,
19 oh yeah."}
20 So they decide to bait her,
21 and **they're like**,
22 <breathy, higher pitch> {"Minna.
23 What are you wearing underne:ath?"}
24 And **she was just like**,
25 <higher pitch> {".h::
26 My purple bra and underwear!"}=
27 =She starts taking it o:ff,
28 **We're like**,
29 <lower pitch> [1{"No:1]:::."}
30 Claire: [1@@ 1]
31 Christine: [2@ 2]
32 Claire: [2You know,2]
33 [3@ 3]
34 Christine: [3"Go: away3][4::." 4]
35 Mary: [3Oh my go3][4:d. 4]
36 Claire: [4 Don't want to— 4]
37 Oh yeah,
38 that was the other thing.=
39 =[(She had something) about nakedness,]

40 Christine: =[**She's all**,
41 <breathy, higher pitch> {"That's a:ll!"}]
42 Claire: she liked to be naked.

This example involves several instances of quoted speech with negative stance taking, primarily introduced by *be like* (or *be just like*). Yet at the climax of the narrative, Christine switches to *be all* in line 40 to give voice to Minna's failed attempt at sexiness. Her morally indignant stance at this inappropriate behavior is once again accompanied by special prosody, which also occurs throughout the narrative.

As example (11) indicates, the use of *be all* to take stances did not preclude the use of other quotative markers to do the same sort of interactional work. For students whose linguistic repertoire did not include the use of *be all*, *be like* performed this function perfectly well. In example (12), the two "normal" girls Erin and Iris are discussing the frustrations they experienced in doing a class project requiring each student to work with a classmate outside of school.

(12) 1 Iris: Ugh.
2 Trust [$_1$me,
3 Erin: [$_1$So ma:d. $_1$]
4 Iris: I didn't have$_1$] a very good time with Barb,
5 ei@the@r.
6 Erin: Rea:lly?
7 <food packages rustling; eating>
8 She was just ↑irritating?
9 Or it was hard to write?
10 Iris: She just like,
11 <eating>
12 wouldn't do it.=
13 =It was like,
14 **she was like**,
15 <high-pitched, nasal> {"O:h,
16 I don't wa:nt to.
17 Na:::h."}
18 **I was like**,
19 "This is gonna—
20 This is easy.
21 Let's just sit down and do it,"
22 you kno:w?
23 **She's like**,
24 <high-pitched, nasal> {"No::,
25 let's take a brea:k."}
26 We like w-
27 She watched TV for two hours while I: typed it.
28 Basically.
29 <eating>

30 Erin: [$_2$Oh my goodness.$_2$]
31 Iris: [$_2$And **I was like**, $_2$]
32 <tense, rapid> {"Great."}

Here, precisely the same kinds of features of stance taking occur as in previous examples, but with *be like* rather than *be all*: special voice qualities and prosody (lines 15–17; lines 24–25) and social evaluation of others (lines 31–32). Affect and evaluation are fundamental to talk; the presence or absence of a particular quotative is not crucial to such stance taking, although the additional indexicality of *be all* as a marker of preppy popularity made it an especially rich semiotic resource for speakers who chose to use it.

Conclusion

As participants in an elite white youth style, preppies at Bay City High School claimed a form of social prestige associated with academics and extracurricular activities that endowed them with control of the school's social space and made them high-profile – or popular – figures. Linguistically, preppies outpaced their peers in the use of the innovative quotative marker *be all*, a form that was disproportionately used by European American teenagers.

While at Bay City High School in the mid-1990s *be all* was used by preppy girls primarily as a default quotative marker, it could be used by nonpreppy teenagers as a marker of (negative) evaluation. This situation suggests that some of the ideological meaning of popularity adhered to the form as it moved into other social groups. That is, what indexically tied *be all* to evaluative stance taking may have been its association with popular, preppy white girls. Elaine Chun (2007) has shown that *oh my god!* had a similar semiotic flexibility for students at an ethnoracially diverse Texas high school. Chun found that *oh my god!* could be used by students of color either to mockingly ventriloquate a preppy white girl style or to earnestly engage in the same sorts of high-affect talk that were seen as particularly characteristic of that style. In my own data, such mocking performances do not occur, and it is not clear whether nonpreppy teenagers consciously associated *be all* with preppies. However, given the ideology linking popularity to "meanness," negative stance taking and mockery of others were viewed as practices particularly characteristic of preppy girls.

The *be all* quotative marker was one of a number of semiotic resources for displaying preppiness as a cool mainstream white style. But not all European American teenagers strove for this form of coolness. In the next chapter, I examine how those who embraced a very different style, hip hop, positioned themselves linguistically by rejecting the indexes of preppy youth and borrowing instead from African American language and culture.

6 Pretty fly for a white guy: European American hip hop fans and African American English

Introduction

One of the students who most intrigued me in Ms. Stein's Life and Health class was a boy named Eddie, a wisecracking white sophomore. Every element of Eddie's stylistic choices was flamboyant, from his class-clown persona to his colorful oversized clothing to his loudly advertised musical tastes. But what I noticed most of all was his speech style, which involved numerous phonological and grammatical features of African American Vernacular English (AAVE) as well as lexical items from African American youth slang.

I had undertaken my research with the original goal of studying teenagers like Eddie, European Americans who participated in hip hop culture. By the mid-1990s, hip hop had a significant impact on American (and global) culture generally, yet Eddie was the first white student I encountered at Bay City High who seemed unambiguously to be an aficionado of this style. Other white youth who embraced hip hop were generally much less extreme in their stylistic choices; indeed, I had completed several weeks of participant-observation before I realized that a number of the European American boys I knew were, like Eddie, avid hip hop fans. I soon learned that such students were often mocked by their peers, both black and white. Consequently, many displayed their identities through relatively small, often incremental clothing and speech markers.

By contrast, Eddie's style semiotically matched or even outpaced the trendiest African American boys at the school, although as far as I was able to discover he had no close contact with them – or with other white youth. He and his best friend, an Arab American boy who did not participate heavily in hip hop, remained at the periphery of Bay City High's social hierarchy, hanging out in the region of the courtyard associated with the school's low-status "scrubs." Undeterred by his marginal social status, Eddie was an exuberant adherent of hip hop style. While most white hip hop fans wore caps, either with the brim forward or – more daringly – backward, Eddie was one of the few teenagers of any race to wear his cap rakishly sideways. He was also one of the first white students to adopt the black youth fashion of wearing his jacket hood over his cap, and he was one of only a few European American hip hop fans at the school who wore one leg of his athletic pants pushed up to his knee, a widespread stylistic practice among cool African American boys.

In some cases, Eddie outdid his black peer role models in his stylistic statements: he did not simply carry a pager, a technological trend mostly restricted to African American youth at that time, but instead wore no fewer than three pagers clipped to the waistband of his pants and also carried a cell phone, then a rarity among Bay City High School students. Moreover, while many teenagers of all races brought small Sony Walkman-style audio cassette players to school to listen to music on headphones throughout the day, Eddie brought an oversized boom box, from which he blasted his favorite rap music for all to hear, sometimes even during classes. Eddie's language use was no less ostentatious than these other aspects of his style. Unlike other white hip hop fans I encountered at Bay City High, he made heavy use of a wide range of AAVE features, particularly the most stereotypical and semiotically recognizable forms. Unfortunately, however, I was unable to record Eddie's speech style despite several attempts to interview him.

This chapter examines the language use of white boys at Bay City High who participated in hip hop; I knew of no white female students who were deeply involved in this style. In fact, the participation of girls of any race or ethnicity in hip hop was quite rare at the school in the mid-1990s. As a largely gendered youth style, hip hop offered European American boys a form of cool masculinity that was unavailable within the styles that predominated among white teenagers. In the 1990s, hip hop culture, especially the commercialized version most accessible to white fans, was deeply influenced by gangsta rap, a genre that promotes a hypermasculine ideal of the "hard" (i.e., strong and unyielding) black "thug" or gangster. Nationwide, white adolescent boys' eager consumption of this image of African American masculinity sparked a moral panic among European American adults. The white hip hop fans I knew did not embrace the physically intimidating gangster style, and none belonged to gangs. Nevertheless, the association of hip hop with cool black masculinity opened them to criticism from both black and other white youth.

AAVE was a key resource in the construction of European American hip hop fans' style. None of the white teenagers whose speech I analyze below were fluent speakers of AAVE, nor did they share a linguistically consistent speech style. Rather, each boy employed a small set of linguistic features in everyday speech without adhering to the variety's grammatical rules. Yet even this very superficial use of African American language was highly salient and sanctionable in the eyes of other teenagers.

Racial and stylistic ideologies of hip hop

African American Vernacular English is an ethnoracially specific nonstandard linguistic variety spoken by many African Americans at least some of the time.

For many years, studies carried out on European Americans' use of AAVE features focused mainly on the degree to which white patterns of AAVE use corresponded to black AAVE patterns (e.g., Ash and Myhill 1986; Labov 1980; Labov and Harris 1986). Other scholarship points to the need to take speakers' and community members' own perspectives into consideration when analyzing European Americans' use of AAVE (Cutler 2003b; Hatala 1976; Jacobs-Huey 1996; Sweetland 2002), noting that what counts as authentic AAVE, for whom, and for what purposes is a contested question.

Two competing language ideologies circulated at Bay City High regarding white hip hop fans' speech style: one racial and the other stylistic. According to the racial ideology, which was held by most students at the school, hip hop's AAVE-influenced language was a form of racialized cultural property indexical of black – or at least nonwhite – identity. White male hip hop fans were often viewed as illegitimately appropriating the coolness of black youth culture and the tough masculinity associated with hip hop style. In contrast, European American hip hop fans favored a stylistic ideology, which held that the semiotic practices of hip hop were not indexical of race but rather were available to all participants in hip hop culture.

The stigma associated with white participation in hip hop was so strong that even European American boys who adopted this style at times condemned it as inauthentic – at least as enacted by others. This is the case in example (1), which comes from a discussion of slang with two white boys: Charlie, who had an alternative style, and his friend Jay, a hip hop fan. In an earlier one-on-one interview with me, Charlie was critical of Jay's use of African American-influenced language (example 5 in Chapter 3). In this example, I have asked Jay about his previous use of the term *perpetrate*, an African American slang term that means 'pretend' or 'behave in a false way.'

(1)	1	Jay:	Perpetrate.
	2		Like,
	3		.h
	4		h::
	5		If you're trying to be: something that you're no:t,
	6		du:de.
	7	Charlie:	<creaky voice> {Yea:h.}
	8	Jay:	[$_1$Like,
	9		u:m,$_1$]
	10	Mary:	[$_1$Oka:y. $_1$]
	11	Charlie:	Trying to ma:rk,
	12		<creaky voice> {and like,}
	13		(0.5)
	14	Jay:	Yeah,
	15		like,=

Mary: =Mark?=
Charlie: =Just trying to act like you're something that you
<creaky voice> {ar:en't.}
Jay: <creaky voice> {Yea:h.}
Like,
like a white dude trying to a:ct,
hella bla:ck,
hella ghetto,
you know?
Mary: Okay.
Jay: Not—
well,
I can't really say black,
but you know.
Hella,
[$_{2}$↑hella,
foo:ls,$_{2}$]
Charlie: [$_{2}$Mhm. $_{2}$]
(0.6)
Jay: Fools that are hella,
yeah,
you know,
that have their pa:nts hella dow:n,

In his use of the word earlier in this discussion, Jay produced *perpetrate* with a distinctive sing-song "shout-out" intonation employed by many African American students during athletic events, pep rallies, and similar activities. The intonational contour is in fact not apt for this word. However, Jay often used this contour to mark a term or utterance as indexical of blackness, which may have enabled him to use African American slang terms among his European American friends with less risk of criticism than if he used them as part of his ordinary speech style. Here he similarly pronounces the word with syllable-final stress (line 1), in contrast to my own immediately prior pronunciation of the word with syllable-initial stress. He then offers a definition, which Charlie paraphrases as "trying to ma:rk" (line 11). *Mark* is likewise an African American lexical item; as a verb it refers to mockery or parodic imitation (Mitchell-Kernan 1971), but it can also be used as a noun to refer to wannabe gangsters.

This second meaning of *mark* may be what triggers Jay to provide an example: *like a white dude trying to a:ct, hella bla:ck, hella ghetto* (lines 21–23). Jay's phrasing echoes Charlie's characterization of Jay, in example (5) in Chapter 3, as trying to "talk like" his black baseball teammates: *Sometimes he tries to act pretty ghetto*. However, Jay withdraws his statement connecting "acting ghetto" to "acting black" (lines 26–28). And where Charlie's description of Jay focused specifically on his friend's black-influenced language use, Jay instead highlights fashion, particularly the hip hop style of wearing baggy, oversized pants that sag below one's boxer shorts. (As it happened, Jay also wore relatively baggy, low-riding pants, but in a modified style that generally did not expose his underwear.) Both boys evaluate white youth who appropriate black stylistic practices as inauthentic, but Charlie endorses the racial ideology, while Jay condemns only the most extreme cases of stylistic crossing (as emphasized by his six uses of the intensifier *hella*), rejecting the idea that such crossing is necessarily racialized, and not mentioning language use at all. In his own speech, Jay engages in a similar balancing act, first using stylized African American English prosody and then switching to an unperformed style, to which he appends the address term *dude* (line 6). The precise function of this slang word here is unclear, although it seems to highlight the performed nature of the previous utterance by enacting a different and perhaps whiter youth style (cf. Kiesling 2004). This example illustrates one way that teenagers like Jay managed the risk of being accused of "perpetrating." In addition, it indicates the ideological distance between European American hop hop fans and their peers in evaluating the meaning of their stylistic practices.

The stylistic ideology held by white hip hop fans runs counter to sociolinguists' understanding of AAVE as a unified and structurally complex linguistic system. Instead, in this ideology African American language is treated as a set of largely unrelated linguistic features – including not only grammar but also phonology and lexicon. Ben Rampton (1999: 423) calls such semiotic resources "textual projectiles" that a speaker can combine via bricolage to construct a specific style. At Bay City High, the stylistic ideology was less often explicitly articulated than linguistically enacted as white participants in hip hop claimed elements of African American English for their own uses. Coupled with these linguistic features were practices of self-adornment that allowed European American teenagers to physically embody a hip hop style.

The embodied semiotics of white hip hop

I was initially surprised when European American hip hop fans were characterized by their peers as "talking black." It eventually became clear to me that what these comments oriented to was not simply a way of speaking but an entire style that involved semiotic practices of physical self-presentation, social geography, and language use.

By the 1990s, the practices of hip hop were widespread enough to have influenced many white youth. A number of preppy, "normal," and even nerdy white students, both female and male, told me that they had been marginally involved in tagging, or marking public spaces with one's graffiti name, during their junior high school years but now viewed this practice as a passé childhood fad. Hip hop fans distinguished themselves from these other groups through their long-term, in-depth engagement in at least some aspects of hip hop culture and through their physical and linguistic display of that affiliation. Yet most white hip hop fans at Bay City High participated in hip hop culture only peripherally as consumers of fashion and rap music (although one friendship group also produced "pieces," or large-scale graffiti art, around Bay City and surrounding areas, and several boys participated in tagging, a practice also embraced by some alternative teenagers). By contrast with the central activities of hip hop, which involve cultural production, hip hop fashion and language involve only cultural consumption, and European Americans had access to these primarily through the media: rap music, videos, magazines, and so on.

The geographic dimension of European American hip hop style is seen in the maps of the high school drawn by two white hip hop fans, Willie and Brand One. Willie marks his location on the school grounds with circled Xs – one on the steps of the arts building, which he labels *white*, and one on the Hill, where his "Basketball friends" are, which he labels *black* (Figure 6.1). In Figure 6.2, Willie's best friend Brand One offers a similar though sketchier representation. He positions himself both with Willie on the Steps and across the courtyard on the classroom building steps, with a "diverse" group of students. Indeed, all of the boys discussed in this chapter took up multiple positions within the racially charged terrain of Bay City High.

Table 6.1 lists the clothing preferences of the five white hip hop fans that I observed most extensively. All the boys drew on the same general hip hop style popular in the mid-1990s and widely worn by students of color, especially African Americans: an oversized but meticulously clean-cut look that drew on designer labels like Tommy Hilfiger and Polo by Ralph Lauren. As mentioned in the previous chapter, before this time, such fashions had been more associated with white country clubs than black hip hop clubs (see also Kakutani 1997); though often termed *preppy*, these designers were not favored by preppy teenagers at Bay City High during the time of my study. The basic hip hop uniform was a cap, chunky athletic shoes, an extra-large polo or button-down shirt layered over a white T-shirt, sagging jeans or Dickies work pants that might reveal the wearer's boxer shorts, and – often even on warm days – an oversized jacket. But each boy shaped this style in his own way.

As the table indicates, Al Capone adopted a rugged and outdoorsy look, while Jay, a baseball player on a largely black team, had a more sporty style. Brand One showed the most sartorial attention to detail – he even had a name for his style ("pretty-boy"), which he claimed he and his friend Willie had invented (despite its close resemblance to general hip hop fashion). Unlike most other boys, shopping was one of his favorite activities. Billy, by contrast,

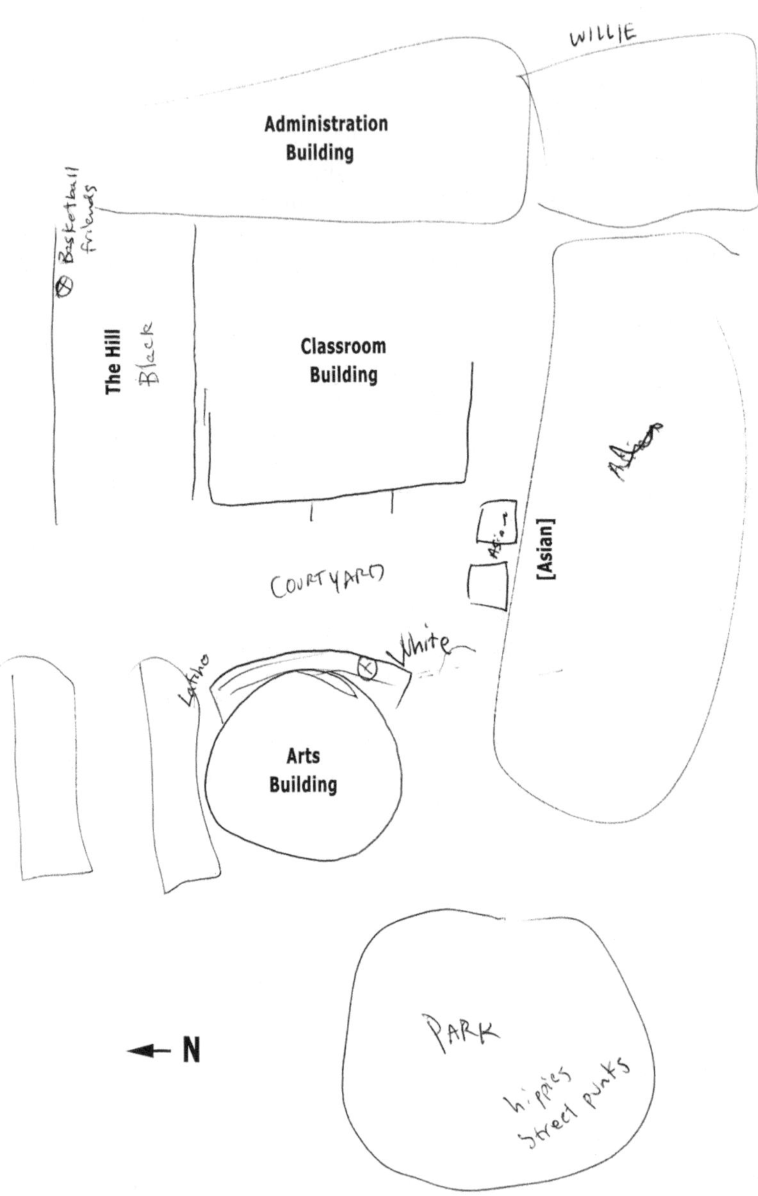

Figure 6.1: Willie's map of Bay City High School

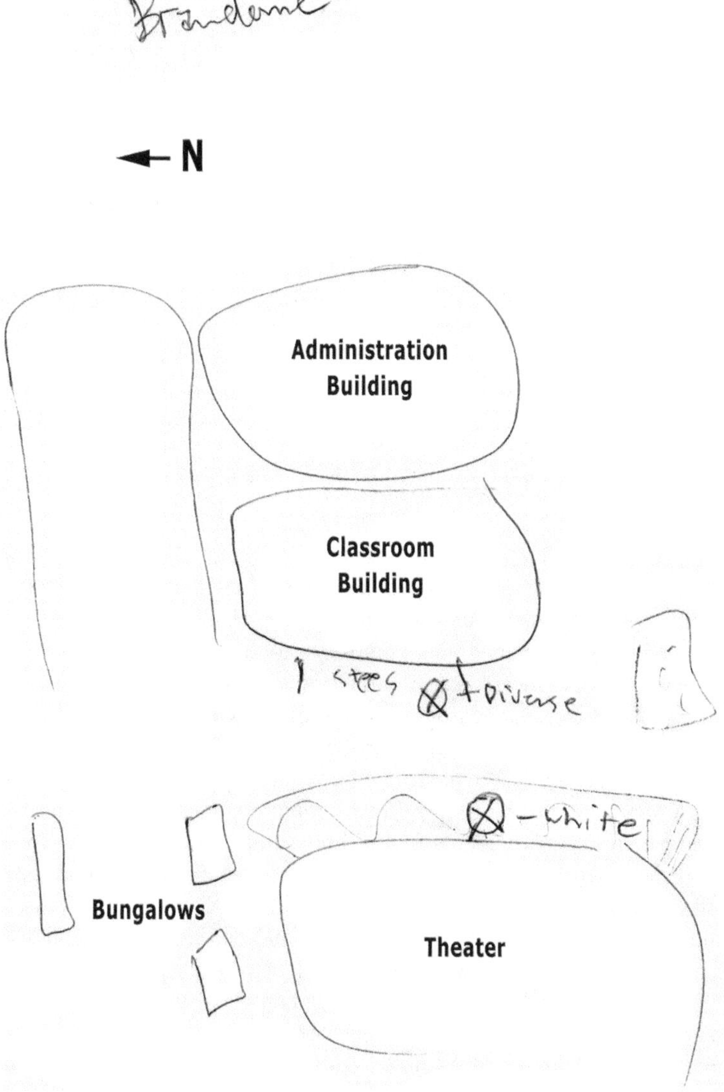

Figure 6.2: Brand One's map of Bay City High School

Table 6.1. *Clothing styles of five European American boys affiliated with hip hop culture at Bay City High School*

	cap	jacket	shirt	shoes
Al Capone	baseball cap with Timberland, Nautica, Hilfiger logo	Eddie Bauer	Polo	Nike hiking boots
Billy	Kangol golf-style cap, knit ski cap, army hat	sports team logo (local), North Face, camouflage jacket	Ben Davis	hiking boots
Brand One	none	North Face, Adidas	Polo	Nike (numerous pairs and styles)
Eddie	Nike baseball cap	Nike	Nike	Nike
Jay	baseball cap with sports team logo (New York and local)	Adidas (?)	T-shirts with sports team logos	Adidas

was very eclectic; in the middle of the school year he shifted from a stoner style to a hip hop style and sometimes combined elements of both. Finally, while Nike was a popular brand with many boys, Eddie's brand loyalty was unsurpassed; I never saw any other company's logo on his clothing.

Economic factors played an important role in these stylistic decisions. Designer fashions were largely out of reach for many black participants in hip hop, and a number of the African American boys at Bay City High wore the same brand-name item often instead of rotating their wardrobe frequently, as many European American hip hop fans could do. Thus even though white boys were marginal participants in hip hop culture, they were more easily able than many of their peers of color to express their identity through hip hop fashion. But there was variation here as well: Al Capone and Brand One were both from solidly middle-class families and had larger wardrobes than Billy, Eddie, or Jay, from lower-middle-class or working-class homes. Like many black teenagers, Eddie was able to maintain his distinctive style only by regularly wearing the same few items repeatedly.

White students' styles also changed over time as they became more involved in hip hop culture. At the beginning of the school year, Al Capone had a bowl haircut, but by May he was wearing his hair shaved short and covered with a cap much of the time. Likewise, as noted above, Billy gradually shifted from a stoner style to a hip hop style. Although he tended toward unkemptness earlier in the year, one day he appeared at school in a pristine hip hop outfit, with a carefully pressed baggy button-down shirt and Dickies pants with sharp seams; from that point on his style was more influenced by hip hop. Beginning as a ponytail in the fall, his hairstyle became gradually shorter, until by the end of the year it was a crewcut, a style that generated a great deal of teasing from other students of all races. Similarly, when Eddie arrived in class with his already short hair in a fade, a hairstyle that originated in hip hop, he was relentlessly mocked by his classmates (see example 3c below).

There were limits to how much these boys participated in the embodied style of their black male peers. For example, many African American boys often wedged an index card or a pen under the side of their cap, and some white hip hop fans emulated this trend. However, no European American boy carried a sports towel or a wooden hairbrush, both popular and highly visible accessories among black boys. And while a few white participants in hip hop, like many African American boys, wore heavy gold chains around their necks, European American hip hop fans did not adopt the black male trend of wearing small gold hoop earrings in both ears (although some alternative boys wore a single small stud). Moreover, while moustaches and long sideburns were not uncommon among African American (and Latino) students, European American hip hop fans had, at most, slight stubble on their upper lips rather than full facial hair. (By contrast, some alternative boys wore full beards or goatees, and preppy, "normal," and nerdy white male students were consistently clean-shaven.) This careful calibration of what was stylistically acceptable seemed tacitly to acknowledge that at least some semiotic resources were the racialized cultural property of black teenagers. To use these resources, especially in the presence of African American students, was thus risky, as indicated by example (2). Here Norman, an African American boy, comments critically and loudly about Al Capone to George, another black teenager:

(2) Fieldnotes

Norman: That patna over there. He got the hip hop stuff. He be geared *up*!

Norman's comment is a form of signifying, an African American discourse genre in which a speaker pointedly but indirectly criticizes another person (Mitchell-Kernan 1971; Morgan 1998). In derisively applying the affiliative term *patna* to Al, Norman indirectly indicates that to refer to his white classmate in this way is as inauthentic as Al's hip hop style. That is, his comment implies that Al thinks he is Norman and George's "patna" but in fact is not. Furthermore, African American linguistic forms proliferate in Norman's utterance in a way that iconically mocks Al's careful adherence to hip hop style: not only does he refer to the other boy as a *patna* but he uses the AAVE grammatical form habitual *be* to indicate that Al is always dressed in hip hop fashion; he also uses a zero form of the auxiliary *has* with *got*, another AAVE grammatical feature. This exaggerated linguistic performance implies that Al's embodied stylistic performance is likewise excessive. Norman thus makes clear that he does not consider Al a patna at all but only a wannabe. Examples like (2) demonstrate the close relationship between fashion and language in hip hop style as well as the controversial nature of white teenagers' use of these resources.

The stylistic use of African American language in white hip hop

What unified the speech style of white hip hop fans was not its linguistic characteristics, which varied widely across individual speakers, but rather the contested yet widely recognized ideological associations of these features. A number of linguistic resources – ranging from lexicon to phonology to grammar – were used by white participants in hip hop culture to position themselves stylistically.

Lexicon

In creating a hip hop linguistic style, one of the simplest strategies for European American students was to use a large number of lexical items associated with African American youth. Unlike grammar and phonology, lexicon was relatively straightforward for white teenagers to incorporate into their everyday speech style because it was easy to identify and did not require mastery of complex structural patterns. Hip hop slang was a particularly important resource in this regard, but speakers sometimes used more general African American English terms as well (example 3):

(3a) Fieldnotes
<Calvin, a black boy, has been telling Brand One about a trick that Tiffany, a black girl, can do.>
Brand One: Tiffany! <wiggles fingers, beckoning her to join him and Calvin>
Calvin: She can put her arms behind her back. <demonstrates, smiling>
<Tiffany folds both arms up behind her back>
Calvin: That's nasty!
Brand One: Damn, **girl**!

(3b) Ethnographic interview
Willie: Like East Coast **fools** <'people, guys'> all have like leather jackets.

(3c) Fieldnotes
<Nick, a black boy, has just commented mockingly on Eddie's new haircut.>
Eddie: <irritably> That's how he cut my hair, **blood**.

(3d) Ethnographic interview
<discussing his friends>
Billy: They're my **homies** <'friends'>, I **give them props** <'show them respect'>.

(3e) Fieldnotes
<G.C., a black boy, tries to return the pen that Billy lent him>
G.C.: Billy! <extends pen>
Billy: **It's all good**. <'It's fine', i.e., 'Don't worry about it'>

(3f) Ethnographic interview
<discussing his white friend Shawn, who is also a hip hop fan>
Al: I mean Shawn'll like,
I'll get into an ar-
a **phat** <'big'> argument with him and,
I mean I know that we're going to still be friends afterwards . . .

(3g) Fieldnotes
<following a dispute between two other students over the ownership of a pen>
Al: If I dropped my pen and somebody picked **that shit** <'that thing'> up, I'd be all over him.

(3h) Fieldnotes
<Priscilla, a white teacher, is trying to organize students to get down to work with their partners on a group project.>
Priscilla: Where's your partner?
Jay: <mock-tearful quality> She left me for another man.
Priscilla: Can you blame her?
Jay: **Scandalous**! <['skænləs]>

(3i) Ethnographic interview
<discussing another hip hop crew>
1 Shawn: They breakdance,
2 and they're in <a local hip hop crew>,
3 but they're not good graffiti writers,
4 but they are graffiti writers,
5 so they'll **hit it up** <'write graffiti'>.

As is common in slang, many of the terms adopted by these boys involve address and person reference (examples 3a–3d), as well as evaluative lexical items (examples 3e–3h). Such forms mark the speaker's stance, while their semiotic associations with hip hop index his style. These teenagers also used slang terms for the central cultural values and practices of hip hop, such as *give props* 'give appropriate respect or recognition to another's status or accomplishments' (example 3d; *props* derives from *proper*), and *hit it up* 'write graffiti' (example 3i). Some terms in example (3) have now entered the American mainstream, but at the time of the study they were understood as black forms.

Address terms were especially powerful – and dangerous – tools for white teenagers' identity work, for they often carry not just semiotic information about stance and style but also semantic information about race and gender. As discussed in Chapter 4, the most problematic term in this regard was *nigga*, which was used by many African American boys at Bay City High as an affiliative or neutral term of address but was off limits to European American youth given its possible use as a racist insult. Thus Eddie in example (3c) addresses an African American boy with *blood*, another widespread term among black male students that indexed racial affiliation but without the potential associations with racism. Eddie's use of this term to an African American could have been taken as a strong (and possibly illegitimate) claim to racialized solidarity, but it passed without remark, perhaps because his classmates were familiar with his speech style. With girls, the situation was a bit different, since neither *blood* nor *nigga* was used toward female addressees. As seen in example (3a), *girl*, a generally affiliative address term used by African American speakers of all ages and both genders, could be used more freely since it lacked the racial semantics of the terms for male addressees. *Fools*, a generic term similar to 'guys' (example 3b) likewise lacked a racial meaning (nor was it necessarily negative).

Other terms were less strongly associated with blackness. In example (3g) Al Capone's emphatic use of *that shit* in anaphoric reference (i.e., reference to a prior noun phrase; here, *my pen*) was a common linguistic practice among African American teenagers, but it is similar enough to nonanaphoric uses of *that shit* by European American youth that it may not have been viewed as distinctively black, while still lending a hip hop flavor to Al's speech.

Speakers could heighten the connection between their own speech style and African American language by calibrating their use of other linguistic features when using lexical items from black youth culture. In (3h), for example, Jay uses a negative evaluative slang term, *scandalous*, that was very popular with African American teenagers but was rare among European Americans, employing African American English phonology (specifically, consonant cluster simplification) as he does so. Indeed, African American-derived lexicon was often coupled with African American English phonology in white hip hop fans' language use.

Phonology

Table 6.2 summarizes the presence of phonological features of African American English in the speech of seven European American participants in hip hop (no frequency counts are provided because Eddie's data are based on fieldnotes). Data are also included from two other boys: G.C., an African American, and Mark, a European American. A fluent speaker of AAVE, G.C. was widely admired by students of all races as an icon of coolness for his hard, affectless style. Mark, a preppy white boy, had no involvement in African American youth culture (his only black friends were members of majority-white friendship groups). The speech of these two boys therefore provides useful points of comparison with the linguistic practices of white hip hop fans.

Table 6.2. *African American English phonological features in the speech of nine boys at Bay City High School (data from European American hip hop fans are shaded)*

	monophthongal /aj/	/ð/ fortition	glottalized /d/	vocalized /l/	vocalized /r/
G.C. (black)	x	x	x	x	x
Al Capone	x	x		x	
Billy	x		x		
Brand One	x		x	x	x
Eddie	x	x	x	x	x
Jay	x		x		
Shawn	x				
Willie	x			x	
Mark (white)	x				

The table lists the five phonological features most widely used by white participants in hip hop. The first is the monophthongization of the diphthong /aj/ in words like *buy* [baː] and *rise* [ɹaːz], which is found in a number of European American varieties throughout the United States, especially the South, as well as in African American English nationwide. All the speakers, including Mark, used some monophthongization, but G.C. and the white boys who affiliated with hip hop did so much more extensively.

The second feature is the fortition of the voiced interdental fricative /ð/ to a voiced alveolar stop [d] in word-initial position, as in *the* [də], *this* [dɪs], and *those* [doʊz]. This feature was less common than monophthongization but was heavily used by some boys. Fortition of /ð/ is characteristic not only of African American English but also of several European American urban working-class varieties on the East Coast; within California, however, it is most strongly associated with black speech.

The glottalization of word-final /d/, as in *good* [gʊʔ], is frequent within African American English but is less stereotypical of the variety than the previous two features. At Bay City High School, glottalized final /d/ was quite salient to white teenagers, as seen in the use of this feature by several boys.

The last two features involve the vocalization of the liquids /l/ and /r/ in postvocalic position. Within African American English, /l/ vocalization may occur in syllable-final position, as in *whole* [hoʊ], as well as before a following consonant, as in *old* [oʊd]. This feature often goes unrecognized by the general population as characteristic of African American English, yet it was part of the speech style of some white hip hop fans. By contrast, /r/ vocalization is a highly stereotypical feature of African American English phonology; perhaps for that very reason it was rarely used by most European American participants in hip hop except in specific slang terms such as *playa* (from *player*; 'male with many romantic or sexual liaisons') and *patna*, both of which are almost obligatorily pronounced with vocalized /r/ by young speakers of all races and ethnicities. In California /r/-less pronunciation is primarily used by black speakers; for a white speaker to use this feature, then, would be to make a strong claim to African American language. The use of /l/ vocalization, on the other hand, may have allowed these boys to signal their affiliation with hip hop without transgressing local racialized linguistic boundaries.

Although most boys used only some of these features, Eddie used all of them, some quite heavily, as well as other African American English phonological forms. Most strikingly, not only did he use vocalized /r/ in unstressed syllables as in *mother*, but he also consistently did so even in stressed monomorphemic words like *sure* [ʃoʊ] and *floor* [floʊ], a pronunciation that was unusual even for most of his African American peers in the classroom setting.

Individual white hip hop fans also used phonological forms that were more restricted in their scope. For example, Eddie regularly deleted the /r/ in *through*, a less familiar feature of African American English phonology that also occurs in some other English varieties. And both Jay and Billy sometimes pronounced /ɪŋ/ as [æ̃ŋ] in words like *thing* and *stink*, a widespread stereotype of African American English. Jay additionally made frequent use of the distinctive "shout-out" intonational contour discussed in example (1) above, as well as stress patterns characteristic of African American English (e.g., *Did you beát her àss?*, jokingly addressed to an African American girl, with primary stress on the verb, as opposed to the more typical colloquial Standard English pattern with primary stress on the object: *Did you beàt her áss?*). Finally, to differing extents several of the boys regularized the definite determiner *a* before a vowel, as in *a attitude* (Brand One), *a accident* (Al Capone), and *a other* (Willie).

Grammar

Previous research on black–white language crossing suggests that grammatical structures and nonstereotypical lexical and phonological features are adopted only by white speakers with extensive cultural integration (Cutler 2003a; Hewitt 1986; Hatala 1976; Sweetland 2002). But despite the fact that most European American hip hop fans at Bay City High School generally were not closely connected to African American students' social networks, some AAVE grammatical features occurred in their speech. This somewhat unexpected finding may have been due to speakers' exposure to AAVE grammar through

Table 6.3. *African American Vernacular English grammatical features in the speech of nine boys at Bay City High School (data from European American hip hop fans are shaded)*

	multiple negation	habitual *be*	3s verbal *-s* leveling	zero aux/ copula	remote past *been*	existential *it*
G.C. (black)	x	x	x	x	x	x
Al Capone	x					
Billy	x		x		x	
Brand One	x					
Eddie	x	x	x	x		
Jay	x	x				
Shawn	x					
Willie	x					x
Mark (white)						

their close attention to rap lyrics, which many fans committed to memory and even recited quietly to themselves as they walked through the halls or sat at their desks. However, white teenagers did not fully master the use of these forms or the complex linguistic system of which they were part.

Table 6.3 summarizes the AAVE grammatical features most commonly used by European American hip hop fans at Bay City High compared to G.C. and Mark. Once again, aside from Eddie, individual boys drew on a small number of grammatical structures in their creation of a hip hop speech style, and most used these only occasionally. It is likely that some used additional features that do not occur in my data set. Notably, all the features in the table were used by G.C., and none were used by Mark except in joking contexts.

The most common grammatical resource for marking a white hip hop identity was the use of multiple negation, as illustrated in example (4):

(4) Fieldnotes
Al: We can't have food in the building no more.

This type of structure was used by all the white hip hop fans in Table 6.3 to at least some extent. Some alternative teenagers also used the structure to stake out a tough, rebellious identity based on the association of multiple negation with working-class speech (Eckert 2000). White participants in hip hop drew on the same feature to align with black youth culture via AAVE. These indexicalities, which exploit the ideology of nonstandard speakers as tough and cool, are overlapping but distinct; the semiotic meaning in each case derives not from the grammatical form itself but from the co-occurrence of this form with other stylistic resources, including other linguistic structures.

Both Eddie and Jay, for example, used habitual *be*, one of the most familiar – and most misunderstood – linguistic stereotypes of AAVE. Non-AAVE speakers generally orient to *be* as an invariant form rather than to its specific grammatical function as a verbal aspect marker of repeated or habitual action. As a consequence, many mocking representations of AAVE incorrectly use invariant *be* in nonhabitual grammatical contexts (Rickford and Rickford 2000; Ronkin and Karn 1999). Remarkably, then, when this feature occurred in white hip hop fans' speech, it was accurately used as a marker of habitual aspect, as in example (5).

(5) Fieldnotes
<Kerry, a white girl, and Jay are looking at the class schedule of required team presentations>
Jay: I don't want to do it.
Kerry: Why not? Isn't your partner here?
Jay: Probably not. She never be coming.

Jay correctly uses habitual *be* to convey a meaning that would be rendered in other varieties of English as *She never comes*. However, the use of this form by white speakers was relatively rare as well as grammatically restricted compared to its use by fluent speakers; it did not reflect the full range of syntactic structures in which habitual *be* may occur (Green 2002).

Two other widely recognized features of AAVE grammar used by some European American hip hop fans were leveling of verbal *-s* in the third-person singular verb form in the present tense (e.g., *She go*) and the use of the zero form of the copula/auxiliary *to be* (e.g., *She going*). Both Eddie and Billy used the first of these features, but only Eddie used the second in my data. Examples of both forms in Eddie's speech are shown in (6).[1]

(6a) Fieldnotes
<In Life and Health class, describing the effects of heavy drinking>
Eddie: It make you do like this. <jitters body> It do!

(6b) Fieldnotes
<In Life and Health class, explaining how pregnancy occurs>
Eddie: When he shoot his nut it go up in there.

(6c) Fieldnotes
<Neil, a white boy, and Eddie are seated in desks facing each other across the central open space of the classroom>
Neil: Why are you looking at me?
Eddie: 'Cause you looking at me.

The other six white boys in the study who were involved in hip hop used AAVE grammatical structures relatively rarely; by contrast, Eddie used numerous features of AAVE grammar at very high rates. His rates of verbal *-s* leveling and zero copula/auxiliary, for example, impressionistically appeared to be close to 100 percent. Such high frequencies should not be taken as evidence that he was fluent in AAVE, however, for as sociolinguists have demonstrated, most fluent speakers systematically alternate their use of these forms with other variants, and thus Eddie's speech exemplifies supercorrection, or the phenomenon of surpassing fluent speakers' rates of use of specific variants (Bucholtz 2001).[2] Stylistically, such supercorrection corresponds with Eddie's flamboyant physical self-presentation to create a spectacular version of white hip hop style.

Two other grammatical features, though equally distinctive to AAVE and well documented by linguists, are less often recognized as characteristic of the variety and perhaps as a consequence were less often used by European American students in projecting a hip hop identity. The first was remote past *been*, which like habitual *be* is a marker of verbal aspect. This form is used to mark an action that has taken place in the relatively distant past but remains relevant to the present. When functioning as an aspectual marker in this way, *been* is obligatorily marked with stress. The examples in (7), taken from an interview with Billy and his friends, illustrate the use of this feature.

(7a) Ethnographic interview
<Billy has just told me that he used to attend Bay City High and now attends it again after attending another school for a year>
Mary: That was sort of how you met people?
(1.2)
Billy: Well,
I'm—
I been knowing everybody,

(7b) Ethnographic interview
<In response to my question about whether he plays sports>
Billy: Um:,
I do spor-
Acme: <clears throat>=
Billy: =I been doing sports,

Whereas many European Americans incorrectly interpret remote past *been* as indicating a completed past action that is no longer relevant (Rickford 1975), Billy uses the form correctly. In both examples, which took place a few moments apart, *been* indicates that a state or activity occurred in the past and is still ongoing; thus (7a) may be paraphrased as *I've known everybody for a long time* and (7b) as *I've been doing sports for a long time*. Despite his correct use of the aspect marker with present participle (*-ing*) verb forms, however, Billy does not employ remote past *been* in other linguistic contexts where fluent AAVE speakers use it, such as with verbs marked for past tense (Green 1998; Rickford 1975). (The fact that Billy twice produces remote past *been* after a self-interruption may also indicate that he is correcting away from Standard English and toward AAVE; cf. Cutler 1999.)

The final grammatical feature of AAVE in Table 6.3 is existential *it*. From a linguistic standpoint, this form is less difficult to master than aspect markers like *be* and *been* because it is structurally less complex, involving a single morpheme, *it*, where Standard English uses *there* in constructions expressing existence (e.g., *It ain't no God*; Labov 1972b). Yet perhaps because it is a minor morphosyntactic phenomenon involving a small, unstressed grammatical morpheme, existential *it* is little recognized by nonspeakers of AAVE. It is therefore not an obvious choice for a white speaker to use to index a hip hop identity, and indeed, only one boy, Willie, who played on a largely African American basketball team, used this form.

(8) Ethnographic interview
<Regarding regional styles of rap music>
1 Mary: So is there like a difference between East Coast and West Coast,
2 'cause some people were saying=
3 Willie: =Yeah.=
4 =[It is.]
5 Mary: =[that there's like a] huge difference.

Willie uses the AAVE form in line 4 in response to my Standard English question in line 1. By contrast with Eddie's frequent use of multiple grammatical stereotypes, Willie's use of existential *it* is by no means a flamboyant assertion of cultural affiliation with hip hop. It may well be that Willie had an especially acute awareness of language that led him to notice and use this easily overlooked form.

For these seven European American boys, mastery of the entire linguistic system of AAVE was not feasible, but fluency was not necessarily their goal. Rather, they were able to project their identities as members of hip hop culture with only rudimentary knowledge of a few grammatical structures, an equally sketchy understanding of several phonological features, and heavy use of African American youth slang. There were also differences in black versus white students' use of these forms in the classroom. Black teenagers used AAVE in situationally sensitive ways, often shifting toward Standard English when addressing European Americans. Some white hip hop fans, by contrast, adhered to their AAVE-influenced speech style in such contexts. This difference may have been partly due to the fact that African American students were sometimes "corrected" by both black and white teachers for using AAVE, but I never witnessed a teacher correcting the spoken language of a European American student, even those who frequently used nonstandard features in the classroom.

Style maintenance and style shifting in white language crossing

Despite instances of linguistic prescriptivism regarding AAVE, most of Bay City High School's classes were very relaxed and informal, with teachers and students of all races using a great deal of colloquial language. Many African American students used AAVE regularly in their classes, not only with their peers but also in interaction with teachers. However, black teenagers, most of whom were bidialectal, were highly attuned to the potential need to shift away from AAVE and toward Standard English in classroom contexts, whether to avoid sanctioning by teachers for their use of nonstandard English or to prevent possible misunderstanding by speakers of other varieties.

Example (9) illustrates the latter situation. The interaction takes place in Ms. Stein's Life and Health course. As part of a class unit on community service, a retired European American man visited the class as a guest speaker to talk about his experiences as a community volunteer. In the example, Evan, an African American boy who was a fluent speaker of AAVE and used the variety frequently in the classroom, asks the speaker a question:

(9) Fieldnotes

Evan: <low volume> How old was you when you started <your volunteer position>?

<white guest speaker indicates that he does not understand>

Evan: How old were you when you started <volunteering>?

When the adult visitor makes clear that he does not understand the question, Evan immediately style-shifts from AAVE to Standard English, even though it may have been his low volume rather than his language variety that has caused the communication problem. Indeed, the very minor difference between his two utterances (the use of *was* versus *were*) suggests that the difficulty was unlikely to be due to his grammar. This swift linguistic accommodation to another's variety illustrates the extent to which African American youth – even rowdy students like Evan, whom Ms. Stein frequently admonished for his irreverent attitude and failure to follow classroom rules – were willing and able to adapt their speech to the school's hegemonic linguistic norm.

By contrast, some European American participants in hip hop did not shift their speech style so readily. As with other elements of the construction of a hip hop style, maintaining one's linguistic style within the classroom was largely an individual matter, and it was generally the teenagers with the most outgoing and outrageous personas – in short, the class clowns – who persisted in their speech style even in the face of possible misunderstandings or sanctions. Among the white hip hop fans in this study were several boys who assumed the class-clown role: in addition to Eddie, Billy and to some extent Jay also claimed this position. Example (10) presents an interaction involving Billy which is in some ways parallel to example (9) above, insofar as it involves a misunderstanding between a European American adult and a student using nonstandard linguistic features. But where Evan in the previous example rapidly switched to Standard English, Billy does not accommodate his interlocutor in the same way:

(10) Fieldnotes
<Natalie, a white teacher's aide, has just read to Billy his lines in a class play>
Billy: It's all good. <[ɪs ɑː gʊːʔ]>
Natalie: It's awful?
Billy: It's all good. <[ɪs ɑː gʊːʔ]>

In response to the teacher's aide, Billy offers a positive evaluative phrase from African American youth slang, *It's all good*, in which he uses numerous features of African American English phonology, including consonant cluster simplification in *it's*, vocalization of the liquid /l/ in *all*, and glottalization of syllable-final /d/ in *good*. When Natalie checks her hearing of this phrase as *It's awful*, Billy repeats himself but without adjusting his phonology in any way that I could detect as I observed the interaction. This particular expression was something of a signature phrase for Billy, a heavy marijuana user who cultivated a laid-back, mellow style (see also example 3e above), and like many other slang items, this phrase functioned as a carrier for African American English phonology among European American hip hop fans. It may therefore have been difficult for Billy to separate pronunciation from lexicon in his production of this expression, or perhaps it would have seemed too jarring – or inauthentic – to use a phrase of African American origin with non-African American English phonology. In any event, Billy does not adapt his speech to Natalie even when it is clear that his pronunciation has led to confusion. This situation differs sharply from Evan's readiness to style-shift with much less evidence of linguistically based miscommunication.

The failure of some European American students to style-shift in situations in which African American students would likely have done so is a form of white privilege. That is, European American hip hop fans' sense of entitlement to appropriate African American linguistic forms is supported by teachers' authorization for them to use these forms in classrooms in contexts where black teenagers ran the risk of sanction if they did so. Teachers may have perceived white youth as deliberately using nonstandard forms for stylistic effect, while assuming that black students "didn't know any better" and required correction. However, not all European American participants in hip hop took advantage of this racial privilege. On the contrary, some students were well aware of the risk of being seen as appropriating African American cultural property, and they therefore seemed to monitor their linguistic practices to avoid giving offense to African American students. The final example involves Al

Capone, who, unlike most of the other boys, was immersed in the cultural production of hip hop and not simply in its consumption. Perhaps not coincidentally, Al was also the most attuned to the racial politics of his identity, as demonstrated in his stylistic practice as well as his discussions of race with me (cf. Cutler 2003a).

Example (11) takes place in the Say No to Drugs class. In an earlier class, the students had composed lyrics for an original rap song about the dangers of drugs, which they were preparing to present to Bay City elementary and junior high school students. Two teachers, both white women, have typed up the students' lyrics and have distributed them to the class.

(11) Fieldnotes
<The teachers, Carolyn and Priscilla (both white), have just handed out photocopies of the students' anti-drug rap song. Calvin, a black student, looks at his sheet.>
Calvin: Why'd you change *talking shit* to *talking dirt*? It don't make any sense.
Al: <low volume> It don't – It doesn't make any sense.
Jay: Al can rap it!
Al: <laughs>
Billy: I can do the beat box while he rap it! <makes rhythmic noises with his mouth into his cupped hands>

Following Calvin's objection to the bowdlerization of the class's lyrics (*It don't make any sense*), Al begins to agree by echoing Calvin's nonstandard formulation, *it don't*. However, he quickly self-corrects and shifts to Standard English *it doesn't*. He speaks quietly and cannot be heard by either teacher, but he can be heard by Calvin, who is seated nearby, as well as by a few other students, both black and white. It therefore seems that Al's concern is not that nonstandard grammatical forms may be sanctioned by the teachers as inappropriate in the classroom context. Rather, he may wish to avoid appearing to imitate Calvin's grammar. Calvin himself may make a partial linguistic accommodation to the teachers he is addressing, since he uses the invariant negative auxiliary form *don't* but not multiple negation (as opposed to the fully AAVE sentence *It don't make no sense*).

By contrast, when Jay loudly issues his proposal for Al to perform the song, he does not adjust his speech style to take into account either the white teachers or the black students in the room. He uses verbal *-s* leveling (*he rap*), a much more AAVE-identified feature than the invariant negative auxiliary *don't*, since the latter but not the former also occurs in European American vernaculars. Moreover, in stepping into his class-clown persona, he speaks loudly to the entire class, much as Eddie does in many of his classroom comments. Thus he is much more on record as using AAVE grammar than either Al or Calvin. By contrast, Billy, himself a class clown, seems to orient to some racialized boundaries in hip hop culture. His suggestion that he and Al perform the rap song is clearly a joke: as long as there were African American male students in the room, they held the primary cultural authority to engage in this sort of hip hop cultural production. Billy's comment is thus both an acknowledgment of and a challenge to the racial ideology of African American youth culture.

Conclusion

At Bay City High School, white teenagers who affiliated with hip hop drew on resources of black youth language and culture to construct their stylistic identities. These speakers were by no means fluent in AAVE, yet they creatively adapted lexical, phonological, and grammatical elements associated with the variety to produce individual hip hop styles. Students at the school viewed these practices through the lens of two competing ideologies of hip hop: the racial ideology of African American youth language and culture as racialized cultural property, and the stylistic ideology, which held that such resources were not racially specific and were legitimately available to hip hop aficionados of all ethnoracial backgrounds.

White hip hop fans' use of AAVE features not only challenged the racial ideology of hip hop but also ignored AAVE's status as a complex and systematic linguistic variety in a number of ways. First, their use was unsystematic and did not conform to the variety's grammatical principles. Second, it was partial, involving only a handful of features of the entire linguistic system. Third, it was superficial, for with a few exceptions, the most accessible features tended to be the most widely used. Fourth, it was stereotypical, with the most widely recognized elements of AAVE being generally preferred. And finally, it was sometimes exaggerated, with supercorrect use of a small set of indexically rich features.

This view of African American language enabled European American hip hop fans to create an identity relation of adequation – albeit contested – with youth of color and especially with African Americans, as well as an identity relation of distinction from other white students. Meanwhile, they sought to authenticate their practices as indexical of hip hop even as their peers worked to position their style as false and inauthentic. In this way European American boys who engaged in hip hop came to represent a highly visible and often problematized form of whiteness in contrast to the more normative and hence unmarked white style of preppy youth.

The next chapter turns attention to another marked white youth style at Bay City High School: nerdiness. Whereas hip hop fans pursued coolness through their use of stylistic resources from black youth culture, nerdy teenagers rejected coolness altogether, thus becoming ideologically hyperwhite according to the school's racial and stylistic order.

7 We're through being cool: white nerds, superstandard English, and the rejection of trendiness

Introduction

On my first day in Ms. Stein's fourth-period class, I could feel the eyes of several students on me. I was particularly aware of a nearby student who was partly facing me, smiling slightly. I smiled in response and then spent the next several minutes covertly staring. I was already becoming accustomed to encountering teenagers whom I was unable to classify ethnoracially, but I was not used to being unable to classify them by gender. I found few clues to settle the question definitively. Long hair might suggest a girl, but many boys at Bay City High wore their hair long. No jewelry, no makeup; strong features and heavy brows; a thin frame clad in nondescript jeans and a loose T-shirt – the student was attractive in a way that quietly evaded gender requirements. It was only when Ms. Stein introduced me to the class and the teenager turned fully toward me, caught my eye, and smiled broadly that the ambiguity was resolved. With a clear view of her face, I could see that the friendly student was a girl.

As I got to know Fred and her group of friends, it amazed me that I had ever had trouble recognizing her gender; certainly, her version of femininity excited no comment or confusion among her peers. It soon became clear that Fred was one of a number of Bay City High School students who were not interested in participating in the high-pressure, rigidly gendered social worlds of cool European American youth. Fred and other teenagers skirted these issues by adopting a nerdy identity that rejected trendy youth styles and instead prized intelligence (especially but not exclusively of a scientific or academic nature), eccentric nonconformity, and a zany brand of humor. Nerdiness resolved several problems for these students: it freed them from keeping up with youth trends, it attenuated the gender differentiation mandated by cool styles, it removed the pressure to engage in practices like drinking, drug use, and heterosexual activity, and it enabled them to pursue their intellectual interests.

Nerds played an important role in the stylistic and racial system of Bay City High, for in spurning coolness they in effect also separated themselves from the local African American youth culture where European American youth trends often originated. Nerdiness therefore had a racialized as well as a stylistic meaning: ideologically positioned as remote from blackness, nerds were often seen as hyperwhite.

Refusing coolness

While nerdiness is often viewed as tied to social exclusion (Kinney 1993), it has been embraced and even celebrated by some recent commentators (Anderegg 2007; Nugent 2008). Indeed, like other youth styles, nerdiness is an actively claimed identity produced through semiotic practices (Bucholtz 1999b; cf. Bakht 2010; Heller 1999); at Bay City High School, being a nerd was not primarily about being unpopular but about being deliberately uncool. Nerdy teenagers often expressed disinterest in, or even contempt for, trendy social practices. They were thus far more oppositional to both preppy and hip hop youth than either group was to the other. Likewise, the contrasting jock and burnout youth categories described by Penelope Eckert (1989, 2000) shared an orientation to coolness despite their antagonism toward each other, but as Eckert notes, nerds stood outside this binary: "If a Jock is the opposite of a Burnout, a nerd is the opposite of both" (1989: 48). At Bay City High, teenagers who affiliated with nerdiness were aware of its stigma, but they did not consider themselves social failures.

Fred's all-female friendship group challenged the social exclusivity and narrow concerns of cool youth through an unofficial club, Random Reigns Supreme, which had no designated activities other than to showcase individual members' offbeat interests, such as a fascination with cows and an almost scientific curiosity about the lifestyle of Mr. Salty, the Nabisco pretzels mascot. ("If you were a pretzel, would you wear a sailor cap?" was one of the club's nonsequitur slogans.) In legitimating the girls' friendship and their untrendy tastes, Random Reigns Supreme made visible a playful alternative to coolness; its members even managed to get a photograph in the school yearbook alongside officially recognized clubs. The club thus subverted the function of many high school organizations and activities as training grounds for corporate life (Eckert 1989).

When I first interviewed Fred, I would not have classified her as a nerd based on her style. I was therefore surprised when she used the term to describe herself and her friendship group:

(1) 1 Mary: [$_1$So— $_1$]
2 Fred: [$_1$We're al$_1$]ways the nerds.
3 We like it.
4 Mary: You@'re the nerds?
5 Fred: We're <creaky voice> {glad} to be the ner:ds,
6 a@nd the squa:res and,

7 Mary: Is that what=
8 Fred: =[$_2$we don't— $_2$]
9 Mary: =[$_2$you say $_2$] you a:re?
10 Fred: <[iʔ]>
11 Well,
12 we don't exactly s:-
13 We don't always say it,=
14 =I: say it.
15 n@
16 Mary: @@[$_3$@ $_3$]
17 Fred: [$_3$But-$_3$]
18 Mary: @ You're [$_4$prou:d.$_4$]
19 Fred: [$_4$you $_4$] know,
20 Mary: [$_5$@@ $_5$]
21 Fred: [$_5$we do:n't— $_5$]
22 We just don't,
23 (0.5)
24 dri:nk,
25 we d[$_6$o:n't,
26 <rapid>{d$_6$]o=
27 Mary: [$_6$ Mm. $_6$]
28 Fred: =any drugs,}]
29 we don't—
30 we just,
31 <smiling voice quality> {get ↑naturally high},
32 Mary: <smiling voice quality> {A[$_7$ha:.$_7$]}
33 Fred: [$_7$@: $_7$]
34 Mary: [$_8$So that makes you nerds?$_8$]
35 Fred: [$_8$We just do: insane $_8$] funny things.=
36 =↑I don't know,
37 maybe.
38 (0.6)
39 Mary: So:,=
40 Fred: =And we're smart.
41 We get <[eʔ]>-
42 good grades.
43 (1.3)
44 Mostly.

Although Fred initially implies that she and her friends willingly accept the label *nerd* for themselves (lines 2, 5), in response to my questions she acknowledges that she has chosen the term for her group and that it is not equally embraced by all her friends (lines 11–14). Hence Fred's statement is less an objective description of her friends' identity than an ideological representation (which I help to co-construct; Bucholtz 2007b). Yet Fred's pithy distillation of her group's practices and values is a kind of "nerd manifesto" that aptly captures the ideological differences between nerds and other teenagers; in its general outline, it accurately identifies differences in practice as well.

Like the members of the Random Reigns Supreme club, other nerdy teenagers had little interest in or tolerance for the preoccupations of their cool peers. One such student, Erich, a fifteen-year-old European American sophomore with glasses and a shaggy mane of dark blond curls, spent his lunch periods reading in the school corridor. Hunched over his book, he was often mistaken for a girl at the school whom he superficially resembled. As with Fred, any occasional gender confusion was the result of Erich's indifference to gender norms, not a conscious subversion of them. It therefore differed from the deliberately gender-bending styles adopted by a few teenagers at Bay City High, mostly girls, who affiliated with punk and goth styles, as well as one or two openly lesbian students.[1]

Despite these fleeting gender mix-ups, Erich was unconcerned about whether he met cool standards of masculinity. He remarked without embarrassment, and even with some pride, that he was a poor athlete, an arena in which, as at other schools, many boys at Bay City High School garnered popularity and sometimes celebrity status: "I'm really horrible at sports. I'm a total klutz. I fall down. I hate sports." He was similarly uninterested in current youth trends; his dismissive attitude toward coolness is evident in a comment he made to me about people who are "fake" during our discussion of slang terms and other lexical items.

(2) 1 Erich: They,
2 they're just not real.=
3 =They're kind of,
4 all,
5 uh,
6 they know what's going o:n,
7 but that doesn't have anything to do with reality,
8 in any [$_1$way.
9 Mary: [$_1$Hm. $_1$]
10 Erich: S$_1$]o,
11 .h they're just kind of,
12 hot ai:r.
13 .h
14 Which is—
15 Like,
16 "O:h.
17 This is what's in sty:le."
18 Mary: [$_2$Mm:. $_2$]
19 Erich: [$_2$And they$_2$] have no ↑idea,

20 what's:,
21 anyth-
22 about anything,
23 but,
24 stuff like that.

Erich contrasts cool teenagers, who "know what's going o:n" (line 6) and "what's in sty:le" (line 17), with those who are connected to reality, such as himself. "I consider myself to be a real person," he went on to say. "I deal with reality rather than all this, uh, *junk*." Being concerned with trendiness, for Erich, was incompatible with being real.

While Erich took a strongly oppositional stance to coolness, other nerdy students were less absolute in their social identities. The following example, previously analyzed in Chapter 5 for its use of quotative markers, illustrates this ambivalence in an interview with Claire and Christine, who identified as nerdy but were moving into cool social crowds. Here the two girls describe the social risks associated with academic achievement:

(3) 1 Claire: It's not,
2 very,
3 popular to be smart.
4 Like everyone goes, <breathy>
5 {"Oh man,}
6 that test was so hard,
7 what'd you get on it?"=
8 =<deeper pitch> {"Oh I got a C: on it."}
9 .h
10 <breathy> {"Well I got a B minus,
11 I was so excited,
12 I thought I was going to ↑f:ail it.}
13 .h
14 What'd you get?"=
15 =<lower volume> {"O:h,
16 I-
17 I-
18 I-
19 I got an A:."}
20 Christine: And everyone [$_1$kind of $_1$] falls silent.
21 Claire: [$_1$"O:h." $_1$]
22 Christine: "O:h."
23 You know like,
24 "Nnn."=
25 Mary: =Mm.
26 Claire: And then you feel compelled to say,
27 .h
28 <higher pitch> {"But it was so ha:rd,

ma:n!"}
[$_2$ I mean, $_2$]
Christine: [$_2$ "I studied $_2$] s:o [$_3$ ha:rd!"$_3$]
Claire: <higher pitch> {[$_3$ "I stud$_3$]ied so hard!"
Mary: [$_4$ Mm. $_4$]
Claire: [$_4$ "O:h! $_4$]
I al-
I-
I stayed up [$_5$ till like o:ne!"} $_5$]
Christine: <lower pitch> {[$_5$ "My tutor helped $_5$] me:."}
[$_6$ @@@ $_6$]
Claire: [$_6$ I know. $_6$]
I know,=
=and then you say,
the magic word,
"I have a tu:tor."
@=
Mary: =Mm:.
Christine: And everyone goes,
"O::::h,"
<lower volume> {and they're all jealous,}
<creaky voice> {and they're like,
"O:h,
wo:w,
I wish I had a tutor."}

Being "not, very, popular" (lines 1–3) is a central issue for these girls' identities. They enact an imagined interaction in which they must obscure their intelligence in front of their cool classmates, accounting for their excellent grades by explaining, "I have a tu:tor" (line 44). In fact, neither Christine nor Claire had a tutor, and they needed no help to excel in school. This scenario thus displays the tension between these girls' academic abilities and their desire not to seem different from their cooler and less intellectually gifted peers, as dramatized in Claire's embarrassed, stuttered confession that she got an A on her test (lines 15–19) and Christine's grunted performance of others' disdainful reaction to such a confession (line 24). Claire's reported attempt to mitigate her shameful high achievement by offering a series of accounts (lines 26–37) also demonstrates this tension. Lexically, moreover, her nerdy use of formal vocabulary in characterizing herself as "compelled" to explain her high grades (line 26) contrasts with her cooler use of the colloquial affiliative marker *man* in self-quotation (line 29).

In this context, the claim to have a tutor is not a flaunting of wealth, since most of Claire and Christine's social group had upper-middle-class parents who could afford to provide their children with such advantages. Instead, it is presented as a deliberate ploy to downplay academic ability (and it may also be a way of mocking their more privileged acquaintances, for both girls came from families that were comfortable but not affluent). Christine and Claire recognized the necessity of such deceptions when they hung out with the cool crowd, but they also insisted on the value of nerdiness. Although they may have hidden this aspect of their identities with cool teenagers, they were unwilling to abandon it altogether.

Despite such tensions, then, nerdy students generally understood their social position at the high school as a choice rather than a curse. They viewed their close-knit friendship groups as evidence of their own social selectivity, not of their social rejection by cool students. Nerds maintained high standards for acceptable friends, and they evaluated those who did not measure up just as harshly as cool students did, although their criteria were rather different. Fred, for example, remarked with a chuckle, "I don't go for stupid people. I just can't get along with them, you know?" Erich expressed a similar intolerance: "I just can't stand people who have all the outward signs of being an extremely stupid person." Yet Erich was also aware that his own often goofy behavior raised eyebrows among cool students; he noted, regarding himself and his friends, "My observation is that other people think we're kind of foolish and crazy for the way we do things." Erich's comments demonstrate the difference between cool students' values and his own: he represents his group's nonconforming practices not as stupidity but as a kind of enlightened "craziness" that marks intelligence. Attitudes such as Erich's and Claire's may be read as arrogance, and in fact nerds are often portrayed in American culture as not merely socially inept but also misanthropic. Yet it was cool teenagers who most publicly engaged in social exclusion and negative evaluation of others (Chapter 5).

If nerds' separation from other groups might be mistaken for aloofness, it could also be misread as social isolation. But nerdy youth were simply comfortable enough with their social status that, unlike their cool peers, they did not closely monitor other social groups. This difference was evident in students' maps of the school. Most teenagers included at least some other socially salient groups, but nerds were less inclined to note the presence of groups with which they did not interact.

Erich, for example, spent a good deal of time constructing his map (Figure 7.1), drawing straight lines with a ruler that he regularly carried with him and joking that his map was not precise because he was not using graph paper or a stencil for the lettering. (Another nerdy student, Bob, shows similar precision, albeit facetiously, in her own map in Figure 5.2a of Chapter 5, in which she provides a mock scale – *1 inch = 30 ft* – and gives ironic credit to the maker of her ballpoint pen: *courtesy of Bic © Clic!*.) Yet in all Erich's attention to detail, he did not indicate any social groups on his map; he marked only the spot on the floor of

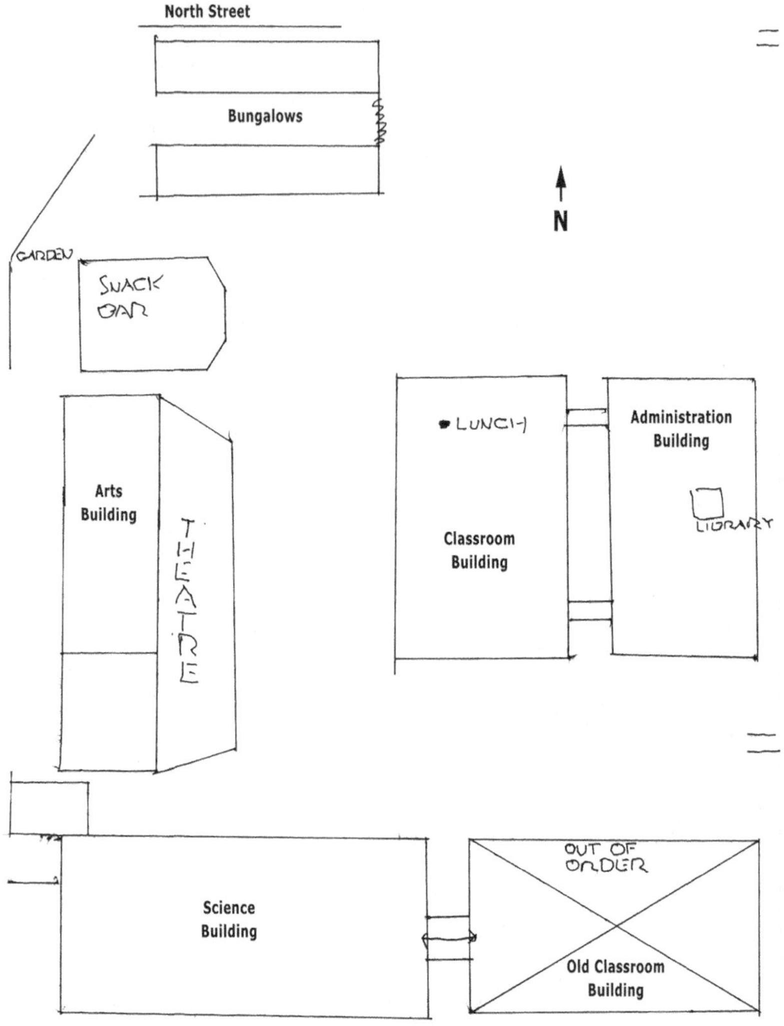

Figure 7.1: Erich's map of Bay City High School

the corridor where he spent his lunch period reading. Claire's map (Figure 7.2) likewise documents in detail her lunchtime location during ninth, tenth, and eleventh grades but does not indicate where other groups hang out. Her map also indicates that during her freshman year her nerdy social group tended to congregate in or near classroom buildings. In general, nerds spent their lunch periods indoors more than cool students, often assembling in classrooms to

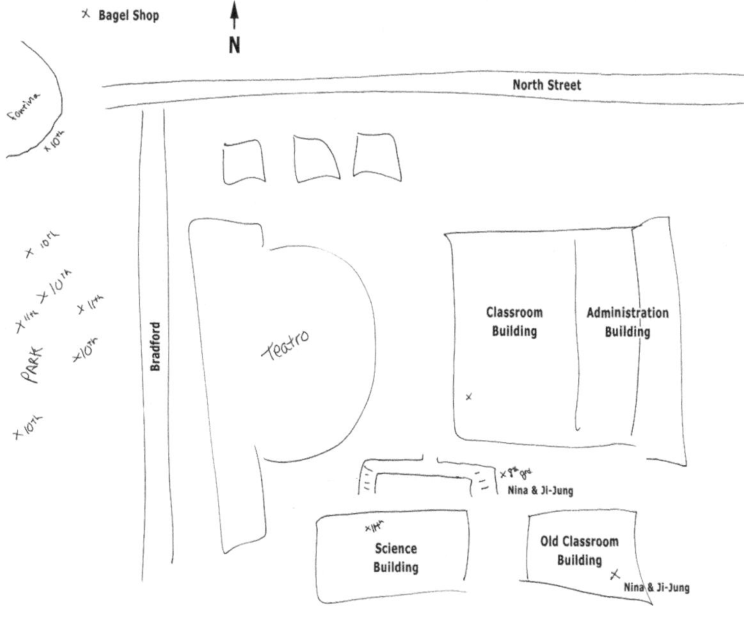

Figure 7.2: Claire's map of Bay City High School

review their homework together. The omission of social detail from these maps does not necessarily mean that nerds were oblivious to the doings of cool teenagers, but certainly they were less invested in the social worlds of trendy youth. Given my standard instructions for the map-drawing activity, "Show me where you hang out and anything else you think is important," nerdy students may have been seizing an opportunity to display their indifference to the geopolitics of high school life.

Moving in and out of nerdiness

Complete separation between nerdy and cool teenagers was often impossible, since in many cases students had known each other for most of their lives, lived in the same neighborhoods, and took many of the same classes; the strong academic reputation of Bay City High School meant that many trendy students were as committed to their studies as were their nerdy counterparts. Moreover, like other social identities, nerdiness shifted over time and across contexts. Some teenagers reported their transition from junior high to high school as a movement not away from nerdiness (Kinney 1993) but toward this style. This pattern is seen in the social trajectories of Bob, Loden, and Kate, all of whom distanced themselves from friends who began to participate in cool practices, and it is even more evident in Fred's case. As discussed in Chapter 5, Fred deliberately chose to leave her former, popular, group of friends in favor of her current, nerdier, group.

Conversely, at the time of the study Claire and Christine were contemplating becoming cooler, a goal that Claire planned to achieve in part by smoking marijuana. Yet Claire had had past experiences both with nerds and with a cool group that made her doubt whether she entirely fit in with either. Likewise, in example (4) Christine states that she does not wholly belong in any group. The example opens as she describes how she differs from her nerdy friends (due to space limitations, brief comments from Claire and me and some small excerpts of Christine's talk are omitted):

(4) sometimes I just feel like, (1.8) that I'm too:, like, (1.3) that I'm too: . . . that I'm too like, s:oi:led or something, you know? . . . Like I'm too:, .h c:ynical:, .h and I'm too:, you know like, unhappy, . . . You have to stay like PG rated @ or they'll just be like, "Oh my go:d." . . . Like I feel way too like, I don't know if j:a:ded is the word, but I feel way too u:h, (1.7) . . . I feel older than them, in a lot of ways and, (0.8) I feel like, I:'m too::, (1.6) I'm too, like, spo:rts oriented, mo:re, and mo:re, uh, you know, there's li:fe other than schoo:l, . . . Whereas, I don't fit in with the people, who, are really really intense on their sports, because I'm— you know, sports isn't e:verything to me:. Um, so I'm a little too, nerdy for the (0.6) jo:cks, I guess you could put it that way, um, . . . I'm too jocky for the ne:rds, . . . I'm too like, pu:re for the truly, you know, the guys who, hang out in the Park a:ll the time, . . . I'm not quite crunchy enough for them, . . .

Christine locates the problem not in other groups but in herself, as shown by her lengthy list of personal characteristics that exclude her from each group, marked by parallel syntactic structure (*I'm too* + adjective). Yet she does not seem to consider herself a social failure; her frustration is instead directed at the rigidity of available stylistic categories (cf. Chapter 3). Social categories have been said to be "protected against induction" (Sacks (1995: 336) in that if a discrepancy is found between a category and one of its members, the category is not redefined; instead, the member is excluded or labeled deviant. Thus, before the example begins, Christine stated that she fails to "qualify" for nerdiness or any other style. It is clear from her remarks, however, that she is not wholly committed to membership in the nerd category. Her description of her nerdy friends is rather patronizing, emphasizing their childlike innocence in contrast to her own more "cynical" outlook. Christine implies, then, that her ambiguous style is a choice in its own right.

As teenagers moving in opposite directions between the ideological poles of coolness and nerdiness, Fred on the one hand and Claire and Christine on the other demonstrate the complexity and fluidity of such identities. Yet all three girls, despite their differences, shared with one another and with other nerdy teenagers a dislike for the cliquishness associated with cool social groups. Moreover, the heightened gender and sexual display required of trendy teenagers was of little interest to nerdy students, especially girls, in part because it was difficult to reconcile with their identities as intelligent nonconformists.

Gender, sexuality, and nerd style

Nerds' rejection of the hegemonic order was apparent in many aspects of their semiotic proctices, which were – often deliberately – uncool. Nerdy youth typically wore comfortable, casual clothing without sports logos or designer labels, and both girls and boys often wore old-fashioned and (at the time) unfashionable Converse Chuck Taylor canvas sneakers in bright colors rather than trendy oversized leather sports shoes or platform sandals. However, nerds often sought to stand out in some elements of their clothing decisions: a boy named Robert, for example, regularly wore a court jester's cap.

Nerd girls in particular tended to challenge fashion norms. Unlike cool girls, they did not wear revealing clothing, and although they sometimes wore items emblazoned with Sesame Street characters or other emblems of childhood, these did not exhibit the combined infantilization and sexualization of cool white girls' clothing (Chapter 5). In fact, female nerds often seemed not simply to ignore but consciously to subvert conventions of feminine self-adornment. Whereas preppy girls preferred pastels and girls with other cool styles often favored black or dark clothing and makeup (cf. Eckert 1996; Mendoza-Denton 2008), many nerd girls delighted in unfashionably bright, even mismatched colors. Their jewelry tended toward plastic Crackerjack rings, and their use of makeup was generally limited to painting their fingernails in alternating colors of red, blue, yellow, and green. In their playful personal style, nerds were also distinct from self-described "normal" teenagers, who often assiduously avoided calling attention to themselves by wearing unremarkable clothing. When "normal" students did venture to wear more dramatic styles, these were usually of the trendy or sexy variety.

By opting out of trendiness, nerdy students largely opted out of the school's heterosexual market (Eckert 1996) and its attendant pressure to engage in sexual activity. The disengagement of nerds from sex and romance was not total, but the ideology of nerds' nonsexuality meant that nerds in romantic relationships could face disapproval from their friends (Bucholtz and Hall 2004: 501–503). Nerds' disregard of sexual and gender norms was especially evident at the spring prom, a formal dance that is an annual tradition in US high schools and is a veritable celebration of heterosexual romance (Best 2000). Most Bay City High School students attended the prom in heterosexual couples or double dates; many nerd girls, however, attended with their female friendship groups. And in contrast to popular girls' glamorous, sexy, and expensive gowns, nerd girls' prom dresses struck a rather different note. Bob, for example, wore a childlike sunflower-appliquéd gingham sundress, and Claire, who studied dance, chose to wear an old-fashioned ballet dress with full tutu from a used clothing store. The pressure of the prom is different for boys, given that the ideology of romance is marketed overwhelmingly to girls (e.g., Christian-Smith 1990). But at least one nerd boy (the flamboyant Robert, once again) subverted the usual formal dress requirement by renting a musical-comedy-style tuxedo, including top hat, tails, and cane.

Besides challenging Bay City High's normative gender and sexual arrangements, nerds also subverted the school's valorization of academic achievement and extracurricular participation. Nerds fulfilled these expectations but in ways unanticipated by teachers and administrators. Their intellectual ability was a source of institutional pride when statewide standardized test scores were reported, but it was also an embarrassment to teachers whose errors they regularly caught and publicly corrected. And their extracurricular activities were often not viewed by their peers as accruing greater glory to the school: chess club, not cheerleading; badminton, not basketball.

Gender played a role here as well. Nerd boys in gym class confronted the masculine norm to perform well in sports. Conversely, although boys were also sanctioned for displaying their knowledge too readily, the problematic nature of being smart was especially acute for girls, and unlike sports, this dilemma was not limited to a single class but to all their academic courses throughout their high school careers. It was often difficult for cool girls to balance the interactional requirements of hegemonic heterosexual femininity with their desire to compete and achieve academically, a double bind that continues into college (Holland and Eisenhart 1990). By withdrawing from conventional femininity and its obligations, female nerds were able to display their intellectual ability without apology (see also Heller 1999: 202–209).

The linguistic construction of nerd identity

Nerds' tendency to resist conventional gender displays carried over into language. In academic contexts, nonnerdy high-achieving white girls often hedged their statements when displaying knowledge, but nerd girls generally made knowledge-based assertions baldly and without mitigation. A number of female nerds had lower-pitched voices than those of their cool counterparts, which were often almost babyish, and nerdy girls with high-pitched voices, like Loden, did not seem to be trying to sound cute or feminine. This rejection of the linguistic trappings of hegemonic femininity was evident even in students' pseudonym choices for this study. Cool girls selected names like *Lumière* (with requisite French pronunciation), *Zoe*, or *Tiffany*, in contrast to nerd girls' choices such as *Fred* and *Bob* – the full pseudonym of the girl who chose the latter name is *Bob, Conqueror of the Universe*. What is striking about these names is that they are not simply masculine but masculine in an unexpected way: they evoke affable Everymen rather than macho he-men. Hence, Fred's and Bob's pseudonyms seem to indicate not an affiliation with masculinity but a tongue-in-cheek disaffiliation with conventional femininity.

Nerdy students drew on linguistic resources at multiple levels, from phonetics to discourse, to display an identity that was simultaneously associated with intelligence, humor, and a resolute refusal to be cool. As seen in earlier chapters, the practices of distinction in which nerds engaged often involved avoiding trendy linguistic forms like current slang and innovative quotative markers. Nerdy practices of adequation, meanwhile, included the use of superstandard English, an interactional emphasis on intelligence and knowledge, and an orientation to words and word play.

Superstandard English as a stylistic resource

Nerds' linguistic style set them apart from their trendy peers through the use of elements of superstandard English, a highly and sometimes exaggeratedly formal version of Standard English (see also Wolfram and Schilling-Estes 2006). The superstandard style was distinguished phonetically by careful articulation and especially resistance to processes characteristic of colloquial speech, like consonant cluster simplification and the reduction of unstressed vowels. These careful pronunciations were coupled with lexical formality as well as extremely standard grammar. The style called attention to its own standardness by going beyond traditional norms of prescriptive linguistic correctness, to the point of occasionally extending prescriptive rules to contexts to which they did not apply. Such linguistic overgeneralization, or hypercorrection (as opposed to the phenomenon of supercorrection discussed in Chapter 6), was prescriptively incorrect, but because it involved rules that were strongly associated with standard language use, it too contributed to the superstandard style.

Superstandard English, unlike Standard English, was a marked linguistic variety among Bay City High School students, evoking the registers of scholarship and science. Even a slight use of such forms could therefore suffice to yield a semiotic distinction between nerds and other teenagers. In the following examples, nerdy students draw on elements of superstandard English in talking to me about books they have read or are reading for pleasure. In (5a), Erich describes Neal Stephenson's 1992 bestselling cyberpunk science fiction novel *Snow Crash*, and in (5b), Claire and Christine jointly offer details about *Smilla's Sense of Snow*, a mystery novel by Peter Hoeg published in 1993. (The connection to snow in the titles of both books is entirely coincidental.)

(5a)
Erich: U:h,
Hong Kong is a franchise too.=
=Mr. Lee's Greater Hong Ko:ng <[hãŋ kãŋg]>,
<sniff>
Mary: Is it meant to be a f:unny book,
or is it [$_1$sort of a:, $_1$]
Erich: [$_1$Yeah.
I:t's$_1$] meant to be somewhat <[sʌ̃mwʌt]> humor.=
Mary: =Yeah.=
Erich: =Bu:t,
it's very good.
It's very fun.=
Mary: =<lower volume> {It sounds good.}=
Erich: Sumatran compu:ter virus.
@@
<smiling quality> {Yeah.}
It's,
a <[ej?]> com↑pu-
it's:,
that's,
(some),
who:le,
long involved plot about these things called namshub <['nãmʃʊb]>.
Which is kind of like a computer program that will program your
brai:n.
<sniff>
And uh,
(0.6)
Mary: Oka::y,
[$_2$@ $_2$]
Erich: [$_2$It's:,$_2$]
it's very complicated.
@@
You have to really read the book to unders:tand it <[ɪt]>.

(5b)
Claire: I can't <[kʰæ̃nt]>,
quite deal with it yet but,
it's (keeping) [$_1$more and more.$_1$]
Mary: [$_1$What ↑is $_1$] it?=
=I've <lower volume> {never heard of it.}
Claire: It's,
it's this wei:rd book,=
=It takes plac:e i:n,
(0.7)
Christine: Ice[$_2$land $_2$] <['ajs'læ̃nd]> or something.
Claire: [$_2$Den-$_2$]=

12 Denmark.
13 Christine: ↑Denmark?
14 Claire: Yeah.
15 Christine: Oh.
16 Oh,
17 she's from Iceland <['ajs'læ̃nd]>.
18 Claire: Yeah.
19 She-
20 she's [$_3$from $_3$]=
21 Christine: [$_3$Okay.$_3$]=
22 Claire: =Greenland <['gɹĩnlɛ̃nd]>,
23 actually <['æktʃəlij]>.
24 Christine: Greenland <['gɹĩːnlə̃nd]>.

At several points in these examples, both Erich and Claire use a careful enunciation style in which stops are fully released rather than being unreleased or glottalized as in more colloquial speech (example 5a: *somewhat*, line 8; *it*, line 34; example 5b: *can't*, line 1). In addition, Erich's speech shows some influence of spelling pronunciation in line 3 (*Mr. Lee's Greater Hong Ko:ng*), where he pronounces the *-ng* of *Kong* as [ŋg] rather than [ŋ] (in *Hong*, the following [k] makes it difficult to determine the pronunciation of the final segment). Likewise, Erich, Claire, and Christine all resist the reduction and deletion of segments: in *a com↑pu-* (example 5a, line 18), where the *a*, though pronounced in a rather clipped way, is given its full phonetic value [ejʔ]; in Claire's pronunciation of the consonant cluster of *actually* with a fully articulated [t] (example 5b, line 23); and in both of Christine's productions of *Iceland* (example 5b, lines 10 and 17), where each part of the compound is given nearly equal syllabic weight. (Christine does, however, produce a more reduced pronunciation of the second syllable of *Greenland* in line 24, following Claire's use of a lax mid vowel in this word in line 22.)

These teenagers' resistance to colloquial speech forms did not merely mark them as untrendy, as did resistance to current slang or to innovative quotative markers. Additionally, it played the more important role of positioning them as intelligent. The association of this precisely enunciated speech style with intelligence may be due in part to its relationship to literacy: nerdy teenagers frequently used something akin to "reading style" (Labov 1972d) even in their spontaneous conversations.[2] Indeed, as shown in Erich's pronunciation of *Hong Kong*, nerdy students occasionally employed pronunciations based on spelling rather than speech (e.g., [folk] for *folk*), as well as noncustomary pronunciations of words they encountered in their extensive reading but had not heard uttered aloud: for example, Loden pronounced her pseudonym as ['lɑdn̩] rather than the more usual ['loʊdn̩]; the name came from a text she had read for a class assignment.

There was an intimate connection between nerdiness and reading: nerds were the only students I knew who admitted to reading for fun, and they often carried mass-market paperbacks or library books along with their schoolbooks, frequently science fiction or fantasy novels but also classical authors such as Victor Hugo and Homer. Several nerds also regularly spent their lunch hour and other free time during school reading. By contrast, for cool youth, reading was so remote from their lives that when, at the end of class one Friday afternoon Ms. Stein urged her students, in her usual litany of advice for the weekend, "Read for pleasure!" several cool teenagers laughed. Trendy students often browsed sports or fashion magazines at school, but they did not generally read books unrelated to their coursework. Importantly, nerds' passion for reading was not an escape either from reality or from social interaction. Instead, it was a pleasurable individual activity that could also be extended into the social realm with sympathetic (and often nerdy) others, as shown in the above examples.

The link between reading and careful speech, moreover, forms the basis of a secondary link between careful speech and intellectual ability, via the ideological association of advanced literacy and extensive education with high intelligence. In short, for nerds the practice of avoiding casual pronunciation in favor of a literate-based speech style reflected a language ideology that tied formal speech register to intelligence. And intelligence in turn was associated, at least by nerds, with independent thought: a refusal to go along with the crowd whether in fashion or in phonetics. Erich invokes this association in example (6), in which he explains why he thinks the term *sophisticated* applies to himself and his best friend, Micah. He asserts, "We're not sophisticated in a *bad* sense, . . . we're much more advanced, . . . in terms of . . . our ways of perceiving things." After I ask what he means, he offers the following example:

(6) 1 Erich: U:h.
2 i-
3 w-
4 i-
5 we don't think—
6 I don't think of anything in a n:or:mal wa:y,
7 [$_1$.h $_1$]
8 Mary: [$_1$Mm.$_1$]
9 Erich: like,
10 uh,
11 a:nd,
12 I don't <[dõnt]>,
13 I use much more,
14 (0.8)
15 I don't know how to describe it,
16 I don't use all the abbreviations for wo:rds?

17 Mary: ↑Hm.
18 Erich: Like,
19 most people abbreviate the—
20 cut off half the words?
21 Mary: [$_2$↑Hm. $_2$]
22 Erich: [$_2$For no p$_2$]articular reason?
23 And I don't do: that.
24 [$_3$@@@@@@ $_3$]
25 Mary: [$_3$Like,
26 do you have an example of that?
27 Or,$_3$]
28 Erich: U:h,
29 (0.7)
30 uh,
31 t-
32 they,
33 the-
34 they cut off the G: on the en[$_4$d of "t$_4$]rippin:g" <['tɹɪpĩŋːg]>,
35 Mary: [$_4$M:m. $_4$]
36 [$_5$Right.$_5$]
37 Erich: [$_5$and, $_5$]
38 (e:nd,)
39 N a[$_6$pos$_6$]trophe.=
40 Mary: [$_6$Right.$_6$]
41 Erich: =<higher pitch> {It makes,
42 m-
43 makes} no sense to me.

Erich connects sophistication, in its positive (i.e., nontrendy) sense, both to an "advanced" and unconventional perspective (line 6) and to careful pronunciation (line 16). From the more elevated position that sophistication affords, the cool colloquial speech style simply "makes no sense" (line 43). Here Erich displays a rather clinical knowledge of slang even as he distances himself from it, as seen in his fastidious pronunciation of the slang word *tripping* (originally, 'in an altered mental state'; hence, 'behaving in a disoriented or nonsensical way, experiencing strong emotions, overreacting'). He articulates the word, typically pronounced as *trippin'*, not only with the standard *-ing* suffix but with a hypercorrect final [g] (line 34), a pronunciation that seems to function as the linguistic equivalent of holding a particularly distasteful scientific specimen between thumb and forefinger for inspection before it is discarded.[3] This blending of casual and formal language allows Erich to display knowledge of current slang without embracing an accompanying orientation to coolness. Aware of my interest in language, Erich takes a researcherly analytic stance toward his own and others' linguistic styles.

Related to the phonetic formality of nerdy speech was its lexical formality. Nerds often chose highly formal polysyllabic words of Greco-Latinate origin over more colloquial Germanic monosyllabic terms, a longstanding stylistic distinction in the history of English. These teenagers also frequently used abstract nominalized constructions, another characteristic of formal and especially scholarly registers (Biber 1988). Such lexical items may position the speaker as smart or learned. Thus the analytic stance that Erich takes in (6) is also manifest in several of his remarks quoted earlier in the chapter, in which he discusses his view of nonnerds in terms that suggest they are the subject of his own empirical study. He achieves this stance largely through lexical choice: *I just can't stand people who have all the* ***outward signs*** *of being an extremely stupid person*; ***My observation*** *is that other people think we're kind of foolish and crazy for the way we do things*. Likewise, in example (7) Claire uses a similarly analytic speech style to respond to a question from me about what term she uses for male high school students:

(7) 1 Claire: Well I—
2 I—
3 I tend to r-
4 to refer: to,
5 (0.7)
6 the who:le,
7 (0.7)
8 Christine: Ev[erybody as a guy:.]
9 Claire: [um,
10 Y chrom]osome,
11 as a guy:.

Claire's lexical choices are formal: *tend*, *refer* (lines 3, 4). And in invoking the register of biology (*the who:le, (0.7) um, Y chromosome*; lines 6–7, 9–10) she participates in the same nerdy practice of scientific discourse already exemplified by Erich. The deliberateness of Claire's choice (and perhaps her effort to reach for the appropriate term) is suggested by the fact that it stands in its own intonation unit, which brackets and highlights the phrase (line 10). Like Erich, Claire seems to understand our interaction as a shared intellectual enterprise, and she repeatedly displays her ability to engage in the scientific discourse of research. Undoubtedly, my role as a researcher triggered this analytic style in some students, an issue that Christine and Claire explicitly noted when they pointed out that they talked differently to me than they did to their friends. But nerds also employed the superstandard style in everyday interaction with peers, a practice that cool teenagers engaged in only in jest.

Nerds also engaged in more overt intellectual displays by making direct claims to knowledge or intelligence. Students might explicitly assert their intellectual abilities or accomplishments, such as in Claire's comment to me, "I take *really hard* classes" or Fred's remark, "It's just – it's a known fact, when I- when I do math I'm being reminded, I'm not being taught. It's – that's how I feel." Or such displays could be enacted through the authoritative presentation of knowledge, such as Erich's lengthy impromptu lecture to me about the relative merits of the computer programming languages Pascal and C. Even seemingly idle conversational topics such as the origin of sesame seeds or where popular students shop for clothing could generate playful knowledge contests, some of them quite extensive (Bucholtz 1999b, 2007a). Such claims to knowledge and intelligence were supported by other nerdy interactional practices, particularly distinctive uses of metalinguistics and language-based humor.

Metalinguistics and linguistic humor

Nerdy students manifested an extraordinarily playful attitude toward language: they had a high degree of metalinguistic awareness, and they took pleasure in manipulating linguistic forms for humorous effect. Thus, although Fred and her friends were either unable or unwilling to supply definitions of many of the slang words popular among trendy teenagers at Bay City High (Chapter 4), she volunteered their definition of a word they had invented:

(8)
Fred: Oh,
and we make up wo:rds,
l@ike,
@@
Okay,
every day Kate and Bob have to go retrieve their violins?
From thei:r,
arts building lockers,
up on the second floor of the arts building?
Mary: [$_1$Uh huh.$_1$]
Fred: [$_1$So we s$_1$]aid,
"We need a new ve:rb,
that means to retrieve one's vio[$_2$lin."$_2$]
Mary: [$_2$@@$_2$]
Yeah,
really.
@@=
Fred: =So,
we go schnar:fing every da@y [$_3$a@fter school.$_3$]
Mary: [$_3$@@@@ $_3$]
Fred: .h:
And there's another verb,
because this other girl's coming with us,
who got her u:m,

25 (0.8)
26 <ice jingling in glass> {(<bike> ↑helmet every day after school.=
27 =So to retrieve one's helmet is to na:rgle. <ice jingling in glass>
28 Mary: You na:r:[$_4$gle.$_4$]
29 Fred: [$_4$S- $_4$]
30 Yeah.
31 So we schnar:f and we nar:gle together.}

The longevity of the term *schnarfing* among Fred and her friends was remarkable, and it was so much a part of their regular discourse that it appeared on several of the maps that the girls drew for me. The term therefore operated, like slang, as "anti-language" (Halliday 1976) signaling ingroup membership; however, in a reversal of slang's usual value as a marker of trendiness, this word gives priority to nerdy practices and activities. Such coinages were not entirely analogous to slang, since they were restricted to the group and did not circulate more widely. The term's phonological structure too is unlike most contemporary slang. The /ʃ/ + consonant onset is associated with Yiddish loanwords into English that currently have a humorously negative rather than hip connotation, such as *schmuck* and *schlock* (cf. Bluestein 1989); for this reason *schnarfing* sounds funny but not cool. And Fred's parody of a formal dictionary definition (*to retrieve one's violin*; line 27) is quite different from the colloquial and often slang-filled explanations of slang terms that cool teenagers offered.

When nerdy teenagers did adopt or coin slang terms, they were quite conscious of doing so. Such reflexivity is illustrated in (9), in which Claire and Christine are discussing *granola*, a local term for a hippie-influenced youth style:

(9) 1 Mary: Are those the grano:la people you were [$_1$talk$_1$]ing about?=
2 Claire: [$_1$Yeah.$_1$]
3 Christine: =Yea::h.=
4 Mary: =Okay.
5 (0.8)
6 Claire: I never use that word except that,
7 . . .
8 Christine used it,
9 the other day,
10 and now,
11 @ it's just,
12 so apt <[æpt]>.
13 (0.5)
14 Christine: Yeah,
15 and,
16 they're very kumbaya:,
17 too@.
18 [$_2$I l@ove those little$_2$]=

19 Mary: [$_2$@: $_2$]=
20 Claire: [$_2$I know.@ $_2$]=
21 Christine: =wo@@rds like <whispered> {[$_3$that.@@ $_3$]}
22 Claire: <breathy> {[$_3$I kno:w.@ $_3$]}
23 Christine: [$_4$They're so$_4$] descripti@ve,
24 Claire: [$_4$@@ $_4$]
25 Christine: [$_5$And they're$_5$] very evo@cative.
26 Claire: [$_5$#:@# $_5$]
27 Christine: [$_6$@@@ ↑@@$_6$]
28 Claire: [$_6$Yeah. @ $_6$]
29 @
30 Christine: ↑@
31 I mean they [$_7$say $_7$] exactly what I'm trying to say.@@
32 Claire: [$_7$Yeah.$_7$]

While cool teenagers tended to comment only on the semantic and social meanings of slang terms and category labels, here Claire and Christine discuss – in depth and at a fairly elevated lexical level – the aesthetic pleasure they take in using a particularly "apt" (line 12) or "evocative" (line 25) term, such as the local slang term *granola* or the adjective *kumbaya*, meaning 'laid-back' or 'peace-loving.'[4]

Attention to linguistic form was also the basis of a great deal of nerdy humor such as punning and other joking activity. Punning was an unremitting part of nerdy teenagers' interactional practices, and nerds frequently seized opportunities to work word play into conversation, as in example (10):

(10) 1 Claire: So,
2 where was my trai-
3 My train of thought got derailed.

Here, Claire makes a pun as soon as she sees her chance, going so far as to interrupt and recast her utterance in order to incorporate it. Indeed, nerdy students were often attuned to very subtle details of linguistic form, a level of attention that allowed them to find humor even in syntactic structures. In example (11), Fred and her friends are discussing their club, Random Reigns Supreme:

(11) 1 Mary: So it's you four plus:,
2 Carrie and Ada?
3 Bob: And some[$_1$times$_1$] Melinda.
4 Loden: [$_1$Yeah.$_1$]
5 Mary: <lower volume> {[$_2$Sometimes Melinda.
6 Fred: ↑.n@
7 Mary: Okay.$_2$]}

8 Loden: [$_2$Well,
9 she's not in the club.$_2$]
10 Fred: [$_2$@↑@@@@ $_2$]
11 Kate: Wha@@@t?
12 Loden: Wha@t?
13 Bob: @@
14 Fred: @:
15 That was like A E I O U@ and <breathless> {sometime[$_3$s $_3$]
16 [$_4$Y.@@ $_4$]}
17 Kate: [$_3$@@@ $_3$]
18 Loden: [$_4$@@@ $_4$]
19 Bob: [$_4$@@@@ $_4$]
20 Mary: @@@@
21 All: <6.2 seconds of laughter>

Fred's hilarity may be baffling to nonnerds (and is even initially confusing to her own friends), yet it signals a high degree of linguistic sophistication. She recognizes in the structure of my and Bob's jointly constructed list of group members (lines 1–3) the familiar list of English vowels taught to beginning readers. Moreover, by drawing a parallel between the two, Fred indicates the extent to which her identity rests on an appreciation for the world of learning and education.

A final example of identity construction through metalinguistic humor is shown in (12). Here, in a discussion of the word *popular* during the lexical activity portion of a group interview, Bob persistently redirects the interaction through purposeful misunderstanding:

(12) 1 Bob: Isn't that a kind of tree?
2 (0.9)
3 Fred: N[$_1$o,
4 that's a popla:r.$_1$]
5 Loden: [$_1$No,
6 that's po:p$_1$]la@@r.
7 Kate: [$_2$Po:p$_2$]la:r.
8 Bob: [$_2$Okay.$_2$]
9 Whatever.
10 @@@@
11 <potato chip bag rustling>
12 <36 lines omitted>
48 Bob: I think they're popular.
49 Fred: Okay.
50 Kate: Who:?
51 Bob: ('Cause-)
52 [$_3$Eliza Hudson $_3$] and like Brittany:.

53 Fred: [$_3$(I kind of think that—)$_3$]
54 Bob: <lower volume> (All them.)=
55 Loden: =Oh yeah.=
56 Kate: =O:h,
57 yea:h.
58 Mary: What are they like?
59 Bob: [$_4$They're okay.$_4$]
60 Fred: [$_4$(Okay,)
61 are $_4$] they ↑Steps people?
62 Bob: S-
63 ↑W:hat?
64 Fred: Do they,
65 [$_5$Are they,
66 can they,
67 be (other) Steps people? $_5$]
68 Bob: [$_5$O:@h,
69 I thought you were talking about like my step relatives.$_5$]
70 <laughter>

In line 1 Bob deliberately mishears *popular* as *poplar*. It is clear that her error is feigned: it is not plausible that I would be asking students for information about botany, and in any case the word is written on a slip of paper. Although she eventually goes on to engage seriously with the topic (line 48), when Fred asks if Eliza Hudson and Brittany's group are "Steps people" – that is, high-profile preppy students who sit on the steps of the arts building during lunchtime – Bob again pretends to misunderstand, this time through a repair initiator token produced with highly exaggerated prosody to display bafflement (*↑W:hat?*; line 63), and she again offers an implausible but amusing alternative interpretation. Besides its clearly humorous function, this word play also problematizes the very terms of the ongoing discourse. Bob's reluctance to admit words like *popular* or *Steps people* into interaction with her friends recalls her similar subversion of slang terms like *blood* in Chapter 4. Such metalinguistic play is more than a simple source of amusement: it is also a form of political work that negotiates the boundaries of identity. However, nerdiness positioned those who embraced it not only in relation to coolness and popularity but also in relation to whiteness.

The whiteness of nerds

For white nerds, rejecting coolness meant first and foremost separating themselves from cool European American students. However, at Bay City High School, coolness had a racial warrant, based on the cultural authority of African American teenagers, who often influenced white youth styles. Thus nerdiness was ideologically viewed as an extreme version of whiteness, one in which African American culture and language did not play even a covert role.[5]

Nerdy teenagers' deliberate avoidance of slang, for example, displayed their remoteness from both black and white youth trends, since African American slang was a primary source of European American slang. Likewise, the use of superstandard English worked to separate nerdy teenagers from their trendy white counterparts who generally spoke a more colloquial variety of Standard English, but it also enforced a division between white nerds and most black students at Bay City High, who used African American Vernacular English among their peers. Colloquial Standard English was less semiotically distinct from AAVE because it included casual phonological and grammatical forms. By contrast, superstandard English reinforced the racialized linguistic divide by highlighting and even exaggerating the elements of Standard English that distinguish it from nonstandard varieties, including AAVE. After all, Standard English has meaning only in contrast to those varieties not recognized as standard (Bex and Watts 1999); this is true of superstandard English to an even greater extent. Additionally, unlike nonstandard varieties, Standard English is largely conservative, resisting linguistic innovation (Labov 1994). And as the language of institutional power, it supports dominant rather than subordinated forms of cultural production: Standard English is the language of academia, just as AAVE is the language of hip hop culture. In using superstandard English, then, nerds at Bay City High came to embody for their cool peers not simply whiteness but hyperwhiteness, a marked and exaggerated form of whiteness that was uncool precisely because it was so completely unblack. This ideology of nerdiness as whiteness could be seen, for example, in cool teenagers' imitations of nerdy speech with a nasal, exaggerated rhotic quality that has long been associated with European American speech (Rahman 2007).

Moreover, nerdiness was a class-based as well as a race-based style. Nerds' tendency to link intelligence to education and to value analytic, scientific, and academic skills projected a working future firmly within the professional middle class. Indeed, some nerdy practices depended on class privilege, such as access to computers and to classes that taught students how to program them. And because at Bay City High social class was also tied to race, class divisions also reinscribed racial divisions. Although in theory any student could use the school's computers, teenagers of different races were directed into different scholastic tracks. Classes on programming languages and computer-based graphics mostly enrolled European Americans and East Asian Americans, while African Americans, Latinos, and Southeast Asian Americans predominated in courses that provided vocational training in data entry and other clerical tasks.

But although nerdiness was ideologically associated with the middle class, individual nerdy students were not necessarily in the higher socioeconomic strata of the school. Erich was working-class, and Christine and Claire, though from middle-class families, were painfully aware of the contrast between their own limited financial resources and the ample spending money available to some of their classmates. Nerd identity, then, was linked not to class status but to class identification (Eckert 1989, 2000).

However, nerds' adoption of a style often viewed as hyperwhite did not necessitate that they embrace hegemonic whiteness. During my fieldwork, a great deal of political debate in Bay City and around the state centered on the dismantling of affirmative action in California's higher education system through the ballot initiative Proposition 209. Erich was part of a group of Bay City High School students who organized large-scale protests against the measure; meanwhile, many European American students whose styles drew heavily upon African American youth language and culture did not participate in these political demonstrations. The wholehearted, or even halfhearted, appropriation of black cultural forms did not guarantee that trend-conscious white teenagers would also adopt a political perspective that was sensitive to African American concerns.

Conclusion

For some teenagers at Bay City High, taking on a nerd identity was an agentive choice that allowed them to escape the pressures of the school's social order and position themselves as intelligent through linguistic practices such as superstandard English, intellectual display, and metalinguistic humor. But in avoiding current slang and embracing superstandard English, European American nerds separated themselves not only from their cool white counterparts but also from most African American students. Consequently, nerdiness was ideologically positioned by other youth as a racially marked, hyperwhite style.

While cool European Americans oriented to African American students either as models or as foils for their own styles and identities, nerds were equally disinterested in both cool blackness and cool whiteness. But as I discuss in the next chapter, despite the diverse styles of European American students at Bay City High School, such teenagers shared a set of discursive practices for talking about race and thus displaying white identities. Chapter 8 examines how European American youth of all stylistic orientations constructed themselves as unaware of racial difference and hence nonracist in talk about cross-racial friendship.

8 "Not that I'm racist": strategies of colorblindness in talk about race and friendship

Introduction

During a unit on race and ethnicity in the Life and Health course, Ms. Stein asked her students if they had ever been in an "interracial romance." Based on the racial divisions I had observed at the school, I was not surprised that relatively few students of any race reported that they had ever been or were currently in an interracial relationship. In sixth period, however, Lauren, a quiet, rather mousy white girl, volunteered that she had a black boyfriend. Heads swiveled sharply to stare at her. To her classmates of all races, this otherwise nondescript student had suddenly become much more interesting.

Interracial dating at Bay City High – especially between African Americans and European Americans – could be controversial, and most white teenagers in my study dated only within their own racial category. This was an issue especially for white hip hop fans, several of whom told me that they found black or Asian girls more attractive than white girls. Yet I knew only one white boy with a hip hop style who had a girlfriend of color, a Latina. This may have been due to the perceived risks of cross-racial dating: one European American hip hop fan expressed the fear that if he pursued an African American girl he was interested in, African American boys would beat him up. Although this perception was based more in ideology than reality – there were in fact a number of interracial relationships at the school, including several involving white boys and black girls – it may have kept some European American students from entering into such relationships.

Friendships between students of different races or ethnicities, though less controversial, were nevertheless marked. As with dating, friendships between black and white teenagers were particularly uncommon but by no means unheard of. Thus in talking to me about interracial friendship, most European American youth confronted a dilemma. On the one hand, they typically had few or no African American friends, but on the other hand, they did not want to be seen as racists. In the extremely liberal and multicultural San Francisco Bay Area, racism was strongly condemned as morally repugnant, a view that these teenagers shared. Bay City High's white students, growing up in generally liberal families and attending schools with progressive, multicultural curricula, were highly attuned to potential racism in others' statements or actions and were quick to deny harboring any racist attitudes of their own. Given this constant monitoring for racism, merely talking about race could be seen as perilous.

In this chapter I examine how several European American teenagers at Bay City High managed the delicate topic of race in talking to me about their own friendships. Due to the sensitive nature of race at the school, not all white youth discussed the topic with me in detail (and in some cases, they did not discuss it at all). I focus primarily on interviews with five white students in which race and friendship were extensively discussed; this approach allows for an in-depth examination of how racial rhetoric unfolds in real time within interaction. The discursive strategies I discuss here, however, were common among European American youth at the school and also correspond to practices of white racial discourse analyzed by other researchers. Talk about race at Bay City High thus was not only a product of the local context but also participated in broader racial ideologies and discourses.

Colorblindness as a racial discourse

Over the past several decades, the dominant public racial discourse among European Americans has shifted away from foregrounding race to downplaying its relevance and significance (Bonilla-Silva 2003). Earlier stages of racism in US history during the slavery and Jim Crow eras drew racial distinctions based on biological essentialism, a belief in natural and inherent differences between racialized groups. In the wake of the civil rights movement, the crudest forms of racism – racially motivated violence, overt discrimination, racial slurs, and explicit assertions of the inferiority of people of color – were censured in most public discourse. In place of such obvious forms of racist practice, often popularly conceptualized as "'real' racism" (Billig 2001), a new racial discourse gained ascendance, rooted in broadly liberal political ideals of equal opportunity and individual rights. This discourse served as the foundation for basic principles of racial fairness that were inscribed into American law. But ironically, it was appropriated as part of a new conservative discourse of race, in which the ideology of egalitarianism came to be used to promote white interests over those of people of color (Wellman 1993).

In this new conservative discourse, which is held by most European Americans regardless of their political affiliation, efforts to redress longstanding racial inequality through affirmative action are rejected as giving an unfair advantage to minorities and infringing on the rights of European Americans. Indeed, from this perspective the fundamental source of inequality is seen not as racism but as race itself. Raising concerns about race-based inequality is therefore condemned in much public discourse as furthering racial division precisely because it calls attention to race (Omi and Winant 1994). Likewise, the liberal goal of racial "colorblindness" – the hope that race might become nonsalient as a factor shaping social, economic, and political opportunities and outcomes – was originally put forth as a way to promote equality for people of color. In the current, conservative version of colorblindness, whites advance their own interests when they argue for treating people as raceless individuals rather than as members of racialized groups for purposes of allocating resources. The problems with the conservative viewpoint are twofold: first, due to the well-documented structural inequities that people of color continue to face, they do not compete with whites on a "level playing field" (to use a common cliché of colorblind discourse) but encounter systematic disadvantages even if all else is equal; second, all else is typically not equal under so-called colorblind policies, which define race neutrality in ways that in fact favor whites. Moreover, in current conservative racial discourse, distinctions between racialized groups are understood not in explicitly racial terms but instead as essentialized cultural differences. As with colorblindness, this perspective exploits and distorts what was originally a progressive political move – in this case, to frame race via culture rather than biology (Gaudio and Bialostok 2005). To be sure, culture (like other concepts sometimes used to replace race, such as social class) is closely tied to race; the conservative cultural discourse of race, however, is invoked not to understand racial processes but to rationalize and justify a host of racial inequities.

As many researchers of racism have argued, to ignore, deny, or misattribute the causes of real racial differences in such areas as income, education, housing, and health does little to eliminate racism and in fact further reinforces racial disparities (Brown *et al.* 2003; Feagin and Vera 1995; Omi and Winant 1994). Colorblind racial discourse can thus perpetuate racism even as its proponents sincerely disavow racist beliefs. This process is fueled not only by public policies and discourses but also by individuals' colorblind talk about race (Bonilla-Silva 2003; Gallagher 2003). Such talk is both "color-evasive" and "power-evasive" (Frankenberg 1993: 14–15) in that it does not acknowledge the continuing social and political significance of racial categories. Consequently, colorblind discourse is enacted through its silences and omissions as much as its words. For discourse analysts, race talk invites close examination to uncover the rhetorical strategies that maintain the discursive and material dominance of whiteness in the face of whites' heartfelt disclaimers of racist intent.

Race talk, research, and structural racism

Discourse about race, ethnicity, and racism, or what has been called "race talk" (or "racetalk") (e.g., Anderson 2008; Bonilla-Silva 2003; Myers 2005; Pollock 2005; van den Berg *et al.* 2004) has been a topic of great scholarly interest in the United States and elsewhere (e.g., van Dijk 1987, 1993a; Wetherell and Potter 1992; Wodak and Reisigl 1999). Most studies of race talk examine how white speakers use racial reasoning to take positions on a variety of issues involving racialized groups, especially minorities.[1] This body of research often seeks to expose and eradicate individual prejudiced or racist beliefs. The colorblind ideology, however, makes it difficult to combat racism by confronting individual racism.

More fundamentally, as noted in Chapter 1, race is not simply a dimension of social classification but more importantly an ideological and institutional system for legitimating social inequality. Hence racism is not perpetuated in the first instance by individual intentions or attitudes, since most individuals have little power to shape large-scale social processes on their own. Racism relies instead on institutionalized structures of inequity and their supporting racial ideologies. Regardless of individual good will, through structural racism members of the ethnoracial majority systematically benefit from white privilege and cannot simply choose to give it up. It is in the interest of European Americans who reap the benefits of their racial category to understand their superior structural position as natural and justified by individual merit rather than due to structural racism. Yet white people who adopt such a viewpoint do not necessarily do so out of cynical self-interest. Rather, because white racial hegemony is widely represented as mere "common sense," it is difficult for many European Americans to imagine other ways of understanding race. To be sure, not all individual whites are advantaged vis-à-vis all people of color in every domain, and a number of prominent proponents of colorblind policies are themselves people of color, such as Ward Connerly, the mixed-race businessman who spearheaded the Proposition 209 initiative eliminating affirmative action in California. But focusing on individuals rather than larger racialized patterns is part of what makes structural racism difficult to recognize.

Given that individuals alone cannot dismantle this system (and often have difficulty even recognizing it), it is of limited analytic value to apply the label of *racist* to individuals who engage in race talk that upholds race-based inequality. A more productive approach is to examine precisely how such talk contributes to wider racial discourses and thus inevitably implicates even well-intentioned individuals – including researchers of race and racism – in structural racism. For this reason, I do not characterize the racial discourse analyzed in this chapter as racist, a term whose blunt force as a label for individual attitudes may miss much of the nuanced complexity of race talk and its intersection with larger sociopolitical processes. Nor do I consider the participants in this study to be racist to any greater or lesser degree than the average white American, myself included. Nearly all members of US society are implicated in some way in the perpetuation of racial ideologies and disparities toward one group or another, often without their conscious awareness. My purpose, then, is not to denounce individuals as racists but to undertake the more challenging task of examining, sympathetically yet critically, how European American teenagers in my study, often with my support and collusion, drew on a wide variety of readily available and highly problematic resources for talking and reasoning about race. Such an approach complicates simplistic characterizations of evil white oppressors and helpless minority victims and thus helps to imagine more effective ways of combating racism as a deeply rooted element of social structures and processes.

The data in this chapter are taken mainly from ethnographic interviews, but the explicit focus of the interactions was friendship rather than race. Because of my concern not to appear overly preoccupied with the school's racial tensions, my general strategy as an interviewer was to follow up on students' mentions of race rather than to introduce the topic into discourse myself. The lexical activity portion of the interview also provided an opportunity for race to enter the discourse, often obliquely via the racialized associations of particular terms. As a consequence of my decision not to ask directly about race unless the topic had already arisen, some students never discussed race with me in interviews, while others did so occasionally or frequently. One of the key contexts in which race came up was in discussions of various social groups at the school, which could lead to the fraught topic of interracial friendship. This issue was extremely delicate, because if a white student stated that she or he had no friends of color, this fact could be taken by others as evidence of prejudice or racism. White teenagers without close friends of color therefore used various discursive strategies to present themselves as nonracist by constructing a stance of colorblindness – a displayed lack of orientation to or awareness of race.

My own displayed stance toward race also influenced the unfolding interaction. I did not openly challenge or question how white youth talked about race, as some activist researchers advocate (e.g., Guerin 2003). My general orientation as an ethnographer was one of openness to whatever students wanted to tell me, but my deep interest in race coupled with my awareness of the local sensitivity of the topic undoubtedly had an effect on the way I responded to my interviewees. Moreover, my position as a white adult researcher with the institutional backing of both the school and my university certainly influenced students' views of me. Thus, my own interactional participation as well as my broader social positionality both authorized and shaped the race talk and the white identities that were produced in these situations.

Racial evasion

The interactional delicacy of talking about race and friendship at Bay City High was evident in white students' circumlocution and inarticulateness around this topic, or what I term *racial evasion*. Such evasiveness has been found in other scholarship on whiteness: "white people's equivocation about their whiteness [is] dramatized in their discourse. Literal equivocation as stammering, hesitation, and verbal backtracking in response to questions about interviewees' relationships with people of color . . . can only be read as a sign of the nature of whiteness at this moment in U.S. history" (Frankenberg 2001: 90; cf. McElhinny 2001). Mica Pollock (2005) proposes the notion of "colormuteness" to characterize this practice of avoiding or silencing discourse about race. Like colorblindness, colormuteness is often seen as a nonracist practice by those who engage in it, for it allows them to behave as though the social phenomenon of race did not exist. Scholars have noted that according to the logic underlying this perspective, "racism does not make people talk about race; talk about race sustains racism" (Gordon and Newfield 1995: 382). In other words, this viewpoint holds that eliminating talk about race will eliminate racism. Yet, as Pollock points out, even when speakers do not explicitly use racial categories they may be strongly aware of and oriented to race.

Finally, aside from the school's liberal racial views, race was a particularly delicate matter at Bay City High at the time of my study due to a series of racial problems at the school that had received a great deal of negative attention from the local media. As a result, I hesitated to raise the topic directly with interviewees. Both the sensationalistic media coverage and my own diffidence no doubt contributed to teenagers' racial evasion in interviews with me, especially regarding the question of their own friendships with students of color. In such situations, talk about race was frequently couched in indirectness and disfluency, a general conversational resource for signaling that the speaker is negotiating some sort of interactional trouble. I examine two different forms of racial evasion: erasing race, or using nonracial terms to talk about racial categories; and delaying race, or introducing racial labels relatively late into discourse about race, marked by pauses, self-interruptions, and other strategies.

Erasing race

In many of my interviews, even when race was the established topic of discussion, speakers sometimes elected not to use racial terms. Some such elisions were likely due to the fact that race could be taken for granted as the discourse topic. Others, however, were more complex, being marked not by elisions but by elaborate circumlocutions. These gaps, in leaving such noticeable traces, put race "under erasure," calling attention to it as an "absent presence" in the discourse (Derrida 1976). Erasure is a powerful semiotic process whereby problematic realities that disrupt dominant ideologies are obscured (cf. Irvine and Gal 2000). In this case, the ideology of racial colorblindness made it difficult for European American youth even to mention race without potentially inviting the inference that they might be racist.

The following example illustrates the kinds of racially evasive wordings that teenagers often produced in discussing racial categories in the context of friendship; it also demonstrates how my own role as researcher facilitated the use of such forms, especially through the discussion of slang and other terms during the interviews. This activity, though not intended to overcome the problem of raising the topic of race, did indeed occasion race talk. Example (1) involves the two relatively nerdy white girls Christine and Claire. Before the example begins, the girls have been sorting through the slips of paper I have given them and discussing the terms printed on them. The term *hip hop* has come up, and after some discussion Christine states, "Not really my thing." In response, I ask a clarifying question:

(1a) 1 Mary: So you don't,
2 n-
3 know people that,
4 would be in something called a hip hop crowd,=
5 =or you wouldn't [use a term like that?]
6 Christine: <higher pitch> [{Oh,
7 I} kno:w them.]

As discussed in Chapter 6, at Bay City High School in the mid-1990s, hip hop was still viewed by most African Americans and European Americans alike as a form of black youth culture that was largely off limits to white teenagers. The mention of hip hop therefore makes relevant some acknowledgment of this racialized boundary. Perhaps signaling my awareness of this situation, my question exhibits some of the same discursive inarticulateness that a number of teenagers displayed when racial topics arose during discussions of friendship, including pausing, disfluency, and circumlocution (*people that, would be in something called a hip hop crowd*; lines 3–4).

This awkwardness may set the tone for Christine's lengthy response (analyzed in greater detail in Chapter 9), which spans over eighty lines of transcription and is replete with vague reference terms for African American students, such as *some people* and *somebody in the crowd*. Her summarizing remarks toward the end of her extended turn continue this pattern of referential vagueness (example 1b):

(1b) 56 Christine: And now I [like] it,
57 Claire: [@]
58 Christine: I like having,
59 friends everywhere 'cause,=
60 =I-
61 I like knowing that I can get along with: people,
62 i:n different,
63 social,
64 groups?
65 Mary: Yeah.

66 (0.6)
67 Christine: Than my own.

In (1b) Christine offers her fullest characterization of the students she has been talking about: *people, i:n different, social, groups? . . . Than my own* (lines 61–67). This characterization and the surrounding talk are produced with disfluencies similar to those found in my turn in (1a): false starts (line 60), pausing (line 66), vowel elongation (line 62), and the incrementally produced characterization of the "hip hop crowd," involving five separate intonation units (lines 61–64, 67). Christine's measured speech style suggests that she is choosing her words with care, and the characterization she finally offers is only slightly less vague than what has come before. Her final formulation of the problematic referent, black teenagers, in terms of "different social groups" takes advantage of the interview's overtly stated focus on this topic while allowing her to avoid racial categories. Indeed, throughout her longer response, Christine mentions race explicitly only once, and that is in reference to herself.

The characterization of race as unspecified "difference" is also found in other European American teenagers' talk about friendship. Example (2) is taken from an interview with the two preppy white girls Zoe and Josie. The girls have been drawing maps of where they and other groups at the school hang out; as she narrates her map, Zoe asserts, "Our school is majorly segregated." After agreeing, Josie counters, "But, I mean it's not completely totally like that at all." Several turns later, I follow up on this comment, remarking, "I've seen people of different races hanging out together." The girls respond with a roughly six-minute-long discussion of the nature and extent of racial segregration at Bay City High, as part of which they comment on their own degree of interaction with students of other backgrounds. Example (2) occurs toward the end of this exchange.

(2) 57 Zoe: Or you have frie:nds.
58 Like,
59 probably for me the friends:,
60 (0.7)
61 that I'm like,
62 (1.2)
63 the most different,
64 (0.9)
65 or-
66 <rapid> {Do you know what I'm saying?}
67 Like the people who are most different from me,
68 <tongue click> who I talk to,
69 are usually people I've met in cla:sses and ↑stuff,=
70 Mary: =Right.
71 Zoe: But,

72 um:,
73 The people who I have like further friendships with?
74 are more similar probably,
75 [in the end,]
76 Mary: [Mm.]
77 Zoe: but in my classes,
78 I probably talk to a lot of people who are different.

Although race has already been the topic of conversation for several minutes, Zoe does not use racial categories or the word *race* itself in discussing her friends and acquaintances of color. Instead, she characterizes them in terms of an undefined "difference" from herself (lines 63, 67, 78), which turns out to be crucial: her interaction with "the people who are most different" from her (line 67) is limited to classes, while people who "are more similar probably" are those with whom she has "further friendships" (lines 73–74). The hedge *probably* in line 74 makes a bit less stark the line separating acquaintances who are "different" from her (i.e., black) from friends who are "similar" to her (i.e., white). Thus without naming race, Zoe is able to distinguish between her friendly acquaintanceships with teenagers of color and her more extensive friendships with other white youth. In such situations, the strategy of erasing race reproduces the discourse of colorblindness by making it possible for students to frame their lack of friends of color as an outcome attributable to nonracial factors.

Delaying race

Even when speakers did overtly use racial categories and terms, by delaying the mention of race they were able to protect themselves from appearing inappropriately racially conscious and hence racist according to the ideology of colorblindness. Example (3), from an interview with the preppy white Jewish boy Mark, exhibits several delaying features in discussing race and friendship. Before this example begins, Mark has been describing his friends to me and has gone on to mention various social groups at Bay City High, but he then adds, "I pretty much only know about the white people." As with Christine in (1a), I take this comment as an opportunity to ask about his own friendships:

(3) 1 Mary: So you don't have any friends who aren't whi:te?
2 Mark: I mean I have—
3 I have—
4 I don't have like,
5 f:rien-
6 Like,
7 <speech error> {<[aðubup]>}
8 the six people I named are a:ll,

9 Jewish.
10 (0.6)
11 A::nd,
12 <coughs>
13 Like I know people,
14 and I'll talk to people and stuff,
15 who a:ren't,
16 (0.6)
17 who aren't white.

The form of my question in line 1 is rather pointed, as I realized to my chagrin only long afterward: not only do I use an extreme-case formulation with negative polarity and emphatic stress (*you don't have any . . . ?*) (cf. Pomerantz 1986), but I also present my characterization as a logical inference from Mark's previous comment (*So*). Given the racial tensions at Bay City High, Mark may well have taken my question as an accusation rather than a neutral request for information, which may partly account for the inarticulateness of his answer. But given that students used similar resources in talking about race regardless of how or whether I prompted them, the form of his answer is also likely rooted in the more general problem of discussing race and friendship.

Mark's turn contains several indicators that he has difficulty formulating his response, including multiple instances of self-interruption and self-repair (lines 2–7, lines 15–17) as well as hedging (line 2: *I mean*; line 4: *like*) and pausing (line 16). In addition, like Christine in (1b) above, Mark initially uses an unmodified vague reference term, *people* (line 13), to refer to his nonwhite peers: *I'll talk to people and stuff . . .* (presumably, the generalizing form *and stuff* is an extender of *talk*, despite its syntactic placement next to *people*). Indeed, although he has voluntarily and unhesitatingly brought up the topic of "white people" a few turns earlier, Mark appears reluctant to talk equally overtly about people of color here, as signaled by his multiple hesitations and delays before he eventually echoes my original formulation, *friends who aren't white*, in lines 13 through 17 (*people . . . who a:ren't, (0.6) who aren't white*).

If naming nonwhiteness is problematic for European American teenagers in talking about friendship, as seen in the preceding examples, naming whiteness can be equally difficult, especially when students admit to not having friends of color. The following example takes place just before example (2) above, after the topic of race has already been established. When Josie and Zoe state that their friends are "all the same," I seek clarification, asking if they are "all white" or "of different races." Example (4) is the second part of Josie's reply.

(4) 25 Josie: See:,
26 like,
27 (0.9)
28 the majority of people,

29 i:n like,
30 the higher track classes,
31 parents have gone to college,
32 and have pushed them into the tracks?
33 Mary: Ri:ght.
34 Josie: And,
35 um,
36 Those are the people I meet every single da:y?
37 and these peopl:e,
38 their parents are ↑white.
39 Mary: Mhm.
40 Josie: So they're white.
41 [You know.]
42 Mary: [Right.]
43 Josie: And their parents:,
44 have gone to college,
45 are pushing them to go to college.
46 And so,
47 the majority of people in my classes,
48 are ↑white.

As a high-achieving and high-aspiring student, Josie, like many of her peers, was strongly committed to taking the school's competitive and demanding Advanced Placement (AP) and college-preparatory classes (or, as they were usually referred to at Bay City High, *high-track classes*; cf. line 30). In fact, I once stayed after school to console a tearful Josie after she discovered that she had not done well enough on a placement test to be admitted to the school's AP English class along with most of her friends. Despite her strong personal commitment to academic achievement, in this example Josie attributes her own and her friends' focus on taking high-track classes to the encouragement (or pressure) of their well-educated parents (lines 31–32). Race itself is mentioned only belatedly, and remarkably, it is only after Josie specifies the whiteness of her classmates' parents that she goes on to acknowledge that her classmates too are white (lines 38, 40). This delay in specifying her friends' racial category may indicate Josie's reluctance to talk about race explicitly in this context, but it also performs the important interactional function of attributing the composition of her friendship groups to a shared orientation to education, rather than race. I appear to accept Josie's account unquestioningly through my repeated agreement markers, which may also indicate empathy and encouragement in response to her reticence. (The strategy of downplaying the relevance of race in accounts of social differences is examined further below.)

The strategies that speakers use to talk around rather than about race do not in fact serve to diminish racial awareness, as the colorblind ideology advocates. On the contrary, because these strategies are so highly marked in interaction they call greater attention to race and to the speaker's hyperawareness of racial topics. For European American students at Bay City High, strategies of racial evasion during ethnographic interviews may in fact have been advantageous precisely for this reason. In displaying cautiousness in race talk, these teenagers were able to project themselves as careful, thoughtful, and nonracist to an adult researcher (just as I was able to project myself as a nonjudgmental, understanding, and supportive listener by responding agreeably to their remarks).

Disavowing racism

Whereas racial evasion implicitly aligned the speaker with the ideology of colorblindness, more explicit testimonials of colorblindness also occurred. Overt denials of racial awareness put on record the speaker's asserted ability to transcend racial distinctions; yet once again in disavowing the salience of race, European American teenagers ended up calling even greater attention to it. This commonplace practice of colorblind discourse, often formulated as *I'm not a racist, but . . .* , has been documented by a number of researchers of race talk (Billig 1988; Bonilla-Silva and Forman 2000; van Dijk 1992).

In example (5), which takes place shortly after example (3) above, Mark continues to respond to my original question *So you don't have any friends who aren't white?* by relating a story that uses strategies of colorblindness to provide evidence that he does in fact have friends of color:

(5) 27 Mark: Like,
28 s:ome guy asked me like,
29 (0.8)
30 <deeper pitch> {"Do you have any friends who are bla:ck?"}=
31 =and I was like,
32 (0.7)
33 "No:."
34 (0.8)
35 And I was like,
36 "Yeah,
37 I do."=
38 =And he was like,
39 "Have you ever gone to their ↑house?"
40 (0.9)
41 "Have you gone to someone who's black's house?"
42 And I was like,
43 "No."
44 But then I thought about it.
45 And I thought,
46 like I ↑have,
47 like two or three times.
48 Like different people.

49 I just didn't think of them as black.=
50 =I thought of the[m] as just like,
51 Mary: [Hm.]
53 Mark: John.
53 Mary: Right.
54 Mark: Or whoever they were.
55 Mary: Right.
56 Mark: You know what I mean?
57 Mary: Uh huh.

In this brief narrative, Mark is interrogated by "s:ome guy" (line 28) of unspecified race who asks a series of challenging questions about interracial friendship: *Do you have any friends who are bla:ck?* (line 30); *Have you gone to someone who's black's house?* (line 41). This story was likely triggered by my own challenging question to Mark in example (3) above. In the present example, Mark-in-the-story initially answers in the negative and then belatedly realizes that this answer is in fact incorrect (in this way the story also functions to repair his previous claim in example (3) that he does not have black friends). Here the discourse of colorblindness is quite overt, as Mark denies that he had even noticed his African American friends' race (line 49: *I just didn't think of them as black*). Such rhetoric has been found to be widespread among whites, who often mention their acquaintances of other races as evidence both of their own liberal racial attitudes and of the ordinariness (which often appears to mean 'similarity to whites') of these particular individuals of color. Moreover, Mark's answer suggests that his social connections to black students are more than incidental, as he states that his visits to his African American friends' homes are, if not frequent, then at least repeated (line 47) and that he has visited not just one black friend but "different people" (line 48).

Again, my whiteness shapes this interaction. Although my own initial stance toward Mark could be seen as confrontational (as shown in example 3), in response to his story I offer not only an acknowledgment token (line 51) but also repeated backchanneled agreement markers (lines 53, 55). Finally, Mark seeks confirmation that I understand what he has said (perhaps because his explanation is a bit unclear or because he is seeking greater reassurance or agreement than is provided by my minimal responses), and I respond affirmatively (lines 56–57). In repeatedly aligning with Mark rather than questioning him further or showing skepticism about his claimed lack of attention to race (especially considering how frequently he initiated racial topics throughout the interview), I seem to accept his self-proclaimed colorblindness as both plausible and understandable and thereby offer a kind of racial solidarity.

At times students made their disavowals of racism even more explicit, as shown in example (6), which occurs around five and a half minutes prior to the examples in (3) and (5) above. Just before example (6) begins, Mark, at my request, has been drawing a map of the school and the hangout areas of his own and other social groups (see Figure 3.1 in Chapter 3). He has just indicated the location of the Hill, remarking, "You know about that. African Americans. Majoratively. . . . And:, one or two white people." This comment presupposes the ideological salience of the Hill as an "African American" space both for students and for the adult researcher. (At the time of the interview I had been doing fieldwork for six months.) In response, I follow up with a question about Mark's connection to students who hang out on the Hill:

(6) 1 Mary: Do you know people over on the Hill?
2 Mark: Not es[pecially.
3   I don't—
4   I don't—]
5 Mary: [You don't hang out there.   ]
6 Mark: No.
7   (2.0)
8   <lower volume> {Not that I'm r:acist or anything.
9   @@@}

Before turning to Mark's explicit disavowal of racist intent in line 8 it is useful to consider some of the other interactional work being accomplished in this brief exchange. My question regarding Mark's acquaintance with black teenagers is a bit less pointed than my later question in example (3) above. However, given the emphatic stress on *know* (line 1), my question is not entirely neutral, implying some doubt that Mark might have African American friends or acquaintances. The distal adverb *over* further heightens the separation I seem to be positing between the largely black social space of the Hill and Mark's usual hangout area. (At the time of this recording, Mark and I were in the school library, but my use of *over* may have been due to the Hill's symbolic distance as much as its physical location relative to us.) Yet even as I highlight racial distance and separateness in the form of my question, I also occlude the visibility of race by using a circumlocution – *people over on the Hill* – to talk about the racialized group that Mark has already introduced, African Americans. In this way I reconfigure the school's racial divide as a geographic divide and downplay the salience of race as a reason for group boundaries. Despite not personally subscribing to the ideology of colorblindness, in this moment I interactionally exploit the ideology in order to minimize my interest in race.

My reformulation of race as geography persists as the interaction continues. Mark hedges his negative response to my question (line 2) and goes on to initiate a rather disfluent explanation (lines 3–4). But before he finishes his utterance, I offer a candidate completion (line 5) that again focuses not on the people who spend time on the Hill but on the place itself. In a number of ways, then, my contributions reframe the interaction as being about space rather than race. Yet as noted above, colorblind strategies of circumlocution may end up foregrounding the topic of race. In this case, Mark remains attuned to the specifically racial implications of his remoteness from the Hill's social scene, and after a lengthy pause he adds an overt denial of racism, *Not that I'm r:acist or anything* (line 8). This utterance is produced in lower volume and followed by laughter, features that seem to frame the comment as a joking aside rather than an earnest effort to deflect any suspicions of racism. The lighthearted keying of the utterance implies that to charge Mark with racism is so improbable as to be laughable. Moreover, race is so salient in this interaction that Mark denies racism even though the topic of race itself is not entirely on the surface of the discourse.

The same dynamic may be found in my interviews with other white teenagers. Example (7) is the first part of Josie's explanation for why she does not have nonwhite friends, the second part of which was presented in example (4) above.

(7) 1 Josie: People.
2 Like,
3 whose parents go to ↑college,
4 who:,
5 who live in like—
6 And I'm not saying,
7 I'm not—
8 I don't mea:n,
9 <smiling quality> {And I,
10 know it sounds really like,}
11 racist when I say that,
12 but-
13 that-
14 and,
15 um,
16 that like-
17 people-
18 other people don't-
19 par-
20 whose parents don't go to college?

In example (4) above Josie restarts and develops her argument more explicitly: that the parents of nonwhite (and given the context, specifically African American) students are not well educated and so do not push their children to take high-track classes where she might meet them. In the present example she rather inarticulately initiates this economic account of racial separation by pointing to racial differences in housing patterns, although the exact nature of this difference is unclear because she does not complete her utterance (line 5).

Josie is able to activate race even though she has left it unnamed up to this point, instead using circumlocutions to characterize her white friends (lines 1–3), in implicit contrast to black students who are not her friends. Apparently recognizing that this contrast may be offensive, she first attempts several abortive denials (presumably) of racist intent (lines 6–8) and then overtly acknowledges that such an intent could be inferred from her comments (*And I, know it sounds really like, racist when I say that*; lines 9–11). Yet by specifying that her statement "sounds really … racist" she implies that it is not so in fact. The risk of racism that Josie orients to here seems graver than the risk Mark confronted above, perhaps because she has ventured to offer generalizations about racialized groups, although like Mark she takes a somewhat joking tone. Whatever the reason, and as I discuss below, she goes on to issue further denials.

Such disavowals of racism inoculated speakers against potential accusations of harboring racist sentiments. It is not clear, however, whether either Mark or Josie was in fact concerned that I would level such an accusation. In both cases, I had directly and somewhat pointedly asked whether they had friends of color, and given the hyperawareness of racial divisions at the school, this question alone could have led them to worry that I was trying to reveal them as racists. On the other hand, both students knew me well and were very friendly with me, and nothing in the interactions or in my fieldwork indicates discomfort with me or my research agenda. It seems likely, in fact, that it was precisely these teenagers' familiarity with me that allowed them to raise the issue of racism in the first place, for they could feel reasonably safe that I would not misinterpret their comments. Thus as with other strategies of colorblindness, denying racism might not counter a genuine risk of being perceived as racist but might instead demonstrate the speaker's sensitivity to racial concerns – that is, denying racism could be used to claim a fundamentally nonracist outlook.

Displacing race

A final discursive strategy that allowed European American students at Bay City High to deny the significance of race in their friendships involved the displacement of race onto class and culture, which were identified as the "real" causes of the school's racial divisions. Race was thus positioned as a red herring, a merely incidental characteristic that distracted from the true reasons for social separation. This strategy has been dubbed "anything but race" (Bonilla-Silva 2003: 62–63), for it leads those who use it to invoke a wide range of explanations for racial inequality other than the social reality of race itself. More generally, displacing race involves any discursive move to minimize racial factors and replace them with social factors deemed less problematic.

Example (8) presents several instances of racial displacement. Here Claire brings up the same issue that Josie discussed in example (4) above: the difficulty of making friends of color in high-track classes. Before this example (from a separate interview that took place before the examples with Christine), Claire has been telling me that Bay City High is different from other high schools in that students do not simply cluster in homogeneous cliques but have wider-ranging friendships, although she quickly corrects herself to say that this is only true of her own friends.

(8) 1 Claire: Everyone has really different groups of frie:nds.
2 (0.7)
3 Actually I shouldn't say that.
4 Most of my friends have,
5 (1.6)
6 really:,
7 (1.4)
8 diverse group of friends.
9 Mary: Mhm.
10 Claire: And I don't mean diver:se as in,
11 (0.9)
12 ethnically,
13 but just diver:se as in,
14 everything.
15 Mary: Hm.
16 (0.6)
17 Claire: You [$_1$know?$_1$]
18 Mary: [$_1$Like $_1$] intere:sts and-
19 Claire: Yeah.
20 You know.
21 Comple:tely diverse.
22 (1.4)
23 [$_2$But-$_2$]
24 Mary: [$_2$Is i$_2$]t also ethnically diverse or is it,=
25 Claire: =↑U::m,
26 Mary: (How would you describe it?)
27 (2.4)
28 Claire: S:omewhat.
29 I mean,
30 I'd like to say it was more but,
31 (0.8)
32 the f:act of the matter is that,
33 it's true,
34 I'm in high tracked cla:sses,
35 it's v:e:ry,
36 (1.6)
37 it's v:ery white looking.
38 And,
39 I don't meet,

40 other people.
41 You know,
42 I-
43 I-
44 I definitely ha:ve frie:nds,
45 (0.6)
46 who: are,
47 of different races,
48 and different ethnic backgrounds than,
49 me:,
50 but it's just hard,
51 because I don't,
52 meet a lot of people.
53 And the people:,
54 I mean the people in my classes,
55 that I—
56 I mean I always talk to,
57 but so:meti:mes,
58 we click and sometimes we don't.
59 And it's comple:tely,
60 interest,
61 related,
62 I think,
63 about your frie:nds.
64 Mary: Uh huh.
65 Claire: Because people who have,
66 different interests just can't be friends.
67 I've tried it,
68 doesn't work.

Claire first asserts that at Bay City High School "everyone has really different groups of frie:nds" (line 1). She then self-corrects, saying, with contrastive stress, "Most of my friends have really:, diverse group of friends. And I don't mean diver:se as in, ethnically, . . . but just diver:se as in, everything" (lines 4–14). Here Claire replaces the general idea of "difference" (a term that, as shown above, could be used to downplay race and ethnicity) with the more politically fraught notion of "diversity." At Bay City High in the 1990s, *diversity* was a catchword of the multicultural discourse circulated by the administration and teaching staff to encourage students to celebrate their own and others' ethnoracial heritage (Chapter 2). It is thus a far from neutral synonym for *difference* in this context. Moreover, at the same time that she makes this lexical switch, Claire states that she is not using the term in the school's usual sense, but instead is using it to mean "diverse as in, everything." This redefinition of *diversity* to explicitly exclude ethnicity (and race), the very core of the term's local meaning, is a form of racial displacement that positions other forms of difference as essentially equivalent to ethnoracial difference. In particular, as the omitted parts of Claire's discussion indicate, her primary concern here is with differences in youth style, a highly salient parameter of distinction for her as a student who participated in multiple, largely white, groups with different styles.

When I ask Claire about specifically ethnic diversity in her friendship groups (line 24), she raises the issue of the relative lack of students of color in her high-track classes. Her response contains several discursive strategies of colorblindness, including both erasing race (e.g., lack of racial specificity: *I don't meet, other people*; lines 39–40) and delayed mention of racial categories through pausing and self-interruption, as well as the implication that her classes may appear more white than they in fact are (e.g., *It's v:e:ry, (1.6) it's v:ery white looking*; lines 35–37). Her remarks again displace race by attributing her lack of friends of color to a lack of shared interests (lines 59–61) rather than to racially specific experiences that might have led to these differences in the first place. As she crisply states, such friendships cannot succeed (lines 65–68). Through racial displacement, Claire redefines diversity as separate from race and ethnicity and locates friendship in the shared interests of individuals rather than in ethno-racially shared sociocultural experiences.

The focus on individuals over groups is only one way of displacing race, for even when speakers attend to social groupings, they may dismiss the role of race in shaping processes of difference and exclusion. Example (9) is the final excerpt from Josie and Zoe's discussion of why they do not have friends of other racial backgrounds. As seen in earlier examples, Josie has been building an argument that her friendships are based on who she meets in her high-track classes. While acknowledging racial imbalances in such classes, she argues that this asymmetry is due to differences in parental guidance, which in turn are due to differences in parents' educational level. In the following example, Josie explicitly displaces race in favor of an economic explanation for her lack of opportunities to form friendships with students of other races. The first two lines of the example are repeated from the end of example (2).

(9) 77 Zoe: but in my classes,
78 I probably talk to a lot of people who are different.
79 Josie: Oh!
80 Yeah.
81 Completely.=
82 =And I don't want to sound like,
83 (0.8)
84 mea:n or,
85 (1.1)
86 like [wr:o:ng]=
87 Zoe: [Mhm.]=
88 Josie: =or anything.
89 Mary: Right.

90	Josie:	But I just think that that's—
91		I don't think it's a race thing.
92		I just think it's an economics:,
93		like,
94		[s:ocial thing more.]
95	Zoe:	[Unconscious kind of thing] too.=
96	Josie:	=Unconscious.
97	Mary:	Yeah.
98	Josie:	A:nd,
99		I think,
100		um,
101		(0.8)
102		It just so happens in Bay City that the majority of people whose parents
103		are pushing them,
104		the majority of people whose parents like,
105		<lower volume>{who've gone to co:lleg:e,
106		are ↑white.}
107		And it's just.
108	Zoe:	Yeah.
109	Josie:	I don't kno:w,
110		I mean I—
111		I just think that's tr-
112		I—
113	Zoe:	Yea:h.
114	Josie:	I think it's ↑true.

Like Claire, Josie draws on several strategies of colorblindness, including delaying mention of racial categories (lines 102–106) and disavowing racist or malicious intent, here formulated in more general terms of moral and logical failing (lines 82–88). In addition, she displaces race by dismissing racially based accounts of social inequality. First, she explicitly discounts the relevance of race in the low numbers of students of color (especially African Americans) in Bay City High's most academically demanding classes: *I don't think it's a race thing* (line 91). It is not clear whether this comment is a rejection of old-style racist arguments that students of color are inherently unqualified to take demanding classes or a rejection of claims that students of color are systematically excluded due to deliberate racist intent by the school. She then offers an alternative, socioeconomically rooted account (lines 92–94), which Zoe amplifies (line 95). Josie further displaces the role of race in her next turn, suggesting that any racial asymmetry in advanced classes is a mere coincidence (*It just so happens . . . that the majority of people . . . are ↑white*; lines 102–106). She then draws the topic to a close by reiterating the truth of this assertion (line 114), though only after a good deal of disfluency and delay. For my own part, I once again offer agreement markers throughout (lines 89 and 97), apparently endorsing her position.

Here both Josie and Zoe discount racial explanations for social disparities, but they also make some first tentative steps toward recognizing structural factors behind such inequities. Josie foregrounds the role of socioeconomic class and limited educational opportunities in perpetuating racial inequality (although she does not acknowledge that such opportunities may not be equally available for people of all races, nor that parents who did not attend college might strongly encourage their children to strive for this goal). And Zoe points to the fact that racial divisions are largely constructed unconsciously rather than deliberately, an important awareness that racism is a social rather than an individual process. Yet the girls' arguments are somewhat self-serving in that by contributing to the hegemonic racial discourse of colorblindness they could be used to absolve European Americans of any individual responsibility to redress racial injustice.

Making color visible and audible: interracial friendships

When Claire in example (8) above asserted that her own friends were "diverse," she made clear that she meant something other than ethnoracial diversity, implying that friendship across any category of difference (such as youth style) was equivalent to cross-racial friendship. To be sure, friendships between students with different stylistic orientations had challenges of their own, but they were by no means unusual, and they certainly did not attract the same degree of comment and even suspicion as did friendships across racial boundaries – and particularly those between black and white students. Yet a number of European American students at Bay City High in fact had close friendships across ethnoracial divisions, often risking peer sanctions in order to do so.

Example (10) is taken from a group interview with Al Capone, a European American hip hop fan, and some of the other members of his crew: John Doe, an African American boy; Peanut, an Asian American boy, and Shawn, a European American boy. The ethnoracial diversity of this friendship group was a central part of their identity, and they took great pride in this distinction compared to other groups at the school. Before the example begins, I have asked the boys a version of one of my standard interview questions: "What makes you different from other groups in this school?" After some preliminary discussion, Peanut and John jointly construct a response focusing on their group's ethnoracial diversity:

(10) 1 John: We're just close.
2 We're all hella close.
3 Peanut: Yeah.
4 There are a lot of other groups,
5 which are,
6 d-

7 separated by rac:e.
8 (1.1)
9 John: [Yea:h.]
10 Peanut: [That] hang out together,
11 and we're—
12 we're just a s-
13 r:eally mixed up group,
14 I mean,
15 [we have,]
16 John: [Yea:h.]
17 Peanut: the m-
18 like-
19 John: All [types of-]
20 Peanut: [Mexi]can Americans in our grou:p,
21 There's A:sians,=
22 John: =African Ame:rican.=
23 Peanut: =African [American.]=
24 John: [Whi:te.]=
25 Peanut: =Whi:te.
26 John: Everything.
27 Peanut: And I mean—
28 To us,
29 it doesn't matter what race you are,
30 as long—
31 I mean,
32 as long as you're just cool with us,
33 and,
34 like you're our frie:nd.
35 Mary: Ri:ght.
36 So you think that's pretty unusual in this school?
37 Peanut: Yeah,
38 I mean,
39 'cause I—
40 like,
41 John: Yeah I—
42 I do.

Peanut responds that what makes his group distinctive is that it is "a . . . r:eally mixed up group" (line 13), in the sense that his friends are of different ethnoracial backgrounds. He and John go on to co-construct a list of the various ethnoracial categories represented in their crew, a list that John sums up as "Everything" (line 26). Unlike the students in the previous examples, Peanut and John demonstrate no interactional difficulty in using racial labels or the term *race* itself. It is striking, however, that it is John, the sole African American member, who collaborates with Peanut in this interaction. While it is evident that he takes great pride in his friendships with the other boys, I also learned in talking to him individually that he faced scorn from his black peers for having primarily nonblack friends. Interracial friendship, then, did not entirely eradicate racial division. But within interracial friendships, race was not such a delicate topic, and teenagers could speak more openly about ethnoracial problems and issues without fear of being viewed as racist.

Conclusion

Although Al, Peanut, John, and their friends explicitly named and celebrated racial diversity in their own group, for most European American teenagers at Bay City High School, the discursive strategies of colorblindness discussed in this chapter – the evasion of racial terms, the disavowal of racism, and the displacement of race by other issues – were important tools that allowed them to navigate the dangerous waters of race in interacting with an adult researcher (who used and supported these strategies during the interviews as well). Far from minimizing race, as the ideology of racial colorblindness advocates, the interactional use of these strategies called attention to it by enabling white youth to simultaneously position themselves as attuned to racial issues – but not inappropriately so – and as nonracist. But these teenagers were not simply parroting racial views they had picked up from their parents or other sources. Instead, they were actively "doing nonracism" as a form of identity work.

The next chapter turns to race talk in a rather different discursive context: narratives of fear, conflict, and resentment. Such discourse draws on some of the same strategies of colorblindness examined in this chapter. At the same time, however, these narratives render race hypervisible by calling attention to racialized tensions at Bay City High. Through such narratives, European American teenagers accomplished the discursive feat of racial reversal, positioning themselves as racially disadvantaged and disempowered in relation to African American youth.

9 White on black: narratives of racial fear and resentment

Introduction

On October 16, 1995, Louis Farrakhan, leader of the politically controversial African American Muslim organization Nation of Islam, assembled the first Million Man March in Washington, DC, to focus attention on the problems facing African American men. Most of Ms. Stein's African American students were absent, many in support of the march. The class's daily journal assignment was to write about some aspect of race in their lives. "I always try to tie this in to Martin Luther King Day or Malcolm X's birthday," she told them, "or today, the Million Man March." After the students had spent several minutes writing, Ms. Stein asked for volunteers to read or describe what they had written. In every class, European American teenagers took the topic of the day as an opportunity to talk about their racialized fear and resentment of their African American schoolmates. As the few black students present looked on, white youth voiced a litany of complaints about the problems they faced as European Americans.

In the fourth-period class, which had the largest number of white students, Finn raised his hand. A tall, solidly built European American boy with shoulder-length fluorescent pink hair, wearing heavy black Doc Marten work shoes and a T-shirt emblazoned with the name of a local punk rock band, Finn seemed to me the least likely student in the class to express fear of African Americans, or of anyone else, but he did so. He reported that he avoided blacks based on personal experience: a group of "black guys" had beat up his friend because they said he looked like a "faggot." "I look just like him," Finn concluded by way of explanation for his fear. As was her practice, Ms. Stein did not comment on Finn's report of his journal entry, but moved on to what another student volunteer had written.

Finn's brief story, like most such stories told by white youth that day, was about more than race. Fear, anger, frustration, and resentment permeated many European American teenagers' narratives. On a day of national attention to the experiences of black men, what social conditions – in the classroom, the high school, the community of Bay City, and the nation – enabled white youth to tell such stories so openly and apparently unself-consciously in a racially mixed setting (cf. Perry 2002)? Although the absence of most (but not all) African American students perhaps gave European Americans greater freedom to talk about race, the stories that white teenagers told participated in a larger set of discourses about race at Bay City High School and in the United States generally.

In this chapter I discuss how European American teenagers at Bay City High used race talk to make sense of their place in a rapidly shifting ethnoracial order in which they were neither numerically dominant nor stylistically authoritative with respect to most youth of color. Conflict-themed racial discourse circulated widely among white students, teachers, and parents, many of whom perceived whiteness as a disadvantaged and even perilous condition at the school and viewed blackness as both privileged and powerful. Based on my fieldwork, I considered this perspective to be an implausible discursive reversal of the actual situations of European American and African American students at Bay City High. The majority of black teenagers lacked the economic and educational opportunities that most white teenagers took for granted, and black students were far more vulnerable than their white peers to being problematized and punished by teachers for allegedly disruptive behavior, even when they had done nothing to warrant such penalties.

Yet despite such (to me) obvious asymmetries, European American teenagers were unquestionably sincere in their beliefs, which derived from everyday interracial interactions rather than the larger structural consequences of racial inequality. These "sincere fictions" of race thus helped to sustain the racial order by ignoring structural racism (Feagin and Vera 1995: 135). Race talk in particular insulated white youth from acknowledging the clear advantages they held over their black peers by focusing attention instead on the ways in which sharing space and resources with African American students within the school was often uncomfortable and sometimes even frightening for them. A variety of discursive strategies emerged in white students' race talk, including complaints of reverse racism, tales of racialized fear, and interracial fight stories. Through these strategies European American youth discursively reconfigured the relative power of blackness and whiteness at Bay City High School.

Racial reversal in discourse of racial conflict

White teenagers' discourse about negative experiences involving African Americans stemmed from a far-reaching ideology of "reverse racism" (or "reverse discrimination"), which maintains that whites are oppressed by people of color and their supposed institutional benefactors. Like the ideology of colorblindness, reverse racism permeates white racial discourse nationwide. But where colorblind discourse is used to erase racial difference, the ideology of reverse racism highlights racial difference in order to call attention to perceived racial asymmetries that allegedly place whites in a one-down position. And while colorblindness is viewed by its proponents as nonracist because it is unconcerned with race, the ideology of reverse racism is argued to be nonracist precisely because it explicitly appeals to race in order to challenge what are claimed to be racist policies and practices directed against whites, such as affirmative action. Reverse racism is therefore an important component of the broader ideological process of racial reversal investigated in this chapter.

A great deal of race talk hinges on majority group members' generalized and usually negative statements regarding minority groups (e.g., Bonilla-Silva 2003; Bush 2004; Myers 2005; van Dijk 1987; Wetherell and Potter 1992). These generalizations are often bolstered by narratives of specific incidents designed to provide evidence for racial claims and complaints. Teun van Dijk reports, for example, that "stories about minorities are often stories about *whites as (self-defined) victims* of acts of minority group members or of ethnic relations in general" (1993b: 127, original emphasis). Narratives lend rhetorical weight to racial generalizations by offering both authenticity and vividness, as the protagonist's personal experience is rendered in dramatically chosen details of place, time, participants, and unfolding events. As analysts have long recognized, a narrative presented as an accurate account of a past event may or may not be grounded in actual truth, and even if it is, it may have been subject to considerable embellishment and editing. The primary analytic concern, then, is not to check the narrative's accuracy (which is generally difficult if not impossible to do) but to understand its function as a powerful tool for "representing reality" (Potter 1996).

Because storytelling is an act of representation and not straightforward reporting, the narrator holds considerable power to select, frame, interpret, and even invent the narrated action. Narration is therefore a type of identity work that allows narrators to position themselves and others within a social drama directed to and constructed for a specific audience (e.g., De Fina 2003; Georgakopoulou 2007; Ochs and Capps 2001). In narratives of racial complaint, gauging the audience is especially important, for such discourse both violates the ideology of colorblindness and puts the narrator at risk of charges of racial prejudice for taking a negative stance toward other racialized groups. For European American youth to talk about racial conflicts and resentments in my presence therefore assumed a certain level of solidarity, based on our friendly relationship as well as our shared whiteness.[1]

White teenagers' race talk included both complaints of reverse racism and narratives of potential or actual confrontations between racialized groups, especially African Americans and European Americans. Fear and a sense of danger were primary themes of such narratives. In early variationist sociolinguistics, the elicitation of fight stories was a methodological technique for capturing the vernacular among African American youth (Labov 1972e).[2] Unlike such fight stories, the narratives in this chapter were not formally elicited but arose during ethnographic interviews in the course of students' talk about social groups at the school. Such stories often involved a perceived threat that does not materialize fully within the telling.

European Americans' narratives of cross-racial danger and conflict often perpetuate dominant racial ideologies (Kiesling 2001; Labov 1990). Scott Kiesling (2006) argues that for members of dominant social groups – in his data, middle-class heterosexual white men – narratives can reinforce the narrator's hegemonic social position, even if this is not the ostensible (or even consciously intended) purpose of the story, by invoking well-established ideologies that are familiar to the audience. In the following data, the racially hegemonic position of European American speakers and their audience members (i.e., other white teenagers and the white researcher) is constituted through discursive reversals that represent whites as subordinated to the greater power and privilege of blacks. By asserting their disempowerment vis-à-vis black youth, white teenagers paradoxically reproduced their own structural position of power. Such discourse provided a warrant for policies and practices designed to protect European Americans and their interests, ranging from the statewide abolishment of affirmative action to the installation of police officers to patrol the Bay City High School grounds. Through strategies of racial reversal, then, white students' perceptions of themselves as racially oppressed were facilitated and validated by the state, the media, the community, the school, their families, and other institutions in their lives.

Racial resentment and the rhetoric of white disadvantage

In their race talk, white youth did not point to specific examples of reverse racism that they or their peers had experienced at the school, instead offering more generalized statements of racial resentment. That is, although European American teenagers may not have been able to report many (or any) clearcut cases of reverse racism, they nonetheless presented themselves as its victims.

The ideology of reverse racism challenged Bay City High's official multicultural discourse, which heavily informed the school curriculum, especially through the controversial Multiculturalism class. This course garnered considerable criticism from European American students, many of whom felt that it portrayed whites as racial oppressors and thus licensed students of color to treat their white peers with open hostility. In example (1), Claire and Christine express their scorn for the school's multicultural discourse, and Claire goes on to offer her own experience in the Multiculturalism class as evidence that this discourse is hypocritical.

(1) 1 Claire: It's so like,
2 Christine: <sniff>
3 Claire: "We a:ll got to show each other respect."
4 It's like,
5 "Yeah well,
6 you should be doing that [$_1$anyway.$_1$]
7 Christine: [$_1$<sniff> $_1$]
8 Claire: We don't need to,
9 make a big,
10 deal: out of it.
11 We shouldn't make [$_2$people go: and,$_2$]"
12 Christine: [$_2$A big politi$_2$]cal campai:gn,
13 a[$_3$bout giving people re$_3$]spect,
14 Claire: [$_3$I kno::w. $_3$]
15 Christine: it's [$_4$like, $_4$]
16 Claire: [$_4$It's like, $_4$]
17 <whisper> {Multi[$_5$culturalism,}
18 oh my$_5$] go:d,
19 Christine: [$_5$"Why don't you just,
20 do it."$_5$]
21 Claire: Teach people how to hate white kids.
22 Mary: Oh yeah?
23 Claire: I'm really bitter about [$_6$that class.$_6$]
24 Mary: [$_6$@@@ $_6$]

The girls' complaints are framed not as specific narratives that illustrate their grievances but as a series of typifications (Agha 2007) and evaluations of a general state of affairs. Thus Claire introduces the quoted speech in line 3 with a structure that marks it as a general characterization (*it's so like*; line 1) rather than a quotation tied to a specific episode or speaker. This typifying utterance is in turn negatively evaluated via quoted speech (lines 4–6; 8–11; 15, 19–20). Similarly, in line 17, Claire introduces the topic of the Multiculturalism class without either characterizing it or offering an explicit evaluation, although her whispered voice quality and use of the affective marker *oh my go:d* (line 18) highlight the dramatic significance of this topic. She then provides a general characterization of the Multiculturalism class (line 21), followed by a negative evaluation (line 23).

Like many other white students at Bay City High, Claire and Christine consider the explicitly multicultural discourse at the school overblown (lines 8–10; line 12), more talk than action (line 6; lines 19–20), and coercive (line 11). This last issue seems to lead Claire to bring up the Multiculturalism class. Her view of the course as a training ground for racism against European Americans (and especially the "white kids" at Bay City High; line 21) was shared by many

European American teenagers. For example, one white girl, Erin, remarked during the discussion of race in Ms. Stein's class that the Multiculturalism course "was hell for me," although she did not provide any further details, and she reported that an African American boy had referred to the class as "Revenge 101."

I later sat in on Multiculturalism and similar classes in the company of Sweet Pea, a black girl who had found in them a sense of ethnoracial pride and purpose that helped transform her from an at-risk student to a popular leader taking special classes in preparation for attending college in Africa. The transformative power of the multicultural curriculum for Sweet Pea stood in stark contrast to the viscerally negative reactions it incited in white youth such as Claire and Erin. And contrary to the horror stories I had heard from European American students, I found that the Multiculturalism teacher, an African American man, was in fact quite respectful of students of all ethnoracial backgrounds while challenging them to think critically about race. I could easily imagine that such a course could be extremely discomfiting for white youth (and for teenagers of color), given its focus on racialized power and identity as well as the teacher's pedagogical strategy of calling on individual students and asking often pointed questions about their experiences and attitudes regarding race and racism. But I could also see the course's value for raising awareness of these issues among Bay City High's ethnoracially diverse student population.

The school's multicultural curriculum was not the only source of white students' complaints of reverse racism. The anti-affirmative-action movement that took hold both in California and nationwide during my fieldwork also shaped European American teenagers' views of their racial position. Thus in a discussion in Ms. Stein's Life and Health class concerning students' post-high-school plans, Erin volunteered that her mother had warned her that she would face considerable obstacles in securing a slot in a good college because "as a white female I have enough going against me," a comment that remained unremarked upon by either the teacher or other students as the discussion continued. Such statements demonstrated the role of parents in fostering the discourse of white disadvantage among their children. Yet the perception among some European American teenagers that they faced an uncertain future due to their racial category was by no means borne out by the evidence. On the contrary, the considerable gap between the college placement rates of European American and African American students at Bay City High was public knowledge and an ongoing target of criticism of the school by the local press.

It appeared that because the discourse of white disadvantage was so firmly entrenched among many European Americans at the school, complaints of reverse racism did not require explanation or supporting evidence. Even when I encouraged students to elaborate further, as in line 22 of example (1) above, they offered few specific details. Following example (1), for instance, Christine tells a lengthy story about a fight that broke out in her Multiculturalism class in which an African American girl was physically attacked by a boy of unspecified race, an incident that Christine found terrifying but in which she herself was not a target of violence. Claire then goes on to complain that Multiculturalism was not academically demanding enough and that she was able to trick the teacher into exempting her from doing any coursework for the entire semester. Apparently such stories were more tellable than those illustrating the claim that the class promoted racial hostility. While I have no doubt that these girls and many other white students did indeed feel uncomfortable, even victimized, in Bay City High's multicultural classes, I heard of no specific instances of such moments during my research.

Narratives of racial fear

Perhaps even more widespread among white youth at Bay City High was the discourse of racial fear, which similarly positioned European Americans as subordinate to and oppressed by African Americans. This discourse relied on a widespread racial ideology of white vulnerability to black violence (Armour 1997), yet, as with the discourse of reverse racism, the perception of physical peril was rarely grounded in specific personal experiences. For example, Shawn, a European American boy, told me that an older friend who had graduated from the high school promised him that he would "take care of" anyone who bothered him. Asian students also participated in this discourse. For example, Joe, an Asian American boy, said that he and his (Asian and white) friends feared being hassled by black students and so spent their lunch period in a small paved area hidden by surrounding classroom buildings. But when I asked both boys if anyone had in fact harassed them at the high school, the answer in each case was "No." Additionally, when specific stories of interracial conflict did occur, they were more often about perceived close calls and verbal confrontations than actual incidents of violence.

In my data, the discourse of racial fear often interacts with the ideology of colorblindness, so that racial others are not always straightforwardly labeled as such in white students' race talk. Yet if blackness often goes unnamed in these narratives, whiteness is frequently mentioned, a reversal of the general European American view of blackness as marked and hence nameable and whiteness as unmarked and hence unmentioned (cf. Trechter and Bucholtz 2001; Whitehead and Lerner 2009). At the same time, the narrators often emphasize the value of forming friendly acquaintanceships with African American youth as protection from interracial conflict, as seen in example (2). The example takes place during a discussion of the term *hip hop*. In response to a question from me about whether she knows people in the "hip hop crowd," Christine, a junior, links the term to her own past experiences of being harassed by black students as a freshman. (The first seven lines of example (2) were analyzed as example (1a) in the previous chapter.)

(2)	1	Mary:	So you don't,
	2		n-
	3		know people that,
	4		would be in something called a hip hop crowd,=
	5		=or you wouldn't [$_1$use a term like that?$_1$]
	6	Christine:	<higher pitch> [$_1${Oh,
	7		I} kno:w them.$_1$]
	8		I know,
	9		I know some people.
	10		(0.8)
	11		Which helps alleviate situations so@me↑@times,
	12		B@ut,
	13	Mary:	↑Hm.
	14	Christine:	they're not like my f:rie:n:ds.
	15	Mary:	What do you mea-
	16		it helps alleviate situations?
	17	Christine:	Oh,
	18		I don't know.
	19		Like,
	20		I-
	21		I've,
	22		N:ot so much recently,
	23		but,
	24		especially freshman year,
	25		I found that like,
	26		I got picked o:n,
	27		because,
	28		you know,
	29		I'm a li-
	30		<higher pitch> {small white girl.}
	31	Mary:	[$_2$Mm.$_2$]
	32	Christine:	[$_2$And $_2$] it's like,
	33		sometimes,
	34		if I knew s-
	35		if I know somebody in the crowd,
	36		I'll be like,
	37		"Oh,
	38		↑hi:!"
	39	Mary:	[$_3$Mm. $_3$]
	40	Christine:	[$_3$(And they'll—)$_3$]
	41		You know,
	42		it'll be oka:y.=
	43	Mary:	=[$_4$Mm.$_4$]

44 Christine: =[$_4$If I $_4$] kno:w,
45 <sniff>
46 (0.5)
47 If I know them they don’t p@ick o@n ↑me@[$_5$@@,$_5$]
48 Mary: [$_5$Hm. $_5$]
49 Christine: for @one thing.

In Chapter 8, I noted Christine’s use of referential vagueness in this example (e.g., *them*, lines 7, 47; *some people*, line 9) as well as the fact that she need not explicitly name the racial category of blackness to be understood by Claire and me. Although she does not racially identify the “hip hop crowd,” as discussed in the previous chapter this label at Bay City High School generally indexed African American youth (or those who emulated their style). Moreover, Christine’s racialized description of herself as a “small white girl” (line 30) makes plain that it is African Americans to whom she is referring with vague terms like *they* and *somebody*.[3] Given that black and white students were the school’s two largest groups, whiteness contrasted most saliently with blackness; moreover, because of the ideology of black-on-white aggression, a European American teenager’s narrative specifying that a victim of violence or harassment was white generally implied that the perpetrator was black. In this way Christine adheres to the discourse of colorblindness even as she signals to her audience the racial dimension of her talk.

Christine is similarly reticent regarding the topic of racialized conflict. She raises the issue in discussing the “hip hop crowd,” but once again in vague terms (*I know some people. (0.8) Which helps alleviate situations so@me↑@times*; lines 9–11). Moreover, laughter tokens are embedded in the final part of her utterance, displaying that the problem is not a serious concern, or at least that she has the situation under control (Jefferson 1984). Likewise, when I ask Christine to elaborate, she hedges repeatedly and emphasizes that the incidents in question mainly occurred two years earlier (lines 22–24). Nor is the narrative she produces highly detailed. Instead, she uses generalization to typify rather than specify the situation she is reporting, and she continues to linguistically obscure the identity of her antagonists, in this case by using an agentless passive (line 26). Yet in the middle of her discourse she self-repairs from the generalized past to the generalized present, thus implying that the situation has not entirely abated (lines 34–35).[4]

In example (3), the phrase *watch your back* is similarly interpreted in implicitly racialized terms by Zoe and Josie. *Watch your back* can function either as a threatening warning or, more positively, within a social code in which friends are expected to look out for one another – that is, to watch one another’s backs. These girls, however, took the phrase as quite literal advice to “watch your backpack.” This interpretation launched a series of narratives about thefts from backpacks that occurred as students moved through the school’s crowded hallways; example (3) is the third in this series. The girls viewed such incidents as expectable rather than exceptional, but they also considered them significant criminal acts. As Josie asserted in initiating the narrative sequence, “There is organized crime at Bay City High,” by which she meant that two or more students sometimes collaborated to engage in petty theft. I have no evidence of such occurrences being commonplace, apart from often-retold stories by these and several other students. I myself never had anything stolen from my own backpack, despite my frequent failure to heed warnings from European American students and teachers about the perils of leaving it unzipped or unattended.

(3) 1 Zoe: Also one time I was walking with my friends to math class?
2 and this guy:,
3 like,
4 h:e was,
5 on my-
6 on my:,
7 (1.0)
8 Anyways,
9 he was like on the right side I guess?
10 And so he started walki:ng,
11 like,
12 to the left,
13 like,
14 sort of like,
15 pushing me o:ver,
16 and I (was like,)
17 <breathy> {“Ah!”}
18 you know?
19 Mary: Wo[$_1$:w. $_1$]
20 Zoe: [$_1$Um,$_1$]
21 and,
22 and,
23 the—
24 like,
25 this guy that we were walking with,
26 like we know him and stuff?
27 And,
28 ’cause he kn:ew.
29 Like,
30 h:e realized that someone was behind us.
31 And he—
32 he said later,
33 he was like,
34 “Yea:h,
35 I was afraid they were going to do something to me.”

36 But I was totally oblivious.
37 Mary: [$_2$Mm:. $_2$]
38 Zoe: [$_2$So like,$_2$]
39 I: don't know,
40 I think it's different for,
41 guys:,
42 <lower volume> {↑also.}
43 [$_3$A little more.$_3$]
44 Mary: [$_3$Oh really?
45 In$_3$] what sense?
46 Zoe: It's,
47 like,
48 more intense for them,
49 I,
50 guess.
51 Mary: [$_4$Hm. $_4$]
52 Zoe: [$_4$Because,$_4$]
53 I mean,
54 he was so awa:re.
55 Li:ke,
56 he was just,
57 Like [$_5$I was- $_5$]=
58 Mary: [$_5$Wo:w. $_5$]=
59 Zoe: =[$_6$I was just$_6$]=
60 Mary: =[$_6$Why? $_6$]=
61 Zoe: =[$_7$wa:lking to cla:ss, $_7$]=
62 Mary: =[$_7$That-
63 that seems like $_7$]=
64 Zoe: =[$_8$I was totally oblivious— $_8$]
65 Mary: =[$_8$ it's the opposite. $_8$]
66 Zoe: Yeah.
67 Well like for w-
68 (1.0)
69 Yea:h.
70 I don't know.
71 For a white,
72 guy?
73 I don't know.
74 [$_9$I think so. $_9$]
75 Mary: [$_9$Oh really? $_9$]

Like Christine in example (2) above, Zoe uses referential vagueness to talk about racial danger without naming the racial other. Thus the supposedly threatening student is referred to only as *this guy:* (line 2), remaining otherwise undescribed. It is only when Zoe – albeit with numerous hesitation markers – specifies the racial category of her male friend (lines 67–72) at the very end of the discussion that race enters the discourse. Yet for all participants race is ideologically salient from the very beginning of the series of narratives, given the topic of danger and theft.

No overt threat emerges in Zoe's story; what constructs the episode as dangerous is the white protagonists' evaluation that it was. These evaluations occur via quoted thought and speech, which help recreate the emotion experienced in the narrated moment. Zoe reports that when she realizes that another student is menacing her, she reacts in alarm (lines 16–17), and she quotes her male friend as saying, "I was afraid they were going to do something to me" (line 35). Yet it is not clear that she and her friends were in imminent danger. Due to the overcrowding at Bay City High School, jostling in the hallways was a regular occurrence, as was being closely followed by other students, and thus another person's mere proximity was insufficient to establish criminal intent. To be sure, a small number of teenagers of any race or ethnicity might take advantage of this situation to grab a wallet out of an easily accessible backpack. But European American youth tended to have a much stronger perception of danger than the facts generally seemed to warrant.

What made white teenagers' stories of racial danger tellable was the potential threat they narrated, and thus details that emphasized this threat were important to include. In several places in Zoe's narrative, details are added that enhance the drama but do not fully cohere. Is the "someone ... behind us" (line 30) the original purported aggressor or a second antagonist, as perhaps implied by Zoe's quoted speech of her friend? And given Zoe's own reported realization of a potential threat in lines 16 and 17, why does she later state that she "was totally oblivious" (line 64) and characterize herself, in contrast to her friend, as "just wa:lking to cla:ss" unaware of any danger (lines 59, 61)? Whatever the reason, this reframing of the narrative from a shared experience of racial fear to one undergone only by her male friend allows her to introduce an important rhetorical point: "it's different for, guys:" (lines 40–41). Zoe develops this point by characterizing herself as unaware and her male friend as hyperaware of an impending danger from one or more (presumably) African American boys. When I express surprise, grounded in my own feminist perspective, that a male might be more attuned to potential physical danger than a female, Zoe specifies that it is particularly "for a white, guy" (lines 71–72) that such situations are so "intense" (line 48). Her narrative thus reproduces a simultaneously racialized and gendered ideology of African American students as dangerous.

Ideologies of masculinity in narratives of interracial violence

Despite white teenagers' expressions of fear of potential black aggressors, physical fights and other forms of confrontation between Bay City High

School's students were far more often intraracial than interracial (cf. Shuman 1986). Indeed, it may have been precisely their rarity that made episodes of interracial conflict especially tellable. Whereas girls' racial narratives, like those of Christine and Zoe above, focused on verbal confrontation or a vague sense of danger, some boys' narratives featured actual violence.[5] In such stories, the ideology that "it's different for guys" found ample illustration. This difference was partly due to many European American boys' perception that, as suggested by Finn's story at the beginning of this chapter, they were open targets of African American male violence. Moreover, for many boys, being able to fight was closely tied to an ideology of masculinity as physically powerful. Hence, male narrators' stories of physical conflict with boys from other racialized groups involved ideologies of gender as well as race.

Although the hegemonic power of middle-class masculinity does not rely on physical strength, physicality continues to be a measure of masculine power (e.g., Connell 1995; Edley and Wetherell 1997; Kiesling 1997) and is especially associated with working-class styles of masculinity (Connell 1995; Willis 1977). Physical masculinity is also often racialized, resulting in the long-standing ideology of black masculinity as hyperphysical and hyperviolent, due to white exploitation of black labor first through slavery and later through low-wage, physically demanding jobs (Collins 2005; Ferguson 2000; Jackson 2006). Likewise, a complementary ideology positioning Asian masculinity as physically deficient emerged from complex political and economic factors in US immigration history (Eng 2000; Espiritu 1997; Shek 2006). These ideologies participate in a system of gendered racial logic that upholds white masculinity as normative, even as it is positioned in some local contexts, especially among youth, as physically inferior to black masculinity (cf. Staiger 2006).

European American boys at Bay City High drew on these ideologies in narratives of interracial conflict in order to construct themselves as occupying an intermediate, "normal" position within a racial hierarchy of masculinity (the term *normal* here does not refer to the mainstream style of some white youth but rather to being socially unmarked – that is, these narrators were "doing 'being ordinary'"; Sacks 1984). Boys' fight stories invoked this ideological hierarchy in several ways: through overt racial references, through physical descriptions of African American boys, and through evaluations of the relative physical prowess of males of different racialized groups.

Racial labels

In sharp contrast to the colorblind strategies of most other race talk I encountered at Bay City High, boys' interracial fight stories introduced the race of the combatants early on and did so in a direct, on-record way, without hedging or disfluency. Given the ideological importance of the racial hierarchy of masculinity in such stories, it was crucial for the narrator to establish the race of the combatants right away in order to lay the groundwork for an account of any physical shortcomings that might be attributed to him based on the narrated events.

The examples in (4) are the openings of three different fight stories. Example (4a) is the beginning of a narrative about an African American student's attempt to steal from the narrator's backpack, a theme also found in the stories by Josie and Zoe discussed above. Example (4b) comes from a series of stories about interracial fights, and example (4c) initiates a narrative illustrating how "real friends," as opposed to "so-called friends," provide support in difficult situations. The first two narrators, Brand One and Mr. Frisky, are white; Brand One is also Jewish. The third narrator, Nico Caen, self-identifies as Puerto Rican but due to his blond hair, blue eyes, and pale skin, he was often viewed as white at Bay City High, an issue he himself acknowledges in example (8) below. Although he did not consider himself white, I include his narrative here because his apparent whiteness is relevant to his story, part of which he co-narrates with a European American boy, Billy.[6] All the boys affiliated with hip hop except for Mr. Frisky, who had an alternative style.

(4a) 1 Brand One: two months ago this du:de,
2 um,
3 (1.5)
4 <tongue click>
5 I was walking up to u:h,
6 to:,
7 the bus stop,
8 and he—
9 he was in my backpack right?
10 This,
11 this black dude was like s:ix,
12 maybe like,
13 fi:ve ten,
14 he was big,
15 he was a lot bigger than me, . . .

(4b) 1 Mr. Frisky: Tim was talking shit,
2 a:nd,
3 suddenly,
4 it seemed,
5 <higher pitch> {out of the woodwork,}
6 once agai:n,
7 the uh,
8 @
9 you know,
10 suddenly about fifty to,
11 you know,

12 sixty,
13 bl:ack kids suddenly swarm after him.

(4c) 1 Nico Caen: Over in the Park,
2 like,
3 beginning of this year,
4 we uh:,
5 <[tʃ]>
6 some little Asian fools tried to start,
7 f:unk with me and my friend,
8 just two of us,
9 and like thirty of them,
10 you know?

In each example, racial labels occur early in the narrative (4a, line 11: *this black dude*; 4b, lines 10–13: *fifty to . . . sixty, bl:ack kids*; 4c, line 6: *some little Asian fools*). In examples (4b) and (4c) such a label is used as the first mention of the antagonist. Nor is the production of racial labels marked by the indicators of interactional trouble seen in colorblind race talk. To be sure, some disfluency occurs, but the labels themselves are produced relatively early, easily, and emphatically. By mentioning race, and doing so at the very outset of their narratives, the narrators put their audience on notice that the story they are about to hear has a specifically racial point.

Beyond the practice of racial labeling, narrators used multiple discursive strategies to represent antagonists of other races; these strategies were designed both to enhance listeners' interest in the narrative and to guide the audience to evaluate the story in the same way as the narrator himself. To make a fight story tellable, narrators must establish that they (or the narrative's protagonist) faced a formidable opponent. Thus in example (4a) Brand One highlights the size of his adversary (lines 11–15), while the other two boys foreground (and no doubt inflate) their opponents' superior numbers (example 4b, lines 10–13; example 4c, lines 8–9). In all three cases, mention of race occurs in close juxtaposition with mention of the antagonists' attributes. Such descriptions are also found in other sorts of race talk (and especially overtly racist discourse). Indeed, the putative physical threat represented by African American men is such a frequent trope of white racial discourse that it has been dubbed the "Big Black Man Syndrome" (Vogelman 1993), while the description of people of color in example (4b) as "swarm[ing]" (line 13) and the use of other vermin imagery (*out of the woodwork*; line 5) are commonplace in xenophobic and racist diatribes (Santa Ana 2002), although it does not appear that the narrator intends these associations.

These narratives draw on both racial and gender ideologies. For example, where narrators may attribute superior numbers to either African American or Asian American antagonists, they attribute superior size and strength only to the former group. This is illustrated in line 6 of example (4c), where Nico Caen describes his opponents as *little Asian fools* (here *fools* is a generic term like *guys* or *dudes*). Although the adjective *little* may be less a reference to the physical size of Nico's adversaries than a trivializing assessment of the threat they presented, it is unlikely that the term would have been used if Nico had viewed them as physically imposing. Through racial references of antagonists in stories of interracial conflict, these narrators construct a racialized hierarchy of masculinities, with African Americans at the top and Asian Americans at the bottom.

Physical descriptions of the racial other

Even when racial labels were not explicitly used, boys' fight stories included racialized physical descriptions that similarly reinforced the gendered and racial hierarchy. This is seen in Brand One's narrative. In (4a) above, the "black dude" is represented as taking an aggressive stance toward Brand One, rifling through his backpack and then (in a portion of the narrative not shown here) challenging Brand One and calling his masculinity into question. Brand One approaches two African American boys that he knows, Steven and Kevin, who are standing nearby, and enlists their aid (example 5a). The race of these boys is not explicitly stated, but details that Brand One supplies indicate that at least Steven is African American: he is on the almost entirely black varsity basketball team; he may have a "fro" or Afro hairstyle (the hearing of this word is uncertain); and elsewhere Brand One quotes him using African American linguistic features (Bucholtz 1999a). (I also happened to know independently that both boys were black.)

(5a) 74 Brand One: Steven's on the basketball team,
75 on varsity,
76 he's like six <creaky> {three:},
77 Mary: Wo@w,
78 Brand One: big ass,
79 (fool/fro),
80 hella sca:ry,
81 And then Kevin's just,
82 he's like fi:ve ten but,
83 people-
84 he's just—
85 he's just—
86 people are intimidated of him because of who he knows,
87 you know?

Throughout his narrative, Brand One presents physical superiority in terms of height: the threatening "black dude" is "s:ix, maybe like, fi:ve ten" (example 4a, lines 11–13); Steven is "like six three:" (example 5a, line 76), and Kevin is "like fi:ve ten" (example 5a, line 82). (By the time Kevin appears in the narrative, however, 5′10″ is no longer treated as an impressive height, and he is only intimidating "because of who he knows"; line 86). In addition to providing these highly specific if clearly estimated measurements, Brand One explicitly evaluates Steven as "hella sca:ry" (line 80). By the end of the story, Steven and Kevin have frightened away the boy who tried to rob Brand One; meanwhile, Brand One rests secure in the assurance of their continued protection (Bucholtz 1999a).

The theme of rescue from a certain thrashing through the intervention of a physically powerful African American protector is also seen in Nico's story. Example (5b) picks up over ten minutes after example (4c). Once again, the narrative focuses on the black rescuer's size, strength, and fearsomeness:

(5b) 1 Nico Caen: Cory came through,
2 he was like=
3 Billy: =Cory is hella [t:all,]
4 Nico: [You know] he's got drea:ds,
5 he's,
6 he's a ra:sta,
7 Billy: He's extre:mely <[strɑ]->
8 if you [see him—]
9 Nico: [He's—]
10 you would not fuck with him if you saw him.

As with Brand One in example (5a), Billy offers details of Cory's height (line 3), and although he does not complete his next utterance, it seems to project a comment on the other boy's physical strength (line 7). Nico confirms Cory's imposing presence (line 10), but his initial description focuses not on Cory's intimidating size or physical power but his rasta – or Rastafarian – youth style, which may seem poorly suited to the immediate concern with fighting ability. As discussed in Chapter 3, at Bay City High the rasta category referred to teenagers, mostly European American, who smoked large quantities of marijuana and listened to reggae music. Many rastas, both black and white, shared the revolutionary political outlook of black reggae icon Bob Marley, but they were usually viewed as mellow and pacifistic rather than threatening. Billy's and Nico's ensuing turns, however, enumerate Cory's physically impressive qualities. Moreover, the narrative suggests that Cory is black, which ideologically implies greater strength. The authentic version of rasta style, like hip hop style, was racialized as black, and the school's primarily European American rastas were often dismissed as "fake rastas" or "wannabes." Nico's non-evaluative mention of Cory's participation in rasta culture indicates that he is in fact African American, as I later confirmed.

In such examples, the absence of explicit racial labels for African Americans may appear superficially similar to the colorblind discourse seen previously. While both practices rely on participants' knowledge of the local racial order, colorblind discourse generally lacks any physical or other description of racial others and evades racial mention, in contrast to the highly detailed descriptions in these examples, in which race is not elaborately avoided but treated as self-evident. Such descriptions do not simply position African American boys as physically superior but use this ideology to further the narrative by implying that their entry into the conflict evens the odds against the nonblack protagonist.

Evaluations of physical prowess

The "racial rescue" storyline seen above focuses on specific African American boys, but in other narratives the ideology of black male hyperphysicality extends beyond particular individuals to encompass all African Americans (or at least all African American males). Such generalizations are found in Mr. Frisky's narrative. In example (6), he digresses from narrating a specific conflict to offer a general assessment of the fighting abilities of African Americans compared to European Americans:

(6) 1 Mr. Frisky: They strike,
2 me,
3 as being stro:nger,
4 more loy:al,
5 um,
6 you know,
7 m-
8 better-
9 better warriors per se?
10 Mary: Mm.
11 Mr. Frisky: Like,
12 you know they,
13 are,
14 <finger snap> {quick} to fight,
15 they're,
16 really hard to knock out and knock down.
17 Mary: Mhm.
18 Mr. Frisky: You know,
19 I've,
20 never-
21 I've been in,
22 a fight,
23 only with one black person,
24 and,
25 it,

26 was over real quick.
27 With me on the ground holding my head going,
28 <higher pitch> {"Ow,
29 that,
30 kind of hurt."}

Mr. Frisky's sweeping characterization of African Americans – "stro:nger" (line 3), "quick to fight" (line 14), "really hard to knock out and knock down" (line 16) – reproduces, with my complicity, the common stereotype not only of black hyperphysicality but also of a black proclivity for violence. Rather than representing these traits as negative, however, Mr. Frisky admiringly presents them as the necessary qualities of "warriors" (line 9). His description elevates African Americans above European Americans in the racial hierarchy of physical power. Nor does he exclude himself from this racialized ranking: he reports that his only fight against a black opponent "was over real quick" (line 26), and although he portrays himself as bemused rather than seriously injured after his defeat (lines 28–30), it is not a flattering self-representation.

Yet narrators' appeal to gendered racial ideologies is designed to inoculate them from being seen as insufficiently masculine, by foregrounding the impossible situation they faced and implying that only a hyperphysical, hypermasculine African American could hope to prevail against such odds. Because they present African American boys as almost superhuman in their physical abilities, narrators position their own abilities as simply normal rather than deficient.

Likewise, interracial fight stories that involve nonblack antagonists allow narrators to locate themselves in relation to other racialized categories in the ideological hierarchy of masculinity. Such rankings may be created through evaluation of the relative physical prowess of various ethnoracial groups. Example (7) narrates a physical conflict in which Mr. Frisky and his friends fight a large group of Filipino boys.

(7) 1 Mr. Frisky: I was,
2 sitting there grinning,
3 you know,
4 just kind of,
5 cackling,
6 at them,
7 a:nd,
8 you know,
9 with this huge grin on my face,
10 like,
11 "Come on,
12 let's do this,"
13 Mary: Mhm.
14 Mr. Frisky: And,
15 suddenly there would be six guy:s all around me,

16 you couldn't really see me anymore,
17 and suddenly two or three of them would just fly back a good
18 three feet onto the [grou:nd.]
19 Mary: [Wo:w.]
20 Mr. Frisky: A:nd,
21 I'd be sitting there in the middl:e,
22 just,
23 swinging and batting fools arou:nd,
24 like little play toys. <sniff>
25 Mary: Wo:w.
26 Mr. Frisky: And,
27 (1.5)
28 it kind of struck me as,
29 you know,
30 (0.8)
31 "Ee:.
32 That's,
33 seven peopl:e,
34 to my one,
35 and that's just Filipino:s.
36 So,
37 (0.6)
38 let's say,
39 uh:,
40 that had been,
41 ↑black men.
42 (1.2)
43 Ouch."

As already noted above, Asians (including Filipinos) are ranked lowest in the hierarchy of masculinity constructed in these narratives. Mr. Frisky's story contributes to this ideology through implicit and explicit evaluations of his adversaries. Given his report that he and his friends were significantly outnumbered, he represents his affect as incongruously lighthearted: he describes himself as "grinning" and "cackling" (lines 2, 5), eager to do battle (lines 11–12). This affective stance contrasts with the apparent gravity of his situation, highlighting his confidence in his physical abilities against such foes. This point is further underscored by Mr. Frisky's characterization of himself as easily able to hold off six or seven attackers at once (e.g., lines 14–18).

The most explicit evaluation, however, comes with Mr. Frisky's self-quotation in lines 31 through 43, in which he remarks that his opponents were "just Filipino:s" and imagines that instead they were "black men," a scenario he sums up with a single word: "Ouch." (This is the only place in my data in which students referred to male peers as *men*, a word choice that seems to further elevate the masculine status of African American boys.) Like previous examples, Mr. Frisky's narrative again positions African American males as physically superior to him. But it simultaneously positions Filipino males as physically inferior. By locating himself, a European American boy, between these two polarized points, Mr. Frisky preserves his masculine standing as a "normal" male.

The final example adds another ethnoracial category to the hierarchy of masculinity. In Nico's fight story he too is greatly outnumbered by Asian American attackers:

(8) Nico Caen: I just put my head down and was just swinging at people,
I-
I was making contact too.
These fools,
all right,
[$_1$all of a sudden $_1$]
Billy: [$_1$them fools $_1$] were like,
[$_2$ ## $_2$]
Nico: [$_2$ all of a sudden, $_2$]
all of a sudden,
yeah,
all of a sudden,
fools were like,
"Oh.
Don't fight,
you know,
don't fuck with him,"
you know?
Mary: [$_3$ Right. $_3$]
Nico: [$_3$ Because, $_3$]
they don't expect,
a:,
fucking,
a-
a white person to be ↑fighting,
you [$_4$ know? $_4$]
Mary: [$_4$Hm. $_4$]
Nico: I'm Puerto Rican,
I-
I look white though,
you know?
They don't expect,
they don't expect the Caucasian person to be fighting,
you know?
Mary: Wo:w.

36 Billy: [$_5$ Yep.$_5$]
37 Nico: [$_5$They$_5$] expect him to get his ass whupped,
38 you know?
39 And I'm not having that.

There are striking thematic and even lexical parallels between Mr. Frisky's and Nico's stories. Both boys describe themselves as "swinging" at "fools" wildly but successfully; this verb in both cases is modified by the emphatic adverbial *just*, which fosters listeners' involvement (Chafe 1982; Erman 1997). In addition, both boys use quoted speech to foreground their own physical prowess, but whereas Mr. Frisky's narrative evaluation comes in the form of a quotation of his own thoughts, Nico quotes the other combatants as calling off their comrades once they realize that they have underestimated his fighting abilities (lines 14–17). And while Mr. Frisky emphasizes his position within a hierarchy of masculinity relative to higher-ranking blacks and lower-ranking Asians, Nico's narrative constructs the hierarchy a bit differently. As a Puerto Rican, he suggests, he has greater physical ability than either Asian Americans (since he forces them into retreat) or European Americans (since his ability to fight belies his white appearance). However, in the end it is an African American boy who saves Nico, as shown in (5b) above. Thus both narrators agree on the superior position of African Americans and the inferior position of Asian Americans on the masculine hierarchy, with their own ethnoracial groups located between these two extremes.

In using discursive strategies to position African American males as having extraordinary physical power, boys of other ethnoracial backgrounds, and especially those who were or appeared white, could ward off the inference that they themselves were physically inadequate. Such narratives, like stories of racial fear and claims of reverse racism, contributed to the discursive reversal of racial disparities at Bay City High School, whereby blacks rather than whites were constructed as advantaged and powerful.

Conclusion

There is no question that many European American youth at Bay City High experienced themselves as beleaguered and oppressed by African American teenagers at the school. Yet white youth were not, as far as I could see, in significant danger from their black peers, and it was European American students who enjoyed considerable advantages due to their racial category. White teenagers tended not to notice the countless ways in which whiteness conferred structural benefits, particularly due to their families' generally higher socioeconomic status. These benefits ranged from greater access to Advanced Placement and college-preparatory courses and extracurricular enrichment opportunities to simply not coming to school hungry, as a number of poor and working-class African American students often did. But what was salient for European American youth was their daily experience of being neither numerically nor culturally dominant, of being afraid to walk through the school's hallways, of being made aware of and sometimes ashamed of their whiteness.

As a white researcher, I was no doubt perceived as sympathetic to the racial complaints and narratives I heard, and having once been a student in a racially divided high school, I did indeed understand the fears and resentments that European American youth confided to me, even as I noted discrepancies between their perceptions and my own observations of race and power at Bay City High. Discourses of reverse racism and racial danger throughout the United States made it almost inevitable that even these relatively liberal European American youth, living in the politically progressive San Francisco Bay Area, would take up such ideologies in making sense of the local racial order of Bay City High School, which they negotiated every day.

White students' discursive strategies of racial reversal reflected their embeddedness within larger American discourses of race, but they were also tied to these teenagers' specific location in a region of the country and in a particular high school in which they were not members of the ethnoracial majority. In the following chapter, I examine how in this context an interview task that I originally thought of as routine – a request for interviewees' ethnoracial self-classification – became an opportunity for white youth to negotiate and push back against a shifting racial order that made it less possible for them to treat whiteness and its advantages as natural, normal, and unmarked.

10 "I guess I'm white": ethnoracial labels and the problem of whiteness

Introduction

A few days after the Million Man March and the classroom discussion of race, Ms. Stein led her Life and Health classes in an activity in which students were instructed to stand up from their seats to indicate their affiliation with a variety of panethnic labels: *African American*, *Asian American*, *European American*, *Latino*, and *Native American*.[1] Many teenagers of all backgrounds – indeed, the majority, in some classes – chose not to stand up to indicate their ethnoracial identity, but rose en masse in response to Ms. Stein's final question, "How many of you prefer not to be racially identified?" The unease these young people displayed about being ethnoracially categorized recalled to my mind a student's comment during the class discussion earlier that week: "I'm white, but I don't really identify with my race."

In the previous two chapters, I examined how white youth at Bay City High negotiated race in talk about friendship on the one hand and in narratives of racial conflict on the other. In this chapter, I show that even the apparently simple act of ethnoracial self-labeling presented similar interactional challenges, particularly for white students. The problem of classifying the self ethnoracially was not unique to classroom activities such as the one described above. Rather, it was an issue that students confronted throughout their academic careers. Although youth at Bay City High claimed a wide range of identities, at the time of the study the official ethnoracial categories used by the school in reporting the demographic breakdown of its student body were far more limited: *American Indian*, *Asian*, *Filipino*, *Hispanic*, *Black*, and *White*, terms that were clearly inadequate to capture the school's racial and ethnic complexity. Outside the institutional context of record keeping, however, teenagers had more freedom to name and negotiate their own identities and often classified themselves ethnoracially either on their own initiative or when called upon to do so by peers. The terms young people used to label themselves and others in such contexts, like the school's labels, reflected the wider ideology of race and ethnicity in US culture (Williams 1989) in variously drawing on such factors as skin color (e.g., *Black*), linguistic background (e.g., *Hispanic*), national heritage (e.g., *Filipino*), and geography (e.g., *Asian*).

The ethnographic interviews that I conducted created another context in which ethnoracial labels could circulate locally. In requesting basic personal information at the beginning of each interview, including age, gender, and grade level as well as race/ethnicity, I invited students to position themselves ethnoracially in a situation that stood apart from both the official institutional context of the school and the informal space of peer interaction but recalled aspects of each. Interviewees thus had to work out for themselves how to understand the situation in order to supply what they considered to be an appropriate answer. At the time, I was largely unaware of the complex interactional and identity work that teenagers were performing in answering these questions. It was only in reviewing the recordings later that I realized that these brief exchanges, which I had considered mere "background information," were worthy of close analysis in their own right (cf. Bucholtz and Hall 2008; Myers 2006; Schiffrin 1997).

Most studies of ethnoracial terms either focus on the broad social outlines of how such terms were historically deployed and currently circulate in public discourse (e.g., Domínguez 1986; Laversuch 2007; Leeman 2004) or examine shifts in the use of and attitudes toward particular labels (Baugh 1991; Oboler 1995; Smitherman 1991). However, scholars have begun to consider how ethnoracial labels are claimed and used in interaction (e.g., De Fina 2000; Kang 2004; Lee 2009; Shenk 2007). Despite the institutional dominance of the US system of ethnoracial classification, white students at Bay City High School were not forced to accept this system wholesale but could creatively adapt it or reject it altogether in their interaction with others, including in interviews with me.

The interview task of self-classification presented problems for students of all backgrounds, given the limitations of Americans' ethnoracial vocabulary and the unstable ground of race and ethnicity. However, it posed special challenges for European American teenagers, for they were compelled to position themselves in a racial matrix in which the category ordinarily assigned to them – *white* – was not entirely equivalent to the others. In the ethnoracial order of Bay City High School, at times whiteness was ideologically associated with cultural blandness and lack of coolness, while at other times it was viewed as the embodiment of racist hegemony. Unlike the identities available to people of color, whiteness was therefore not an identity that could be safely embraced with pride (Perry 2002; Phoenix 1997). Moreover, Jewish teenagers and the small number of first- and second-generation immigrant youth of European descent could claim an ethnic or national affiliation roughly parallel to the identities asserted by many students of color, but such ethnic ancestry was not a meaningful part of the identities of most other white students, whose families had been in the United States for three or more generations and had not retained significant ties to their ethnic heritage. Interviewees dealt with this problem in a variety of ways, either by taking up, elaborating, or ironically commenting on available categories or by problematizing the task of ethnoracial self-classification itself.

Categorizing the self "for the record"

Unlike in Chapters 8 and 9, in which students overtly or covertly topicalized race, in my requests for teenagers' personal information at the beginning of my interviews with them, race and ethnicity were treated not as full-fledged topics in their own right but as background information that bracketed and led into what both my interviewee and I understood as the real business at hand: a more open-ended discussion of students' past and present friendship groups, their social and linguistic practices, and their views of other social groups at the school. These brief, bounded exchanges concerning race and ethnicity contrast with the sorts of interview data examined in much of the previous research on racial discourse cited in the two earlier chapters, in which racial issues are the explicit focus of the interview. Yet in providing ethnoracial information about themselves in this routine context, interviewees negotiated issues of identity no less than in narratives or other more sustained forms of race talk.

Asking about people's own ethnoracial identities during the interviews carried some potential risks, for as a European American researcher at a school that had been harshly attacked in the local press for racial tensions between students, I feared that I would be viewed as yet another sensationalizing outsider if I showed too much curiosity about racial and ethnic issues. But I was in fact deeply interested in how my interviewees classified themselves, for I had discovered early on that my own perceptions of students' ethnoracial backgrounds were often wildly wrong, and I was unable even to hazard a guess as to the heritage of some teenagers. My solution to this interactional dilemma was to ask about ethnoracial identity in the context of a series of questions about the interviewee's personal information: age, gender, and year in school. These questions echoed the bureaucratic forms that students were accustomed to filling out for school and other official purposes. While I needed some of this information about each study participant in any case, the inclusion of gender in my list of questions – something both the interviewees and I took to be obvious – further underscored that this exchange was institutional in nature, since asking questions to which the answers are already known to the questioner is far more typical of institutional talk than of casual interaction (Atkinson and Drew 1979; Sinclair and Coulthard 1975; Stokoe and Edwards 2008).[2] This institutional framing allowed me to ask about ethnicity, which in other contexts might have been seen as intrusive or strange.

I also took other steps to mitigate the potential awkwardness of asking about ethnoracial identity. I framed all my questions as being "for the record," a phrase that implicitly invoked an institutional context beyond the interview, perhaps governed by a higher authority than myself. In addition, I tried to place the question about ethnicity later in the series and often in final position in the list, both to downplay its importance and to allow the interviewee to go into greater depth on this question. Moreover, unless the interviewees themselves questioned the task of stating their ethnicity, I usually accepted whatever responses they gave without follow-up questions or comments, unlike my more engaged style in the rest of the interview. Finally, in posing the question I generally used the term *ethnicity* rather than *race* because the latter was a much more politically contentious term at the school. For some teenagers, however, *ethnicity* was a relatively formal and unusual term, which may have further constructed the question sequence as bureaucratic talk. This word choice inevitably affected the responses I received, as students had to decide whether I was specifically interested in ethnicity or if I was using the term as a euphemism for race. In any event, no one appeared to have trouble understanding the word, and students rarely maintained a strict distinction between race and ethnicity.

By employing such strategies, I ended up positioning myself at this initial stage of the interview as a kind of low-level bureaucrat collecting information not out of any personal or professional interest but for some larger institutional purpose. Thus the ethnoracial labels young people produced in response to my question often differed from labels they used for themselves and others in the heart of the interview and in other interactions.

Interviewees were also constrained by the categories of race and ethnicity that were culturally available to them. Drawing on these categories, teenagers of all ethnoracial backgrounds produced four main types of ethnoracial self-classifications: color labels, race labels, citizenship labels, and ethnicity/heritage labels. The insufficiency of all of these in characterizing students' ethnoracial identities is reflected both in the fact that individual teenagers often used more than one label or type of label to classify themselves and in the various ways that interviewees deployed the terms in their responses.

The color label *white* was the term most widely used at Bay City High to refer to European Americans (likewise, *black* was most often used for African Americans, although the more formal term *African American* was also sometimes used), and it was the most common label used by European American youth to classify themselves both in the "for the record" sequence and in other contexts. However, in the interviews such self-classifications often involved additional commentary and explanation, as illustrated below. The race label *Caucasian*, though originating in a now-discredited biological theory of racial classification, continues to be used in bureaucratic forms that request ethnoracial information. This term was not unusual in the "for the record" sequence but was rare in teenagers' casual interactions with me and with one another. The use of this label therefore displayed an orientation to the interview question as "official business" rather than a more informal request for information. The citizenship label *European American* and other variants had a similarly formal and bureaucratic association. Such labels combine the adjectival form of a continent, nation, or ethnicity with the citizenship term *American* and thus allowed youth to claim multiple subject positions with a single term. By contrast, ethnicity/heritage labels are associated with individual ethnic groups or national heritages, such as *Scottish* or *Swedish*, without the additional specification *American*.

Interviewees were clearly aware of the inflexibility of these categories, for in responding to the interview question, even those who answered unequivocally often provided some commentary or explanation, and others expressed reluctance to answer at all. The following analysis examines the four main strategies that students used in dealing with the question of ethnoracial self-classification: producing an unmarked response that treated the question as easily answerable, elaborating on their ethnoracial identity, commenting ironically on their chosen label, and problematizing the question itself.

Unmarked responses

Many European American teenagers answered the question of their ethnoracial identity more or less straightforwardly, without any overt display of reluctance or additional comment; that is, in conversation-analytic terms, they produced preferred responses (Pomerantz 1984). But it would be a mistake to assume that their interactional compliance signaled a simple relationship between their reported ethnoracial category in this exchange and their identity in other contexts. Indeed, I repeatedly found that my ethnographic knowledge of students' everyday lives did not match up neatly with how they ethnoracially classified themselves in response to the ethnicity question. Thus teenagers' responses do not definitively assign them to static ethnoracial categories but rather reveal how they chose to position themselves ethnoracially at this point in the interview.

Example (1) illustrates the difference between what Bay City High School students reported in response to the interview question and how they positioned themselves at other times and in other contexts. The example (and the recording) begins in the middle of my request for the interviewee's personal information. I have just asked Mark to choose a pseudonym, and I then go on to ask for the other items of information.

```
(1)  1 Mary:  and your ↑age,
     2        sex,
     3        ethnicity,
     4        and year in school.
     5 Mark:  All right.
     6        My name is Mark Levinson?
     7 Mary:  @@@
     8        Oh I get a last name [too.
     9                                   @@]
    10 Mark:                       [I am:,   ]
```

11 @
12 (0.9)
13 u:m:,
14 sixteen years o:ld,
15 (0.6)
16 I am:,
17 (0.6)
18 a boy:.
19 (0.8)
20 I am,
21 white,
22 and I am a junior:,
23 (0.5)
24 at Bay City High School.
25 Mary: Okay.
26 A:nd u:h,
27 Did you grow <higher pitch> {up in Bay City?}

Mark's response, *(0.8) I am, white* (lines 19–21), is unmarked in that it directly answers the question about ethnicity, without hedging or other indications of interactional trouble. To be sure, his response contains pauses, but hesitation markers occur throughout the response, not only in the reply to the ethnicity question. It is unlikely that a student, no matter how reticent to discuss her or his ethnoracial identity, would hesitate to report gender or grade level, which were considered public knowledge. Rather, as other examples also show, the task of answering this multipart question put considerable cognitive demands on interviewees. Hence the slow speech production found in students' responses (e.g., lines 10–24) likely reflects the online processing of the question and the formality of this portion of the interview instead of any reluctance to answer.

Despite the directness of Mark's response, the color term *white* does not fully capture his ethnoracial identity. As I knew from my participant-observation and as he goes on to discuss in detail later in our interview, he displayed a strong Jewish identity in other circumstances, yet this dimension of his ethnicity goes unnamed at this moment. It appears that Mark, like many other Jewish teenagers I interviewed, understood the interview situation (or at least the "for the record" sequence) to be one in which *white* was a more appropriate category than *Jewish*. By contrast, research interviews in which both interviewer and interviewee are Jewish, and Jewishness itself is the focus of discussion, yield detailed and complex characterizations of interviewees' ethnoracial identities (Frankenberg 1993; Modan 2001). Such self-identifications are shaped by both the interactional context and the ethnographic context. Thus, unlike Gabriella Modan's (2001) Jewish adult interviewees in Washington, DC, the Jewish teenagers I talked to at Bay City High uniformly – if at times apparently reluctantly – identified themselves as "white," no doubt due in part to how they were positioned within the school's racial order. This local pattern also reflects the larger historical process whereby Jewishness has undergone ideological whitening in US society (Brodkin 1998; Rogin 1996).

However, Jewish identity is not entirely unexpressed in this initial exchange. In line 6, Mark selects his pseudonym; as my reaction in line 8 indicates, it was unusual for study participants to choose a last name as well as a first name, especially one that was not part of a culturally iconic name like *John Doe* or *Al Capone* (as shown in the next example). What is notable about Mark's invented surname, *Levinson*, aside from the fact that he chose one at all, is that it is associated with Jewish heritage. Thus although he limits the explicit naming of his ethnicity to *white*, through his choice of pseudonym he has already implicitly positioned himself as (also) Jewish.

In other cases, unmarked responses did not underreport the interviewee's everyday ethnoracial identity but overreported it, in the sense that she or he claimed an identity category in response to the ethnicity question that did not appear salient in other contexts. Example (2), which illustrates this phenomenon, opens with my request to Al Capone to state his pseudonym.

(2)
1 Mary: [Your,
2 fake name.]
3 Al: [All right.]
4 My name is Al Ca{po:ne.} <creaky>
5 Mary: Okay.
6 And I need,
7 your age,
8 your year in schoo:l,
9 u:h,
10 your sex and your eth[nicity,
11 for the record.]
12 Al: [.h::::]
13 All right,
14 I:'m s:-
15 I just turned seventee:n abou:t,
16 (0.6)
17 two weeks ago,
18 .h:::
19 Mary: <quietly> {Happy ↑birthday.}
20 Al: Thank you.=
21 =And u:h,
22 .h
23 let's see.

24 .h:
25 I:,
26 (0.5)
27 am: a ↑junior,
28 uh graduating nineteen ninety seven,
29 a:nd,
30 let's see,
31 .h:
32 and I am:,
33 (0.5)
34 Scottish German American.
35 Mary: Okay.
36 A:nd how long have you lived in the Bay Area?

In line 34, Al classifies himself as *Scottish German American*. Such citizenship labels were much more commonly used by students of color than by white students to categorize themselves, and the almost pedantic precision of the response elevates Al's answer to a more formal level than either *white* or a collocation like *Scottish and German* would have done. But this ethnic specificity is not necessarily indicative of Al's ethnoracial identity in other contexts. From what I observed, Al had very little affinity for either his Scottish or his German heritage. Indeed, as his self-selected pseudonym suggests, he was far more interested in Italian American culture, especially as represented in popular stereotypes of Italian Americans as Mafia gangsters. This is not to say that Al did not feel a connection to his own ethnic roots, but only that this connection did not manifest itself in even occasional public displays of ethnic affiliation. By contrast, students of color regularly decorated their school materials with slogans like *Laotian Pride* or *Brown Tribe* (the latter on a folder owned by a Latina student) and talked about their cultural traditions in classes and with peers. Al's self-identification here orients to the interview as a context in which his "official" ethnoracial classification rather than an everyday identity is most relevant.

In one case, the mismatch between a student's response to the ethnicity question and what I knew of her identity based on my ethnographic fieldwork led me to inquire further, violating my usual practice of accepting whatever response interviewees gave. In example (3), I have just asked Fred for her pseudonym and personal information. In response to the ethnicity question, she classifies herself as white, and in surprise I ask her about her Armenian heritage, which she mentioned in a class discussion.

(3) 1 Fred: Okay.
2 I'm Fred?
3 Mary: @@
4 Fred: I':m,

5 <higher pitch> {What's the next thing?}
6 Mary: Oh,
7 whatever,
8 ag:e,
9 Fred: Sixteen,
10 (0.7)
11 [$_1$You have to keep reminding m$_1$][$_2$e $_2$].
12 Mary: [$_1$Year in sk- $_1$]
13 <louder>{[$_2$Year$_2$] in schoo:l,}=
14 Fred: =Junior,
15 Mary: U:h,
16 sex,
17 Fred: Fema@le,
18 Mary: a:nd,
19 ethnicity.
20 Fred: White.
21 Mary: Okay.
22 (0.9)
23 And—
24 <higher pitch> {Didn't you say in class once,
25 that you're Armenian?}=
26 Fred: =Armenian,
27 yeah.
28 A quarter Armenian.
29 Mary: A quarter?
30 What's=
31 Fred: =My grandma.
32 Mary: ↑Hm.
33 [$_3$What's the rest of, $_3$]
34 Fred: <creaky> [$_3${(Was) Armenian.}$_3$]
35 Mary: your background?
36 Fred: European mutt.
37 @::
38 Mary: Okay, …

With prompting from me, Fred offers several different responses regarding her background: *White* (line 20), *a quarter Armenian* (line 28), *European mutt* (line 36); additionally, in a later group interview with her friends she labels herself *Caucasian*, using the same term her friends have previously selected. My followup question to Fred's initial answer (*Didn't you say in class once, that you're Armenian?*; lines 24–25) implies that the label *white* does not completely exhaust her ethnoracial classification. However, my comment, sparked by Fred's impassioned discussion of her Armenian identity in class, may be heard by her as indicating that I consider *Armenian* a nonwhite category. Fred subsequently characterizes the "rest of (her) background" as specifically *European mutt* (line 36), which implies white ancestry. Here I am the one to propose that there is more to the interviewee's ethnicity than can be covered by the term *white*. In most interviews, however, the initiation of a more elaborated account of the interviewee's ethnoracial identity came from the students themselves rather than from me.

Elaborated responses

When an interviewee produced an unmarked response, even if there may have been more to say about her or his ethnoracial identity it went unsaid. By contrast, in elaborated responses to the question of ethnic identity, teenagers first provided what seemed to be an unmarked response and then amplified upon this answer in order to clarify their ethnoracial self-classification, thereby offering a more complete characterization than a single descriptor could convey.

Example (4) illustrates this sort of elaborated response. Just before the example begins, Acme has stated his pseudonym, and I move on to the rest of the "for the record" routine:

(4)
Mary: All right.
(0.8)
A::nd uh-
I need like just for the record,
your a:ge,
your year in schoo:l,=
Acme: =My name's—
uh-
my name—
o:h yeah.@
I'm seven[$_1$teen years old,$_1$]
Rachel: [$_1$@@@@ $_1$]
Acme: and I go to Bay City High School,
and <staccato, creaky> {I am in the <[ði]> twelfth grade.}
Mary: Okay,
a:nd your sex and ethnicity for the record.
Acme: My name is ↑m:ale,
Mary: @[$_2$@@@@ $_2$]
Rachel: [$_2$#### $_2$]#
Acme: Oh,
I'm a ↑m:ale,
(1.1)
and u:m,
I do in fact like sex,
but that's probably not the question,

a:nd,
Mary: We can get into [$_3$that if you want.$_3$]
Acme: <louder> {[$_3$My ethnic$_3$]ity's:,
Caucasian.}
Mary: All right.
So:.
How long you been going to Bay City [$_4$High School?$_4$]
Acme: <louder> {[$_4$I'm Swedish.$_4$]}
(0.7)
Four years.
(0.7)
Mary: Okay.
You live in Bay City?
Acme: Yep.
My whole life.

Acme's recycling of the *My name is* format in lines 7 and 9 and again in line 17, though inapposite since he has already answered the question, indicates his orientation to the task. (His difficulties in responding to my multipart question may be attributable to the fact that at the time of the interview he was smoking marijuana.) His orientation to the exchange as bureaucratic or institutional talk is also seen in his first choice of label, *Caucasian*. He produces this response in a relatively unmarked way (*My ethnicity's:, Caucasian*; lines 28–29). His final consonant lengthening and slight pause before uttering the race label may indicate either processing problems or uncertainty about how to respond, but it does not display any overt discomfort with the question. In line 30, I accept the answer and attempt to close off the sequence with a receipt token, *All right.*

However, Acme continues the exchange, overlapping my next question with a louder elaboration of his original answer (*I'm Swedish*; line 33) before going on to answer my next question in line 35. This expansion may be in delayed response to my use of the term *ethnicity*, which can convey cultural or national heritage rather than race. The race-based term *Caucasian* may thus seem inappropriate, and *Swedish* may be a repair rather than an addendum. In either case, Acme treats his first response as requiring further information.

Example (5) provides another illustration of an elaborated response to the ethnicity question. Brand One has already provided his pseudonym before the example begins:

(5)
Mary: Your age?
Brand One: I'm sixteen.
Mary: A:nd,
for the record,
can you also state you:r,
(0.6)

7 year in schoo:l,
8 sex and ethnicity.
9 Brand One: Um,
10 I'm a junior,
11 (1.2)
12 a:t Bay City High School.
13 And uh,
14 (0.8)
15 I'm white,
16 slash Jewish.
17 Mary: A:nd,
18 Oh.
19 Sex.
20 You're a male.
21 Brand One: Oh that's right,
22 male.

In lines 15 and 16, Brand One characterizes his ethnoracial identity as *white, slash Jewish*. Like other students' responses, his answer displays some orientation to the task as akin to filling out a bureaucratic form. In this case, this orientation is suggested by Brand One's use of the word *slash* as an oral version of a punctuation mark ordinarily used to separate two alternatives or complementary elements in written discourse. This complex ethnoracial label, however, is not produced seamlessly. Brand One pauses briefly not only before producing the ethnoracial label, *white* – as many interviewees did – but also afterward, and then adds the increment *slash Jewish*. Thus although syntactically the two parts of his ethnoracial self-classification operate as a single unit, prosodically the second label functions as an addendum to the first. The word *slash* may either suggest that *white* and *Jewish* are different ways of conveying the "same" ethnoracial identity or that these are different elements of a single complex identity.

This example also illustrates the asymmetry between the gender and ethnicity components of the "for the record" question. As already noted, gender identity is generally understood to be obvious from visible signs alone, and thus I am able to supply this "commonsense" information on Brand One's behalf (line 20) and receive his confirmation (lines 21–22). By contrast, in none of the interviews did I ever venture to answer my own question about ethnicity. The question about gender, moreover, almost always received an unmarked response (or a humorous quip, as in Acme's response in example 4), while answers to the ethnicity question were much more varied, as students negotiated between the strictures of the interview space and the complexity of their identities. Elaborated responses were one way of negotiating this tension, by adding ethnic value to what would otherwise go on record as simple whiteness. Thus an elaborated response suggests that the unmarked response *white* alone is insufficient to characterize the speaker's ethnoracial identity.

Ironic responses

In a few striking cases, interviewees embraced the term *white* as a badge of ironic pride, recognizing that this identity was in fact neither an acceptable nor a desirable source of pride for most European American students at Bay City High School. In mock-celebrating their affiliation with whiteness, these young people wryly commented on the local unavailability of whiteness as a valued ethnoracial identity.

In example (6), I am interviewing Jay for the first time; his friend Charlie, who has been interviewed separately, is also present. I have already initiated the "for the record" sequence, to which Jay launches his reply:

(6) Jay: All right.
Um,
I'm a ma:le,
(0.8)
male,
<[e:j?]>
fiftee:n,
u:m,
Mary: Not eighteen after all.
@
Jay: No,
I'm not really eighteen,
I'm fifteen,=
=U:m,
I'm a sophomore,
(0.5)
What was the other thing?
<Charlie? drumming on tabletop>
Mary: [$_1$ U:h, $_1$]
Charlie: <quietly, careful articulation> {[$_1$## eth-$_1$]
ethni-ci-[$_2$ ty.$_2$]}
Mary: [$_2$Oh,$_2$]
eth[$_3$nicity.$_3$]
Jay: [$_3$I'm a $_3$] <loud whisper> {white boy}!
@
Mary: All right.=
Jay: =I'm white.
Yea:h.
Mary: Oka:y.

Jay has difficulty recalling all the parts of my question and asks for a reminder (line 17) of the last component, the ethnicity question. Charlie is the first to offer a response but stumbles a bit over the pronunciation of *ethnicity* (lines 20–21), an indication that he does not commonly use this term. Meanwhile, I hesitate (line 19) and then use a change-of-information-state marker, *oh*, after Charlie begins to supply the answer (line 22). This somewhat studied disattention to the ethnicity question on my part is in keeping with my frequent efforts to downplay the importance of race and ethnicity in the interviews.

In producing his response Jay does not offer the unmarked response *I'm white* but instead gives a fuller and more animated answer: *I'm a white boy!* (line 24). The addition of *boy* is informationally superfluous, for not only has Jay just stated his gender (lines 3, 5), but this categorization is understood as obvious. His use of this formulation therefore appears to function not informationally but rhetorically, which is also indicated by his reiteration *I'm white. Yea:h* (lines 27–28) after I have already indicated the adequacy of his first answer.

Here Jay does not simply claim the problematic category of whiteness but embraces it with some fanfare. That his stance is ironic rather than sincere can be seen in the exaggerated emphasis of his response. In line 24 he utters the words *white boy* in a loud whisper, as though reporting shocking information, and indeed *white boy* could be used as a term of opprobrium or contempt by students of color at Bay City High, connoting weakness and inadequate masculinity (see also Chapter 9). As a hip hop fan, Jay had to negotiate this ideology on a daily basis. His shift into a cool, nonchalant stance in lines 27 and 28 ironically performs a double-voiced persona at odds with the ideology of what it meant to be a "white boy" in this ethnographic context. He thus playfully reclaims an identity that was often derided in the ethnoracial order of the school.

The phrase *white boy* also occurred in another student's response to the "for the record" question, in a similarly ironic way. Example (7) is taken from my interview with Mr. Frisky:

(7) 1 Mr. Frisky: Um.
2 My age,
3 I'm fifteen years o:ld,
4 .h
5 My sex,
6 I'm male,
7 either that or,
8 female with a rea:lly deep voice,
9 .h
10 u:m,
11 (0.7)
12 <tongue click>
13 .h
14 uh,
15 year in school,
16 I'm in,
17 tenth grade,
18 a:nd,
19 <quietly> {What was it?

20 ↑#?}
21 Mary: Ethnicity.
22 Mr. Frisky: Ethnicity.
23 I'm the <[ði]> whiteyest of the white boys,=
24 =I'm,
25 Russian and,
26 and uh,
27 British.
28 [.h::]
29 Mary: <quietly> {[Okay.]}

Although Mr. Frisky is a very different kind of "white boy" than Jay, having an alternative rather than hip hop style, he too embraces this term as a characterization of his ethnicity. Again, the term's ironic valence is signaled by the exaggerated emphasis of his response: he is not simply "a white boy" but the "whiteyest" of all (line 23), where the neologized superlative form derives from a longstanding negative African American slang term for European Americans, *whitey* (Chun 2001; Smitherman 1994). This self-characterization, like Jay's, invokes and ironically comments on the views of many students of color toward whiteness, and particularly white masculinity. (The corresponding term *white girl* never occurred in response to my requests for ethnic information.) Mr. Frisky goes on to provide two ethnicity/heritage labels, *Russian* and *British*, with a mock-British released /t/ in the latter word (lines 25–27). His rapid movement from declaring himself "the whiteyest of the white boys" to specifying his ethnic background seems to indicate that in his view these European ethnicities are hyperwhite in some sense (see also Bucholtz 2002b).

Although ironic responses were rare, when they occurred they were consistently associated with whiteness. The only other interviewee to answer the ethnicity question ironically was Susan, an outgoing girl of mixed race who described herself, in an apparently oft-used formulation, as a "ploud <i.e., proud>, black woman and a, proud w- white woman who can't da:nce" (lines 37–40). The example begins right after I have asked Susan for her pseudonym:

(8) 1 Susan: Susan!
2 Mary: Okay.
3 Susan: [$_1$@@@ I love that name. $_1$]
4 Mary: [$_1$And-
5 @@ $_1$]
6 ↑Great.
7 Oka:y,
8 And I'll need your:,
9 age,
10 sex,
11 ethnicity,

12 and year in schoo:l,
13 for the record.
14 Susan: U:m.
15 Age,
16 f:ifteen,
17 and,
18 something or other,
19 a few months,
20 or something.
21 A:nd,
22 (1.1)
23 Oh.
24 I'm female.
25 [$_2$That $_2$]=
26 Mary: [$_2$Okay.$_2$]=
27 Susan: =<lower pitch>{would be that whole Susan thing.}
28 Mary: [$_3$@@ $_3$]
29 Susan: [$_3$U:m, $_3$]
30 (0.7)
31 Ethnicity,
32 I'm interracial.
33 (0.9)
34 U:h,
35 I locate with:,
36 many different races,
37 Ploud, <[plaʊd]>
38 black woman and a,
39 proud w-
40 white woman who [$_4$can't da:nce,$_4$]
41 Mary: [$_4$@@ $_4$]
42 Susan: you know,
43 all that—
44 all the stereotypes,
45 (0.9)
46 U:m,
47 and I go to Bay City High School.
48 Mary: Okay.
49 Susan: In California.
50 Mary: Right.

As with Jay's and Mr. Frisky's responses, Susan's answer orients to the risk of expressing pride in a white identity. She humorously undercuts her overt assertion of white pride with an invocation of a mildly negative stereotype of European Americans (line 40).[3] Ironic responses such as these allowed young people to comment on the problematic positionality of whiteness at Bay City High while complying with the ethnicity question.

Problematizing responses

While all the previously discussed strategies of ethnoracial self-labeling negotiate the limitations of available categories in some way, students' dissatisfaction with these labels and their objections to the very act of labeling became particularly vivid in a number of interviews in which the interviewee problematized the ethnicity question itself. Most teenagers complied with the task of ethnic self-classification and left any resistance off-record, in that they did not display overt objections to the interview question. In problematizing responses, however, young people made clear that they rejected the premise on which the question was based (see also Ehrlich and Sidnell 2006; Stokoe and Edwards 2008; Widdicombe and Wooffitt 1995). Notably, all of the interviewees who used problematizing responses eventually self-identified as white (albeit with displays of reluctance). When ethnoracial identity was treated as a problem in the interviews, then, it was a problem specifically for European American youth (Gallagher 1994; Martin *et al.* 1999).

Interviewees who problematized the interview task did so by undermining their own epistemic authority (Heritage and Raymond 2005) to answer the question of ethnicity definitively. That is, in asking the question I positioned students as having greater knowledge than I did about their ethnoracial backgrounds, but in their responses some interviewees abdicated this authority by using evidential stance markers that indicate uncertainty, like *I don't know* and *I guess*. In American culture, such responses violate a strong expectation that an individual of high school age will have certain knowledge of her or his ethnoracial categorization. And indeed, it is improbable, given the prominence of race and ethnicity in US society as well as the evidence of the data, that these teenagers truly did not know which category they were assigned to within the American ethnoracial system. On the contrary, in feigning ignorance, they were able to convey their disapproval of or discomfort with the question itself.

The extent to which teenagers problematized the ethnicity question ranged from brief comments to detailed discussions of the meaning of *ethnicity*. In some cases, their problematizing remarks reflected mild amusement, while in others, the interviewees seemed troubled by the question. Example (9) illustrates a relatively lighthearted problematizing response from Erich:

(9)
1 Erich: All right.
2 U:h,
3 .h:
4 I'm fiftee::n,
5 I'll be sixteen in under a month,
6 Mary: ↑Hm.
7 Erich: U:m,
8 I'm in,

uh tenth grade,
I'm a sophomore,
in other words,
.h:
u:h,
I'm:,
Caucasian,
I guess.
I don't know.
.h
From,
uh,
outward si:gns.
Mary: <quietly> {@
(1.1)
@
[$_1$Oka:y$_1$],}
Erich: [$_1$A:nd $_1$] w-
anything else?
Mary: Oh,
sex.
Erich: Uh,
male.
[$_2$@@@ $_2$]
Mary: [$_2$Okay,
that covers that.$_2$]
All right.

In lines 14 and 15 Erich offers an ethnic self-classification, but in the next several lines he goes on to undercut this response through a series of epistemic hedges: *I guess* (line 16), *I don't know* (line 17), *From, uh, outward si:gns* (lines 19–21). This last remark treats his ethnicity as an empirical question rather than an established fact. The quasi-scientific formulation of the utterance, moreover, contributes to Erich's construction of his identity as a nerd and makes clear that although he undermines his own epistemic authority here (something of great value to nerdy teenagers; cf. Chapter 7), he does so for a higher intellectual purpose, not out of ignorance.

By contrast, Erich answers the other three "for the record" questions without hedging. He provides a high degree of precision in responding to the questions of age and grade level (lines 4–5 and 8–11, respectively), and he responds to the question of gender with some laughter (line 32), presumably because he considers the answer to be self-evident (even though due to his shaggy hair he was sometimes mistaken for a girl by other students). This display of skepticism specifically toward the ethnoracial question is characteristic of all the interviews featuring problematizing responses.

While Erich's challenge to the ethnicity question is mild and somewhat jocular, in other cases interviewees exhibited open discomfort with the question of ethnicity. In example (10), Billy initially tries to answer the question but then abandons the attempt and supplies a different label for himself. In his lengthy response, he displays a strong orientation to the audio recorder and to the interview as a formal speech event through his departure from his vernacular speech style as well as his attempt to attain a more formal or academic register (despite my instructions in lines 8 and 9 to "just, talk normal"):

(10) 1 Billy: All right.
2 (1.6)
3 I-
4 it's on,
5 right?=
6 Mary: =Yeah.
7 It's on,
8 you can just,
9 talk normal.
10 Billy: Okay.
11 (1.5)
12 <louder, careful articulation> {My name is Billy,}
13 (0.7)
14 a:nd,
15 I'm seventeen years o:ld,
16 a:nd,
17 um,
18 I'm a male,
19 (0.9)
20 a:nd,
21 (0.7)
22 my ethnicic- <[ɛθ'nɪsɪs]>
23 my ethnici- <[ɛθ'nɪsɪʔ]>
24 ty <[ti]> is,
25 um I'm Ge:rman,
26 Po:lish,
27 whi:te,
28 whatever,
29 you know?
30 (0.5)
31 How—
32 <smiling quality> {I mean,
33 how-
34 how do I describe that shit?}
35 Mary: <smiling quality> {Howe:ver you wa:nt.}
36 Billy: I have a whole bunch of different like,
37 (0.7)

38 I have a whole bunch of different ethnicities inside my-
39 (1.1)
40 background.
41 Mary: Okay.
42 Billy: You know?
43 (1.0)
44 Mary: [Okay.]
45 Billy: [Bu:t,]
46 (0.9)
47 However you want to describe it,
48 I'm just like=
49 Mary: =Right,
50 Billy: <careful articulation> culturally diverse <['daj'vəɹs]>.
51 Mary: Okay.
52 Tha:t's good.

Although Billy, like Charlie in example (6) above, has some trouble producing the word *ethnicity* (lines 22–24), he does not immediately display any hesitation about answering the question and begins to answer by offering a list of ethnicity/heritage and color labels (lines 25–27). However, he soon gives up in apparent frustration, indicating his inability to answer the question in several ways: by posing a rhetorical question about how to do so (line 34), by noting the diversity of his background (lines 36–40, 48–50), by showing indifference to any candidate classification that might be offered (line 28), and even by ceding epistemic authority to me (line 47). Despite Billy's stiffness and apparent discomfort with the interview situation, it is obvious that his reluctance to identify himself ethnoracially is not due to a lack of understanding of what is being asked or what a possible answer might be. Rather, his reticence appears to stem from his view that any conventional label would be inadequate to describe him; he therefore rather formally offers *culturally diverse* (line 50) as a preferable alternative. Such characterizations of one's ethnoracial identity have been described as part of a strategy of "ethnic abundance" (Lee 2009: 54).

This discursive strategy is also seen in example (11), taken from my first research interview with Claire, another nerdy teenager. The example begins after she has provided her pseudonym.

(11) 1 Mary: A:nd,
2 what is you:r,
3 age,
4 sex,
5 ethnicity,
6 and year in school.
7 Claire: Okay,
8 I'm sixteen years old.

9 (1.6)
10 Female.
11 (1.7)
12 Junior.
13 (1.7)
14 And I guess I'm w-
15 white.
16 @:
17 Mary: @@
18 You guess?
19 Claire: @@
20 Well,
21 @
22 I mean I-
23 I-
24 I hate questions like that,
25 it's like,
26 we:ll,
27 @
28 let's see,
29 if you w-
30 really want to trace my heritage,
31 @
32 Mary: @@
33 Yeah,
34 if you wa:nt.=
35 =I mean however you would describe yourself.=
36 Claire: =I'm a m:utt.
37 Mary: Okay.
38 Mutt:'s good enough.
39 U:m, …

In response to my request for her ethnic self-classification, Claire exhibits the same sort of joking skepticism about her ability to classify herself that Erich displayed in example (9): *I guess I'm w- white. @:* (lines 14–16). I respond with amusement but also with a question that may be heard as challenging (@@ *You guess?*; lines 17–18). In lines 20 through 24 Claire offers a strongly negative evaluation of the original question, though with some markers of hesitation and hedging. She then mocks the very idea of tracing her heritage (lines 29–30), a point I apparently miss, going on to encourage her to do precisely that. She ultimately offers a characterization of herself that is the antithesis of a "heritage" (line 30): she is a "m:utt" (line 36). Claire inserts laughter tokens throughout her turns, which may be designed to keep her remarks from being heard as direct criticism.

I generally did not offer much comment on compliant interviewee responses to the ethnicity question, but problematizing responses elicited a fuller reaction from me. In example (11) I positively evaluate Claire's unconventional responses with laughter at several points and the assessment *good enough* (line 38). I likewise offer a positive evaluation of Billy's response in line 52 of example (10) (*Tha:t's good*), and I laugh in response to Erich's epistemically uncertain answer in lines 22 through 24 of example (9). These evaluations (as opposed to my more usual *Okay*) not only close off the sequence but also indicate a form of interactional trouble within the interview, namely, that the answers these students provided are not what was expected (Antaki *et al.* 2000).

Interviewees who problematize the question of ethnoracial classification are clearly aware that their responses are unconventional. I later interviewed Claire together with her friend Christine, and in responding again to the "for the record" questions, she gave the same initial response to the ethnicity question that she provided in example (11). Her answer suggests that her original response was not due to a failure to understand what a compliant response would entail (example 12a):

(12a) Claire: Clai:re,
(1.0)
sixteen,
junior,
(0.8)
u:m,
(2.2)
What else was it?
(1.0)
Mary: [$_1$U:h, $_1$]
Christine: [$_1$Ethnic$_1$]ity and sex.
Mary: Yeah.
Claire: Female,
(0.9)
Uh,
(0.6)
guess I'm white.
I me@a-
Christine: @@
Claire: @
Mary: @
R@ight,
[$_2$we went through this last time.$_2$]
Christine: [$_2$@
(Whatever.) $_2$]
↑@@@@
Claire: Yeah.

28 @
29 Mary: Probably white.
30 [$_3$@@@ $_3$]
31 Christine: [$_3$Pro@ba@bly.$_3$]
32 .h
33 Claire: Well,
34 I mean when you say ethnicity,
35 (0.5)
36 <clears throat> [$_4$That sort of implies $_4$] a culture.
37 Christine: [$_4$Who knows what it means.$_4$]
38 Mary: Right.
39 Claire: @
40 <higher pitch> {I'm from Bay City.}
41 @@
42 Mary: @@Okay,
43 [$_5$(that sort of) works. $_5$]
44 Christine: [$_5$What kind of white culture i@s (that)?$_5$]
45 Claire: I@ kno@w!
46 [$_6$@@: $_6$]
47 Mary: [$_6$@@@@ $_6$]
48 Christine: [$_6$@@ .h @@ $_6$]
49 Claire: <smiling quality> {I have no culture.}=
50 Christine: =Okay.=
51 Claire: =Thank you very much.=
52 Mary: =Okay.

Claire's response in line 17 (*guess I'm white*) is very similar in wording to her response in lines 14 and 15 of example (11), and again she and the other participants orient to the unconventionality of this answer through laughter. Once again, Claire offers an account that challenges the basis of the question, by noting first that ethnicity implies culture (lines 34, 36) and then stating that because she lives in Bay City, she has no culture (lines 40, 49). And as in example (11), I initially fail to recognize her challenge, accepting her prosodically marked and perhaps double-voiced utterance *I'm from Bay City* (line 40) as a (barely) adequate response to the question (lines 42–43). Christine, however, immediately understands the irony of Claire's statement and offers an elaboration of her friend's point in line 44 (*What kind of white culture i@s (that)?*), which then receives uptake from Claire (line 45). Attending to classificatory responses rather than interactional dynamics leads me to miss the point of this exchange until the very end.

In this example, the two girls align with each other regarding their shared understanding of the ethnicity question as problematic. Yet when Christine goes on to answer the same question compliantly in example (12b), which immediately follows (12a), Claire takes a somewhat different position toward her own ethnoracial identity:

(12b) 53 Christine: =And I'm Christine,
54 I'm six↑teen,
55 I'm a junior,
56 female,
57 (0.6)
58 and I'm pretty much white too:,
59 unless you want to get,
60 (0.9)
61 really complicated.
62 Claire: [$_1$In which case— $_1$]
63 Christine: [$_1$If you want to say I'm, $_1$]
64 Irish Portugue:se,
65 or something like that.
66 Mary: [$_2$Oka:y. $_2$]
67 Claire: [$_2$I know.$_2$]
68 @@
69 Well,
70 I could get into it too:,
71 but [$_3$that would,$_3$]
72 Christine: [$_3$@@: $_3$]
73 Mary: @@@
74 Claire: be off the subject.
75 Christine: It would indeed.
76 Mary: O:kay.

Christine answers the ethnicity question straightforwardly (*I'm pretty much white too:*; line 58); her initial hedge concerns the degree to which *white* completely captures her ethnicity rather than her degree of certainty that she is white. She first uses a color label (*white*) and then elaborates with a "really complicated" (line 61) compound descriptor formed of two ethnicity/heritage labels (*Irish Portugue:se*; line 64). In response, Claire makes clear that it is not in fact a lack of ethnicity that prevented her from offering a more detailed answer of her own (line 70). This jockeying for ethnoracial position was not unusual; in several group interviews, an elaborate ethnoracial display by one teenager spurred a matching display by another. As Claire and Christine agree, however, delving into the details of their ethnoracial identities would "be off the subject" (line 74); in spite of their lengthy excursus about ethnicity, the girls do not in fact see the research interview as focused on such issues. In fact, this comment may suggest that they understand my question about ethnicity as actually being about race.

In these and other problematizing responses, European American teenagers pushed back against the idea that they should be willing and able to answer an interview question about their ethnic identity, thereby expressing skepticism of the available terms and the assumptions underlying them. Yet no student ever flatly refused to answer the question, perhaps because to do so would have been an awkward social breach, whether due to their sense of my greater institutional power or a feeling of solidarity with me as a researcher–friend. Instead, people managed to lodge their complaints on record while continuing to cooperate with the interview task. In this way, they rewrote the "public transcript" (Scott 1990) of the interview record to include their own concerns and priorities.

The problem of ethnoracial self-classification was shared by European American teenagers of all ethnic backgrounds and stylistic orientations. I originally expected that white participants in hip hop would have more difficulty negotiating this question than other students, but the data do not support such a generalization. Among the hip hop fans in the examples above, Al Capone gave an unmarked response, Brand One gave an elaborated response, Jay gave an ironic response, and Billy gave a problematizing response. Similarly, interviewees who problematized the ethnicity question were not stylistically homogeneous: nerds, hip hop fans, and preppy teenagers all produced such responses in my larger data set. And while students of Jewish heritage, who were locally viewed as ethnically marked but racially white, faced particular difficulties in responding to the question, they too produced a range of answers, from Mark's direct, unmarked response to Brand One's elaborated response to Erich's and Claire's problematizing responses.[4] Indeed, my interviews with teenagers of various races and ethnicities as well as my broader ethnographic observations revealed that all students actively negotiated their ethnoracial identity. However, the fact that only white interviewees interrogated the premise behind the ethnicity question indicates the problematic position of this racial category in the ethnoracial order of Bay City High.

Conclusion

For European American students, race and ethnicity were nearly always politically charged issues. The racial tensions of the school and the relatively low value locally placed on whiteness by their peers meant that being made aware of their race in the school context was generally not a pleasant experience for them. Moreover, for many white teenagers, whiteness was not readily available as an ethnicity or culture but rather was often viewed as an absence of culture that could make them feel different from and inferior to their classmates of color, who regularly expressed ethnic pride and participated in school-sponsored ethnically based activities. When pressed, European American youth could indeed produce an ethnic self-classification, often a fairly complex one, yet such categorizations may have had little to do with their day-to-day identities.

My own whiteness also shaped how interviewees responded to the ethnicity question. As discussed in the previous chapter, European American students felt free, even eager, to share with me stories of racial conflict and tension in which they were portrayed as the victims, for which I served as a sympathetic audience. By the same token, as a white interviewer, I may have been viewed as more receptive to European American students' ironic and problematizing responses than had I been a researcher of color (and conversely, students of color may have viewed me as less receptive to such responses). In this situation, my seemingly simple question regarding ethnic identity entered into a local discourse of race and ethnicity in which European American teenagers felt themselves to be at a profound disadvantage. The strategies that interviewees used for dealing with this task suggested that it was not easy for them to produce a satisfactory ethnoracial self-classification within the confines of a brief bureaucratic exchange, or even in a more sustained discussion. Their responses to the question of ethnicity were therefore not perfunctory answers to a banal question but agentive engagements with and commentaries on some of the most high-stakes issues in their daily lives.

In the final chapter of this book, I summarize the major themes of the analysis and reflect on how race and ethnicity at Bay City High School and around the nation have been reconfigured since the time of my original fieldwork, as well as the ways in which linguistic and nonlinguistic researchers can make common cause to investigate the thorny question of whiteness.

11 Audible whiteness

Introduction

It is only by publicly engaging in acts of identity that an individual's identity becomes a social object, visible and audible to others and perhaps even to oneself. This viewpoint most clearly finds support in the case of identities that can be adopted relatively easily, such as the stylistic identities of the European American youth in this book. Teenagers may choose to move from preppy to punk, from nerdy to cool, from an alternative style to a hip hop style, by changing where and with whom they hang out, how they dress, and how they talk.

This perspective may initially seem less apt in discussing more enduring forms of identity, like gender or race, for the signifiers of such categories are inscribed on the body in a far more permanent way than clothing or hairstyle. But I have suggested in the foregoing chapters that in this regard the racial category of whiteness is little different from the stylistic categories of preppiness, nerdiness, and so on: both kinds of identities are built through everyday social practices. When European American teenagers in my study used African American youth slang in a mocking or stylized way, or when they spoke of their fear or resentment of their black peers, they were "doing" whiteness – that is, they were acting in ways that in the local ethnographic and interactional context positioned them as white. This is not to say that such practices will be understood as indexical of whiteness in all contexts, nor that a person who "acts white," or black, or any other racialized category will necessarily be understood by others to be a member of that category. Social actors do not have unconstrained agency to construct their desired identities in a way that others will recognize and acknowledge. The relationality of identity means that identities are not the projects of individuals alone but are constantly co-constructed, supported, negotiated, and challenged by others. Because social categories are protected against induction (Sacks 1995: 336), people who act outside their expected or assigned category may be seen as failed members of that category, as "wannabes" of some other category, or even as "culturally unintelligible" (Butler 1990). This phenomenon is illustrated in the case of European American hip hop fans, whose stylistic choices were interpreted by many of their peers as inappropriately "acting black" given their racial assignment as white, and whose ability to be viewed as authentic participants in hip hop culture was therefore frequently called into question.

As I have argued, the process of identity construction has its genesis in social interaction, especially through the resources of language. In this concluding chapter, I examine the implications of the approach I have taken in this book both for sociocultural linguistics and for research on identity and race. And because the critical study of whiteness has a progressive political agenda in addition to its scholarly goals, I go on to examine the racial agency of the individuals who populate these pages, including the study participants as well as myself as the researcher. I note some places in my data where the social practices and ideologies of Bay City High School students have the potential to dislodge locally entrenched forms of whiteness in favor of transformative racial projects. I also critically reflect on how my own subjectivity as a European American scholar shaped the research process and the ways that I saw, understood, and dealt with my own and others' whiteness. Finally, I turn from the ethnographic past to the present day and locate this study in relation to the changing face of race in Bay City, in California, and in the nation as a whole.

Contributions to sociocultural linguistics

One aim of this book has been to encourage more dialogue between sociocultural linguists and other researchers concerned with race as well as other forms of social identity. These topics are vast and multifaceted, and they require correspondingly multifaceted theories and methodologies. As scholars in different fields converge on shared questions, the opportunity arises to learn from one another's expertise. My own considerable intellectual debt to other scholars should be abundantly evident in the pages of this book.

A second aim has been to combine different approaches to language, culture, and society in a single study in order to bring complementary perspectives to bear on the same body of linguistic data. This book therefore represents one example of how sociocultural linguistics might proceed as an interdisciplinary coalition of fields concerned with the relationship of language, culture, and society. By focusing on a particular social phenomenon – whiteness – rather than a single level of linguistic structure like phonology or lexicon or discourse structure, I have been able to unpack the varied ways in which language works as an integrated whole for creating social identities. This approach involves a holistic examination of the simultaneous working of multiple linguistic resources to accomplish social goals. Consequently, it offers a more contextually complete picture of how language works and the functions it serves than if I had considered a particular linguistic level on its own.

One of the linguistic contributions of this study is to further the theorizing of style within sociocultural linguistics. I have advocated a research focus on the co-occurrence of linguistic resources, including different levels of linguistic phenomena, in stylistic construction, for styles can only be understood if they are examined as complete semiotic packages. A youth style like nerdiness is not created solely through the use of careful articulation, nor through formal-register lexicon, nor through superstandard grammar, but through the combination of all these elements. I have likewise shown the importance of linking these linguistic resources to other semiotic indexes such as clothing and social geography. And I have shown that styles function within a semiotic system of distinction, as seen, for example, in the way that nerdiness takes much of its meaning from its contrastive relationship to the styles of cool youth. Thus what makes teenagers nerdy is as much about what they do not do – from their avoidance of the most current slang or other linguistic innovations to their disengagement from other aspects of trendy youth culture – as it is about what they do. In short, in stylistic analysis, the specific indexicality of semiotic forms can only be arrived at by examining the entire range of resources that social actors have at their disposal.

A second linguistic contribution of this work is its concern with analyzing linguistic forms within discourse, where they take on interactional functions and social meanings. In this book I have advocated a discourse-based form of linguistic analysis, one that takes into account both the structure and patterning of linguistic forms and their discursive deployment in interaction. For instance, in order to arrive at the full social meaning of innovative quotative markers it is necessary to examine both their social patterning and their interactional functions. Quantitative analysis of the quotative marker *be all* yields information about the indexical linking of this form to preppies and especially preppy girls; meanwhile, qualitative analysis shows that *be all* may also be used by other youth for stance taking and especially for negative evaluation of others. More generally, using interactional methods of discourse analysis combined with attention to linguistic forms, I have demonstrated at various points that stance is a basic building block in the construction of social identities, as speakers display their subjectivity toward their addressee and toward the ongoing talk.

A third linguistic contribution is to focus on linguistic forms in tandem with language ideologies. Sociocultural linguistic scholars have generally given attention either to linguistic structure or to language ideologies rather than considering both together (see discussion in Woolard 2008). The linguistic-anthropological concept of indexicality is a powerful theoretical tool for demonstrating how linguistic forms and practices come to be vested with ideologically mediated social meanings that both enable and constrain identity work. Analysis of specific linguistic features as well as their stylistic clustering helps sociocultural linguists to see how these forms come to be implicated in larger ideologies, such as the explicit racialization of white hip hop fans' speech as inappropriately black or the implicit racialization of white nerds' speech as hyperwhite.

Finally and most fundamentally, this book seeks to contribute to the scholarly understanding of language and identity. Once a marginal issue in many areas of sociocultural linguistics, identity has surged to the forefront of scholarship, yet what is meant by identity and how best to study it are far from settled issues. This diversity of intellectual perspectives is to be encouraged, for it keeps the field dynamic and productive, but inevitably I have my own preferred theories and methods for understanding identity as a sociocultural linguistic phenomenon.

Contributions to language and identity

The approach I take to the linguistic study of identity is rooted in interaction and ethnography. The three themes outlined below sketch the main components of this approach and its advantages for the study of race as a social identity that is largely produced through language.

Identities are built in social interaction

Throughout this book, I have emphasized that race is not imposed by some invisible power but rather is built moment by moment through social – and particularly linguistic – interaction. Face-to-face social interaction is the most immediate site for the construction of social identities of all kinds, for it is there that identity projects are assembled and launched, often through explicit talk about social categories and their associated practices, meanings, and perceived social value. Thus ideologies are not free-floating but are anchored to interaction, where they emerge as socially consequential. European American students at Bay City High School did not think of themselves as white because of some abstract ideological force but because of the countless specific instances of concrete ideological work in which they were interactionally positioned as white by their parents, their teachers, their peers, and many other people besides. Nonlinguistic research on race often takes such specific instances of ideology-in-the-making for granted in its focus on broad historical and cultural processes of racial formation. But it is on the ground, in interaction, that such large-scale processes unfold and have effects on people's lives.

In some interactional forms of discourse analysis, especially conversation analysis, researchers seek to understand the social world from the point of view of participants. Thus researchers do not set out to "find" identity, or power, or other macro social categories and processes in their data. By placing participants' viewpoints at the center of the analysis, interactional researchers hold themselves accountable to making sense of talk in the same way participants do, and they remain mindful of the agentive role of individual social actors in creating and negotiating social meanings – including social identities – for themselves and others. My own analytic practice has been influenced by this general principle.

Examining how identities are interactionally forged also has methodological advantages. Interactional analysts have developed a vast store of tools and insights for addressing how social actions are carried out within talk. This sort of analysis goes well beyond the investigation of discourse content to consider the details of discourse structure; in this book, I go beyond most conversation analysts' concern with this issue to include attention to linguistic structure at lower levels as well. Analyzing talk only for its content, apart from its structural organization and phonological, grammatical, and lexical features, or treating it as a transparent informational record about the speaker, may miss the most significant aspects of many interactions. The tools of interactional analysis allowed me to investigate, for example, precisely how white youth managed the delicate task of talking about race and friendship (such as through colorblind practices like evading explicit mention of race), or how they responded to my request for their ethnoracial self-classification (such as by complying with or challenging the question).

Further, interaction-centered scholarship encourages recognition of the research situation itself as an interactional context that is co-constructed by the researcher and the study participants alike. I have shown throughout the book that it is crucial to take into account the specificity of this context in order to make sense of the data it yields. As a researcher at Bay City High School, I was a social actor in my own right, and what I said and did – what I asked, how I responded, when I spoke, and when I was silent – had a profound influence on the talk and other social activities of the young people with whom I interacted. Unlike much traditional social science research, however, an interactional approach does not seek to eliminate this influence, for it is inevitable in any study in which the researcher has contact with the participants. Rather, interactional analysis aims to acknowledge and examine the effects of the researcher as an integral part of the data.

Social interaction is by and large linguistic interaction, and sociocultural linguistics therefore has an important role to play in understanding how identities are socially constructed. This requires researchers to attend to the rich details of linguistic forms – grammatical, phonological, and lexical – and their indexicalities. Variationist sociolinguistics has produced an extensive body of knowledge regarding the distribution and patterning of linguistic structures across social categories. When combined with the linguistic-anthropological theory of indexicality and with interactional methods of discourse analysis, the examination of such forms within discourse reveals how they are semiotically deployed as part of identity work. This process is seen in the linguistic practices that white teenagers employed to create identity relations of adequation and distinction on the basis of style as well as race. For example, the use of a slang term like *patna* with African American English-influenced pronunciation could index a hip hop style that affiliated with black youth culture, while the use of formal, superstandard grammar could index a nerdy style that repudiated trendy coolness.

The interactional investigation of identity, then, must also be a linguistic investigation in order to capture the full range of resources through which social identities are constructed. But if understanding the semiotic tools that social actors use in constructing their own and others' identities requires the close analysis of linguistic forms, then interpreting the indexicality of those forms requires detailed knowledge of their social meaning within the local context. Ethnography is therefore an important component of the approach I have taken in this book.

Identity is ethnographically situated

Ethnography seeks to arrive at an understanding of culture that is congruent with local perspectives. Like interactional analysis, ethnography requires researchers to set aside their own analytic preconceptions and preoccupations in order to give priority to the viewpoints of study participants. This does not mean substituting the participants' perspectives for scholarly analysis. The goal of ethnography is instead to root the analysis in an understanding of how local social practices that the researcher may initially misinterpret – or fail to see or interpret at all – in fact make sense from the participants' point of view. By the same token, an important component of the ethnographic experience is for researchers to reflect on their own positionality and subjectivity.

This ethnographic principle helped me to think more productively about the racial dynamics of Bay City High. I originally perceived much of European American students' discourse about African Americans as inaccurate, illogical, and sometimes even racist, but as I tried to listen more carefully to what they had to say, I came to understand their feelings of racial fear and resentment even as I strongly disagreed with their perspective on race. The teenagers I talked to were to some extent adopting discourses that they had encountered from their parents, the community, or the media, but they were also constructing racial ideologies that helped them to manage the often uncomfortable situation of being white in a racially divided school. In addition, I gradually saw the ways in which my own whiteness licensed certain kinds of interaction between me and my study participants, and at times perhaps invited the sorts of racial complaints that students reported to me. Ethnographic research thus sheds light on the local uses to which the structures and functions of social interaction may be put, including the discursive practices in which speakers engage and the ideologies that they thereby construct, reproduce, or call into question.

An ethnographic perspective is also necessary in order to interpret local semiotic systems. It is not always immediately evident which resources are recruited for indexical work, and in addition the same or similar semiotic materials may be used in different ways by social actors with distinct goals and identities. It took me several weeks of ethnographic participant-observation, for example, before the indexical practices of most European American hip hop fans were legible to me as markers of a specifically hip hop style. At first the styles of these white boys seemed to me very similar to those adopted by some alternative and preppy youth. I had to learn to read stylistic signs in the same way that teenagers themselves did, by attending to such subtle details as shoe color and the precise degree of bagginess of an individual's jeans as well as how these markers clustered together into locally meaningful stylistic packages.

Ethnography also calls attention to the variability and mobility of social identities, something that cannot be fully uncovered by research methods that rely on brief or superficial contact with study participants, like surveys or traditional social science interviews. During my year of research at Bay City High School, I found that whiteness could be a repository of cultural ideologies as well as a resource for social identities, that it included the accumulation of structural power but also the individual perception of white powerlessness or of whiteness itself as a problematic category. I have given attention to all these different dimensions of whiteness throughout this book, as well as to the points where they intersect, in order to demonstrate that whiteness is neither monolithic nor static but rather stems historically from a shared set of sociopolitical structures and racializing processes. Despite this common source, local forms of whiteness vary according to the historically and culturally specific "racial situations" through which they are constituted (Hartigan 1999). As ethnography demonstrates, there is no single form of whiteness; there are many ways of being white and doing whiteness, and these can change across time and place, as well as being refracted through gender, social class, style, and other factors that shape the kinds of racial lives that people live.

Aspects of identity are not separable from one another

In this book I have focused on three local styles of whiteness among European American students at Bay City High School: the mainstream preppy style, which borrowed covertly from African American cultural sources but remained largely remote from African American youth; the nonmainstream hip hop style, which borrowed openly and heavily from black youth culture; and the mainstream nerdy style, which disengaged from both black and white forms of trendy coolness. The stylistic distinctions that teenagers created through their semiotic practices were thus also a form of racial positioning – a way of constructing different ways of being white, especially in relation to blackness. Moreover, youth styles involved gender positioning as well as racial positioning. Hence preppies embraced hegemonic femininity and masculinity, but nerds rejected these strictly regimented forms of gender. And hip hop fans adopted a style that, while highly contested for white boys, was for the most part not even available for white girls.

At the same time, however, white youth with different stylistic affiliations shared a general repertoire of discursive strategies for talking about race, and such strategies helped to construct a shared racial identity across stylistic differences. These teenagers were also united with one another and with youth of color through their shared identities as high school students and as Californians, although these social categories emerged less often as interactionally salient given that they were not a parameter of difference within the peer social order.

The analysis throughout the book has shown that race is not simply laid on top of these other components of identity (or vice versa). In accordance with the theory of social categories as intersectional rather than additive (Crenshaw 1991), I have presented each sort of identity as part and parcel of the others. After all, white hip hop fans at Bay City High School were not simply hip hop fans who happened to be white, for in the local African American-dominated hip hop scene, white fandom was qualitatively different (at least ideologically and often also in practice) from black fandom. Similarly, white nerds were not simply nerds who happened to be white, for whiteness was ideologically integral to the meaning of nerdiness in the school's ethnoracial order. More generally, the many aspects of an individual's social identity are always intertwined and mutually constituting, and so race – or any other dimension of identity – cannot be studied in isolation.

In this book I have illustrated one approach to studying race as a complex, situated, and variable identity. Using the tools of sociocultural linguistics – particularly interactional discourse analysis, variationist sociolinguistics, and linguistic anthropology – as well as ethnography, I have argued that, in people's everyday lives, whiteness is fundamentally a linguistic and interactional racial project. This fact has implications for the investigation of race and ethnicity.

Contributions to language and race

Race is built through language. From the ethnoracial labels that classify individuals and groups, to the racial ideologies and discourses that perpetuate notions of racialized difference, to the indexical processes that tie race to linguistic practices, language brings race into being as a social reality. All of these linguistic forms in turn arise in the first instance through social interaction, and I have argued that it is only by examining the production of such forms in their discursive context that it is possible to see the workings of the linguistic mechanisms that support racial systems, and especially systems of racial inequity in which whiteness remains hegemonic.

Yet the lived experience of being white is distinct from the concept of whiteness. Theories of whiteness both draw on and abstract away from individual situations in order to make broader generalizations about the nature of race, power, and identity. As a theoretical tool, the notion of whiteness is a reification – an objectification – of the innumerable social processes and practices enacted by white people as part of racial projects. Whiteness, then, only gains its power as a global force through its enactment as a local practical accomplishment: whiteness, like all racial categories, is no more and no less than what people make of it and do with it in specific sociocultural and interactional contexts.

Somewhat paradoxically, it is precisely when white identities are at their least audible – whether because they are so taken for granted by social actors or because they are so deeply problematic in a given context – that the tools of sociocultural linguistics are most useful. Amanda Lewis has cautioned that "research on whiteness must not fall prey to focusing on whites only when they are claiming white identities most loudly or explicitly" (2004: 624). Indeed, race may be at issue even when both researcher and study participant believe they are talking about something else (Best 2003). If theorists of race are correct in their position that whiteness permeates and structures sociopolitical relations at every level, then the effects of this ideological saturation should be evident in what people do and say, even when they are not talking explicitly about race. Hence researchers must find ways to uncover the workings of race empirically without simply stipulating its relevance as a theoretical given. It is here, especially, that sociocultural linguistics can make significant contributions to the study of race.

At Bay City High School, for example, white teenagers sometimes used the term *diverse*, a term that was strongly associated with the school's official discourse of multiculturalism, to describe their racially homogeneous friendship groups, thus attending to stylistic rather than racial difference. I interpreted such redefinitions as a tacit form of "doing" whiteness because of the strongly racialized meaning and valorization of diversity in the local ethnographic context. By the same token, one of the central themes of this book is that the youth styles embraced by European American teenagers are also styles of whiteness, yet most of the time this connection was not articulated in so many words by young people themselves. Nevertheless, whiteness was central to the stylistic practices in which they engaged every day – it was the staging ground for indexical action, the context in which styles took on their local social meanings, as seen in the different racial positionalities of preppiness, hip hop, and nerdiness as white styles vis-à-vis African American youth culture. Thus analyses must be attuned to semiotic practices as well as overt ideological statements in order to make whiteness audible as well as visible. Whiteness therefore has an important role within the interdisciplinary study of language and race.

For the most part, whiteness has not been an explicit focus of research within the various branches of sociocultural linguistics until relatively recently. In variationist sociolinguistics, whiteness has mainly entered analysis as a demographic fact, a category to be correlated with linguistic variables in comparison to other ethnoracial categories. Meanwhile, in some forms of discourse analysis, whiteness has been a more or less taken-for-granted subject position that is used to account for acts of discursive power, rather than examined as a social object constructed through such acts, while in interactional analysis, it has remained mostly unexamined (but see Whitehead and Lerner 2009). In linguistic anthropology, whiteness has primarily figured in research through comparison with the practices of nonwhites in contexts of cultural encounter, yet only rarely has whiteness been thematized and problematized in such studies. More recently, however, sociocultural linguists of various stripes, influenced in part by the study of whiteness in other fields, have begun to attend to this issue as a central research question.

The growing body of linguistic scholarship on whiteness builds on the insights of previous work in sociocultural linguistics while extending these findings in new directions. A focus on whiteness, for example, encourages a closer look at language use that has often been seen as marginal, such as the nonfluent use of a linguistic variety by outgroup members. Among European American hip hop fans at Bay City High, the emblematic use of features of African American Vernacular English was highly idiosyncratic and by no means systematic. Such practices differed considerably from the use of AAVE by fluent speakers, as documented by a substantial body of sociolinguistic scholarship. Yet the wealth of knowledge provided by this research tradition enabled me to recognize the often subtle ways in which white hip hop fans adjusted their speech toward an African American linguistic norm. It is precisely the ability of these relatively small linguistic moves to be semiotically meaningful that is important for the understanding of language as a social phenomenon. The social evaluation of such language use by others also demonstrates that there may be competing language ideologies even in a very small place like a single high school, for white hip hop fans' ideology of their semiotic practices as stylistic and not racialized was contested by other students at the school.

As a social construct, race must be sustained not only through the workings of large institutional structures but through the everyday practices of ordinary people. Given the inevitable racialization of all members of American society, each of us is engaged in racial projects of one kind or another. Youth, too, are racial agents. Far from simply being buffeted by racial ideologies beyond their control, young people actively engage these ideologies in their constructions of race as a social reality. I have discussed the many ways that European American teenagers' racial agency supported the existing racial order and dominant racial ideologies of Bay City High School as well as of the United States more generally. But I have also shown that these teenagers did not all do whiteness in the same way. The variability of whiteness in different contexts provides some traction for alternative ways of constructing race.

Doing and redoing whiteness

There were various moments in my research when European American youth enacted whiteness in ways that facilitated racial equity and thus presented a counterdiscourse to local and nationally dominant ideologies of race. Rather than simply "doing" whiteness according to established racialized patterns, these young people were "redoing" whiteness – rethinking it, reshaping it. These counterdiscursive forms of whiteness were not specific to a particular youth style: at different times preppy teenagers, nerds, and hip hop fans all engaged in practices that seemed to offer some leverage for dislodging hegemonic whiteness in favor of a more productive engagement with race.

For example, in their discussion of why they didn't have black friends, the preppy girls Josie and Zoe showed some awareness (however limited) of the structural factors that perpetuate racial asymmetries. Though insufficient in itself as a basis for reworking race and whiteness, the girls' talk about differential access to education could, if fostered, provide a starting point for such a process. One of the limitations of such talk for significantly altering racial ideologies and realities was Josie and Zoe's reluctance to acknowledge their own race as a factor in the greater material advantages they had accrued. Nevertheless, their remarks created a small crack in the wall of whiteness, one that could be widened through ongoing discussions of race and the unequal distribution of socioeconomic resources.

Another example of a potentially transformative form of whiteness was the nerd boy Erich's leadership in organizing demonstrations against Proposition 209, the ballot initiative to abolish affirmative action in California's public universities and state agencies. Erich was not otherwise deeply engaged in political activism, and his own extremely nerdy style was viewed by other students as antithetical to blackness. But he felt strongly that affirmative action was an important tool for correcting the nation's history of racial injustice, and he displayed that belief in a very public way. Erich's racial agency was in sharp contrast to many of the school's white hip hop fans, who did not share his political commitment despite their stylistic investment in black youth culture. Although the proposition ultimately became California law, Erich's involvement in the protests against its passage laid the groundwork for his and other European Americans' possible long-term engagement in direct political action around racial issues.

A third instance of progressive racial agency was seen in the friendship group that included the European American hip hop fans Al Capone and Shawn along with a number of boys of color. This hip hop crew prided itself on the ethnoracial diversity of its membership, which sharply distinguished it from many other white students' friendship groups, given the school's ideologies and practices of racial division. Perhaps not coincidentally, the crew's active engagement in hip hop through graffiti art went well beyond consumption of hip hop's cultural products and appropriation of its semiotic practices by most white fans. For these boys, then, hip hop culture achieved some of its potential to transcend barriers and unify youth around a shared social movement (Alim 2009).

In addition to these three cases, it is likely that the white youth I came to know over the course of my fieldwork at Bay City High School had more complex views of race than are reflected in my research. Even students whose race talk reproduced dominant ideologies in one way or another might not have been strongly committed to these ideologies and might have been open to other ways of interpreting their situation. Moreover, teenagers' ideas about race may have changed over time. My research necessarily documented only a small portion of their lives, and if I had been able to follow them throughout high school and beyond, or into other settings like their homes, churches and synagogues, and after-school jobs, the picture of these young people's racial agency would have been correspondingly more complex. The representation I offer here, then, is by no means a complete account of how European American youth at Bay City High talked about, thought about, and enacted race.

This raises a final issue of racial agency: my own. In planning and carrying out my fieldwork, in analyzing the data, and in writing up the results, I had a tremendous amount of power to shape the ethnographic situation and to represent what emerged. And my power as a researcher was compounded by my whiteness. Like many European American students at Bay City High, I did not experience myself as powerful during the research process. I often felt uncertain about my project and about my relationship with the young people who participated in it. Given the many ways in which I differed from these teenagers, especially in age but often also in my own style of whiteness, our shared racial identity was one resource through which we could achieve adequation with one another. This situation once again had the potential for a transformative reworking of whiteness through a sustained and open dialogue about race. Yet my reluctance to engage my study participants directly on racial topics – in part due to my cognizance that race was an especially fraught issue at Bay City High School – caused me to miss some opportunities to learn more about students' perspectives on racial issues as well as to offer an alternative point of view. I remain ambivalent about whether I should have tried to provide such a viewpoint, for regardless of my good intentions it would have been simply one more racial discourse among the many others in which these young people were immersed, and it would also have been difficult to reconcile with my ethnographic commitment to understand teenagers' racial perspectives rather than to impose my own.

To be sure, these possible or actual moments of intervention into whiteness-as-usual are very small acts of racial agency. Even in the best of circumstances, the politically progressive racial agency of isolated individuals has limited potential to effect larger-scale change at the societal or institutional level. But as these individuals engage with one another in social interaction and come together in larger groupings, they speak with a louder voice, making audible new, more equitable, forms of racial discourse.

The changing face of race

Since the time of my fieldwork, much has changed in Bay City High School, in California, and in the nation. Public discourse about the school has moved away from a concern with "self-segregation" and racial conflict to a focus on educational inequities and the dismantling of the highly racialized tracking system. A host of pedagogical innovations have been introduced in hopes of creating a more stimulating educational experience for all students. Despite this general shift from a discourse of fear and resentment to a discourse of educational equality, some white community members continue to worry that the presence of large numbers of black students at the school will lead to budgetary strain and racialized violence.

Meanwhile, Latinos have surpassed African Americans as the largest minority both in the state and in the nation, though not yet in Bay City itself, nor in Bay City High School. If present demographic trends continue, however, it is likely that Bay City High will have a very different ethnoracial composition in coming years, and some of the issues that have been playing out mainly between African American and European American students may instead become central to a three-way relation among blacks, whites, and Latinos, with Asian Americans figuring in crucial ways as well.

The reconfiguration of the demographic contours of both California and the United States complicates the longstanding US racial ideology focused on a black–white color line. But Jonathan Warren and France Winddance Twine

(1997) argue that even in the nation's rapidly changing ethnoracial order, the ideological poles of blackness and whiteness remain. Thus blackness continues to be a defining point of difference for whiteness.

The present era is marked by another important shift in the relation between blackness and whiteness: the election of Barack Obama as the nation's first African American president. A number of commentators asserted early on that with Obama's inauguration, the United States had entered a new "postracial" era. But despite such claims, the racial issues with which this book is concerned are far from resolved. The 2008 election and the national upheavals since that time show that race remains very much on the minds of voters, commentators, and politicians themselves. During the election, Obama's racially mixed heritage and perceptions of his racial loyalties were frequent topics of discussion and debate among blacks and whites alike. His racial style was much discussed, as well as the pivotal role of language in its construction. And while on Election Day he won a majority of young European American voters, whites were the only ethnoracial group in which he did not win a majority of the overall electorate.

As the son of a black man from Kenya and a white woman from Kansas, Obama has often been said to "transcend" race. But not even the President of the United States can transcend Americans' long-entrenched racial ideologies that the child of one black parent and one white parent is considered black, not white. Obama's ethnoracial classification is a cultural vestige of a racial system formerly enshrined in US law as the "one-drop rule." To the extent that Obama transcends race, then, it is not in his person but in his politics and his policies.

Although the Bay City High School of the mid-1990s and the nation's racial hopes for the 2008 election year are now in the past, they both contribute to the racial conditions and projects of the present. In the preceding chapters I have attempted to make sense of race in one California high school at a specific historical moment, and to demonstrate how European American students' ethnoracial identities and ideologies were shaped by and gave shape to the other identity work – of style, gender, class, and much more besides – that they carried out in that time and place. I have particularly tried to highlight the often overlooked but central role of language in this process. This book, then, is in effect a way of turning up the volume on whiteness. By calling attention to language as a key resource for producing and reproducing the social world, it aims to make white racial identities, in all their complexity and variability, more audible.

Notes

1 WHITE STYLES: LANGUAGE, RACE, AND YOUTH IDENTITIES

1. All names for people and places in this book are pseudonyms. In many cases, study participants chose their own pseudonyms. Other identifying information has also been changed.

2 LISTENING TO WHITENESS: RESEARCHING LANGUAGE AND RACE IN A CALIFORNIA HIGH SCHOOL

1. Attempting to obtain more detailed and up-to-date records from the school district several years later, I was told that all student demographic information from 1995–96 had been lost.
2. Southeast Asian American students were of Cambodian, Laotian, and Vietnamese descent. East Asian American students were of Chinese, Japanese, and Korean descent. There were very few South Asian American students (e.g., those of Indian or Pakistani descent) at the school.
3. Ms. Stein encouraged her students to call her *Olivia*, but typically only white students did so; most students of color called her *Ms. Stein* or *Miss Stein*, or sometimes *Miss Olivia*. I refer to her as *Ms. Stein*, in keeping with most students' practice.

3 CLIQUES, CROWDS, AND CREWS: SOCIAL LABELS IN RACIAL SPACE

1. Age may have been a factor in teachers' tendency to overlook students' stylistic practices. I spent more time with older, more experienced teachers than with younger ones. Novice teachers who had only recently left behind their own high school experience may have been more attuned to youth styles.
2. I never heard any accusations of "acting Asian" or "acting Latino," perhaps because of the smaller size and hence lesser ideological salience of these groups at Bay City High.
3. The concept of coolness originated in African and African American culture, where it refers to the presentation of self as calm and in control (Morgan 1998). More generally, *cool* is a slang term of remarkable longevity that can be used as a positive evaluative term for persons, objects, or situations (R. Moore 2004).

4. White hip hop fans tended to describe their style via practices rather than labels, while their peers labeled them with insulting terms such as *wannabes* or (mocking) hip hop slang like *G's* or *homies*. See note 6 below.
5. In Chapter 10, I examine how individual Jewish students interactionally negotiated the question of ethnoracial classification.
6. The term *G's* (literally, 'gangsters') was often derisively used for white hip hop fans at Bay City High. The term *TAGGERS*, which appears near *G's* in Figure 3.1b, is not necessarily associated with a hip hop style nor with black youth, despite its origins as a hip hop practice. As discussed in the case of Acme in example (1), tagging was a practice in which alternative white teenagers also engaged.
7. One exception, which is not racially marked in Figure 3.1a, is the inclusion of "BCP" (Bay City Posse), an African American group that European American students considered a gang. This detail may have been included due to the adjacency of this group to Mark and his friends, at least in the morning (*IN AM*).
8. John Doe does not label this area ethnoracially, and his lack of familiarity with the group was evident in his pronunciation of *XIV* as letters of the alphabet rather than as a numeral.
9. *African American Vernacular English* refers to a specific linguistic variety that features ethnoracially distinctive grammar, phonology, and lexicon. *African American English* is used here as a cover term for all ethnoracially distinctive linguistic varieties spoken by African Americans, including those that feature Standard English grammar and distinctively African American phonology and/or lexis.

4 SAY WORD?: RACE AND STYLE IN WHITE TEENAGE SLANG

1. This example also illustrates the cultural authority of African American students at Bay City High. Calvin, a not particularly cool black boy, is the first to mock Priscilla for her outmoded slang use, triggering similar teasing from white students, yet the term *stoned* (and related words like *stoner*) still held currency among cool European American teenagers at the school.
2. *Hella* was not considered profanity. Surprisingly, given that *nigga* is a highly controversial and often taboo term, as discussed below, it was not censored by the yearbook's faculty advisor. It may have been overlooked because of the variety of nonstandard spellings used for the word as well as because yearbook messages were often dense and hard to read, with spaces between words removed by their authors in order to squeeze as much text as possible into the limited allotted space.
3. Latina and Latino students rarely used the term in their yearbook messages, which were often composed in Spanish.
4. Mel, who is memorialized in many yearbook messages, was an African American boy from the same age cohort as the graduating class who died toward the end of junior year.
5. *Break yourself* is much more widely recognized than used, and so knowledge of the phrase does not indicate an individual's involvement in criminal activity. However, the expression held racialized associations for at least some speakers. After Brand One offered a definition he added, "A big person like George would say it, not a little person like me." Because George was not only tall and muscular but also African American, this remark may invoke a racial stereotype of African American males as

criminally inclined. See also Bucholtz (1999a) and Chapter 9 on Brand One's narration of racialized violence.

6. More recently, *wacked* has spread among upper-middle-class suburban European American youth in Southern California and white adult speakers in the national popular media.

5 I'M LIKE YEAH BUT SHE'S ALL NO: INNOVATIVE QUOTATIVE MARKERS AND PREPPY WHITENESS

1. For research on changes in the US English quotative system, see Barbieri (2007); Blyth *et al.* (1990); Cukor-Avila (2002); Dailey-O'Cain (2000); Ferrara and Bell (1995); and Romaine and Lange (1991). Studies of quotatives in other varieties of English include Buchstaller (2006a); Macaulay (2001); Stenström *et al.* (2002); Tagliamonte and D'Arcy (2004, 2007); Tagliamonte and Hudson (1999); and Winter (2002).
2. In a study of Californians' views of language in their state (Bucholtz *et al.* 2007), the most frequently mentioned linguistic item was the slang term *hella* (47.4%), with *dude* a distant second (6.5%). *Like* (without any distinction between quotative and discourse marker functions) was the third most often mentioned (5.0%).
3. Null quotatives, or quoted speech not introduced by a quotative marker (e.g., *She called them up. "So when are we going?"*), and the use of *like* without the copula (e.g., *You always see people like, "Didn't I have history with you freshman year?"*) were excluded from the analysis, as were a few other specialized quotatives such as *think*.
4. The statistical method used was Hierarchical Configural Frequency Analysis (HCFA), a statistical procedure used to explore multidimensional frequency tables. HCFAs are based on regular chi-square tests and involve corrections for multiple post hoc tests (von Eye 1990). My thanks to Stefan Gries for his invaluable aid with the statistical analysis.
5. For preppies' use of *be all*, Holm-adjusted $p < 0.001$, $q = 0.031$; for preppy girls' use of *be all*, Holm-adjusted $p < 0.001$; $q = 0.032$.
6. In Waksler's data, *be all* also characterizes a particular state or condition, as seen in line 49 of example (7): *and they're all jealous.*
7. For preppy teenagers, Holm-adjusted $p < 0.001$, $q = 0.024$. For nonpreppy teenagers, Holm-adjusted $p < 0.001$, $q = 0.039$.

6 PRETTY FLY FOR A WHITE GUY: EUROPEAN AMERICAN HIP HOP FANS AND AFRICAN AMERICAN ENGLISH

1. My data from Eddie are limited to his speech in Life and Health class, where, as noted above, he often adopted the role of class clown, and hence many of his statements were designed to amuse other students. In particular, the content of the first two examples is rather sensationalistic, since they focus on Eddie's authoritative statements about alcohol abuse and sex, respectively. I undoubtedly paid more attention to Eddie's outrageous comments than to his more neutral remarks and tended to document the former more than the latter in my fieldnotes.
2. The phenomenon of overshooting a community's speech norm is traditionally called *hypercorrection* (Labov 1972c), a term also used for overgeneralizing a linguistic rule, often due to prescriptive pressure. John Baugh (1992) uses the term

hypocorrection when the reference variety of supercorrection/hypercorrection is a nonstandard dialect such as AAVE.

7 WE'RE THROUGH BEING COOL: WHITE NERDS, SUPERSTANDARD ENGLISH, AND THE REJECTION OF TRENDINESS

1. I was not aware of any openly gender-bending boys at the school, although one boy in my study made a number of comments to me that suggested he was gay and/or transgender.
2. Of course, careful articulation does not have only one social meaning (cf. Benor 2001; Eckert 2003, 2008; Podesva *et al.* 2001).
3. For additional social meanings of (ing) see Campbell-Kibler (2007); Fischer (1958); Kiesling (1998).
4. "Kumbaya" is a standard folk song that was newly popularized in the 1960s and thus came to be associated with the hippie era.
5. As a result of this ideology, youth of color who engaged in nerdy practices were often understood by other students to be aligned with whiteness or "acting white," although they did not view themselves in this way. Ada, the sole Asian American member of Random Reigns Supreme, did not generally participate in the nerdy practices central to the group; her (rather peripheral) membership was due to her friendship with Bob (Bucholtz 2009a).

8 "NOT THAT I'M RACIST": STRATEGIES OF COLORBLINDNESS IN TALK ABOUT RACE AND FRIENDSHIP

1. Race and ethnicity are not necessarily distinguished in such research or in the data it analyzes, given the particular ethnoracial configuration of the United States and other nations in which such research has been carried out.

9 WHITE ON BLACK: NARRATIVES OF RACIAL FEAR AND RESENTMENT

1. A few middle-class East Asian American students also discussed racial issues with me, but in the binary racial logic of the school these students were widely understood as aligned with whites rather than blacks, and their stories often reproduced this division by highlighting their fear of African Americans. Moreover, no African American students spoke to me about interracial conflict, although I sometimes overheard discussions of the topic in classrooms or the schoolyard.
2. This technique has been critiqued for perpetuating racial stereotypes (Morgan 1994), and the elicitation of dramatic narratives in general has been found to be methodologically problematic (e.g., Butters 2000; Wolfson 1976). This early work is important, however, for establishing narrative analysis within linguistics, and it continues to be influential.
3. Christine's reference to herself as a *girl* is not necessarily gendered in the same way that *white* is racialized, for person reference in English often requires gender specification (Kitzinger 2007).

4. Christine seems to interpret my phrase *hip hop crowd* as a physical grouping of (black) people (*if I know somebody in the crowd*; line 35) rather than as a social group with a shared style. Bay City High's classrooms, hallways, and grounds were densely packed with students, and this experience of physical overcrowding may have been more salient to Christine (especially given her small size) than the stylistic meaning of *crowd*.
5. Although white girls at the school also got into fights, the European American girls who were interested in participating in this study were mostly middle-class, academically oriented students who did not seek to gain peer prestige through displays of toughness. One Southeast Asian American girl, a former gang member, told me a number of fight stories, though not with a focus on participants' race.
6. Puerto Ricans were a very small segment of the total Latino population at Bay City High School, which itself was only 10 percent of the student body. The relative rarity of Puerto Ricans in California compared to Mexican Americans and other Latino groups may have enabled Nico to claim an authentic ethnic identity that elsewhere could have been difficult for him to assert without challenge.

10 "I GUESS I'M WHITE": ETHNORACIAL LABELS AND THE PROBLEM OF WHITENESS

1. The classroom activity on "interracial romance" discussed in Chapter 8 took place on the same day.
2. Likewise, I usually used the term *sex* rather than *gender* in asking for this personal information, in part because it is more common in bureaucratic forms and thus was likely to be more familiar to students.
3. Claiming whiteness may have been especially difficult for students of mixed heritage. Another girl whom I knew to be of mixed race classified herself as black in our interview and went to great lengths to keep her peers from learning that her father was in fact white. Bay City High School students of African and European descent whose parents were considered to be of different races were often understood as "mixed" rather than black or white; they could also be classified simply as black.
4. Neither Erich nor Claire mentioned their Jewishness in answer to the ethnicity question, but this information came up in other interactions.

References

Agha, Asif (2007). *Language and social relations*. Cambridge: Cambridge University Press.

Alba, Richard D. (1990). *Ethnic identity: The transformation of white America*. New Haven: Yale University Press.

Alim, H. Samy (2004a). *You know my steez: An ethnographic and sociolinguistic study of styleshifting in a Black American speech community*. Publication of the American Dialect Society 89. Durham, NC: Duke University Press.

(2004b). Hip Hop Nation Language. In Edward Finegan & John R. Rickford, eds., *Language in the USA: Themes for the twenty-first century*. Cambridge: Cambridge University Press. 387–409.

(2006). *Roc the mic right: The language of hip hop culture*. New York: Routledge.

(2009). Translocal style communities: Hip Hop youth as cultural theorists of style, language, and globalization. *Pragmatics* 19(1): 103–127.

Alim, H. Samy, Awad Ibrahim, & Alastair Pennycook, eds. (2008). *Global linguistic flows: Hip Hop Cultures, youth identities, and the politics of language*. London: Routledge.

Anderegg, David (2007). *Nerds: Who they are and why we need more of them*. New York: Penguin.

Anderson, Kate T. (2008). Justifying race talk: Indexicality and the social construction of race and linguistic value. *Journal of Linguistic Anthropology* 18(1): 108–129.

Androutsopoulos, Jannis K. (2000). Non-standard spellings in media texts: The case of German fanzines. *Journal of Sociolinguistics* 4(4): 514–533.

Antaki, Charles, Hanneke Houtkoop-Steenstra, & Mark Rapley (2000). "Brilliant. Next question . . .": High-grade assessment sequences in the completion of interactional units. *Research on Language and Social Interaction* 33(3): 235–262.

Antaki, Charles, & Sue Widdicombe, eds. (1998). *Identities in talk*. London: Sage.

Armour, Jody David (1997). *Negrophobia and reasonable racism: The hidden costs of being black in America*. New York: New York University Press.

Ash, Sharon, & John Myhill (1986). Linguistic correlates of interethnic contact. In David Sankoff, ed., *Diversity and diachrony*. Philadelphia: John Benjamins. 33–43.

Atkinson, J. Maxwell, & Paul Drew (1979). *Order in court: The organisation of verbal interaction in judicial settings*. London: Macmillan.

Bakht, Maryam M. (2010). Lexical variation and the negotiation of linguistic style(s) in a Long Island middle school. Unpublished Ph.D. dissertation, New York University, Department of Linguistics.

Bakhtin, M. M. (1981). *The dialogic imagination*. Austin: University of Texas Press.

(1984). *Problems of Dostoevsky's poetics*. Minneapolis: University of Minnesota Press.

Bannister, Matthew (2006). *White boys, white noise: Masculinities and 1980s indie guitar rock*. Burlington, VT: Ashgate.

Barbieri, Federica (2007). Older men and younger women: A corpus-based study of quotative use in American English. *English World-Wide* 28(1): 23–45.

Barrett, Rusty (1999). Indexing polyphonous identity in the speech of African American drag queens. In Mary Bucholtz, A. C. Liang, & Laurel A. Sutton, eds., *Reinventing identities: The gendered self in discourse*. New York: Oxford University Press. 313–331.

(2006). Language ideology and racial inequality: Competing functions of Spanish in an Anglo-owned Mexican restaurant. *Language in Society* 35(2): 163–204.

Basso, Keith H. (1979). *Portraits of "the whiteman": Linguistic play and cultural symbols among the Western Apache*. Cambridge: Cambridge University Press.

Baugh, John (1991). The politicization of changing terms of self-reference among American slave descendants. *American Speech* 66(2): 133–146.

(1992). Hypocorrection: Mistakes in production of vernacular African American English as a second dialect. *Language and Communication* 12(3/4): 317–326.

Behar, Ruth, & Deborah A. Gordon, eds. (1995). *Women writing culture*. Berkeley: University of California Press.

Benor, Sarah Bunin (2001). The learned /t/: Phonological variation in Orthodox Jewish English. In Tara Sanchez & Daniel Ezra Johnson, eds., *Penn Working Papers in Linguistics: Selected Papers from NWAV 29*. Philadelphia: Department of Linguistics, University of Pennsylvania. 1–16.

Berubé, Allan (2001). How gay stays white and what kind of white it stays. In Birgit Brander Rasmussen, Eric Klinenberg, Irene J. Nexica, & Matt Wray, eds., *The making and unmaking of whiteness*. Durham, NC: Duke University Press. 234–265.

Besnier, Niko (1992). Reported speech and affect on Nukulaelae Atoll. In Jane H. Hill & Judith T. Irvine, eds., *Responsibility and evidence in oral discourse*. Cambridge: Cambridge University Press. 161–181.

Best, Amy L. (2000). *Prom night: Youth, schools, and popular culture*. New York: Routledge.

(2003). Doing race in the context of feminist interviewing: Constructing whiteness through talk. *Qualitative Inquiry* 9(6): 895–914.

Best, Amy L., ed. (2007). *Representing youth: Methodological issues in critical youth studies*. New York: New York University Press.

Bex, Tony, & Richard J. Watts, eds. (1999). *Standard English: The widening debate*. London: Routledge.

Biber, Douglas (1988). *Variation across speech and writing*. Cambridge: Cambridge University Press.

Billig, Michael (1988). The notion of "prejudice": Some rhetorical and ideological aspects. *Text* 8: 91–110.

(2001). Humour and hatred: The racist jokes of the Ku Klux Klan. *Discourse and Society* 12(3): 267–289.

Birnbach, Lisa, ed. (1980). *The official preppy handbook*. New York: Workman.

Bluestein, Gene (1989). *Anglish-Yinglish: Yiddish in American life and literature*. Athens: University of Georgia Press.

Blyth, Carl, Sigrid Recktenwald, & Jenny Wang (1990). I'm like, "Say what?!": A new quotative in American oral narrative. *American Speech* 65(3): 215–227.

Bonfiglio, Thomas Paul (2002). *Race and the rise of Standard American*. Berlin: Mouton de Gruyter.

Bonilla-Silva, Eduardo (2003). *Racism without racists: Color-blind racism and the persistence of racial inequality in the United States*. New York: Rowman & Littlefield.

Bonilla-Silva, Eduardo, & Tyrone A. Forman (2000). "I am not a racist but . . .": Mapping white college students' racial ideology in the USA. *Discourse and Society* 11: 50–85.

Briggs, Charles L. (1986). *Learning how to ask: A sociolinguistic appraisal of the role of the interview in social science research*. Cambridge: Cambridge University Press.

Brodkin, Karen (1998). *How Jews became white folks and what that says about race in America*. New Brunswick: Rutgers University Press.

Brown, Michael K., Martin Carnoy, Elliott Currie, Troy Duster, & David B. Oppenheimer (2003). *Whitewashing race: The myth of a color-blind society*. Berkeley: University of California Press.

Bucholtz, Mary (1995). From mulatta to mestiza: Passing and the linguistic reshaping of ethnic identity. In Kira Hall & Mary Bucholtz, eds., *Gender articulated: Language and the socially constructed self*. New York: Routledge. 351–373.

(1999a). You da man: Narrating the racial other in the linguistic production of white masculinity. *Journal of Sociolinguistics* 3(4): 443–460.

(1999b). "Why be normal?": Language and identity practices in a community of nerd girls. *Language in Society* 28(2): 203–223.

(2000). The politics of transcription. *Journal of Pragmatics* 32: 1439–1465.

(2001). The whiteness of nerds: Superstandard English and racial markedness. *Journal of Linguistic Anthropology* 11(1): 84–100.

(2002a). Youth and cultural practice. *Annual Review of Anthropology* 31: 525–552.

(2002b). Play, identity, and linguistic representation in the performance of accent. In Kate Henning, Nicole Netherton, & Leighton Peterson, eds., *Proceedings of the ninth Symposium about Language and Society – Austin*. Austin: University of Texas Department of Linguistics. 227–251. www.utexas.edu/students/salsa/salsa proceedings/salsa9/papers/bucholtz.pdf

(2007a). Shop talk: Branding, consumption, and gender in American middle-class youth interaction. In Bonnie McElhinny, ed., *Words, worlds, and material girls: Language, gender, globalization*. Berlin: Mouton de Gruyter. 371–402.

(2007b). Variation in transcription. *Discourse Studies* 9(6): 784–808.

(2009a). Styles and stereotypes: The linguistic negotiation of identity among Laotian American youth. In Angela Reyes & Adrienne Lo, eds., *Beyond yellow English: Toward a linguistic anthropology of Asian Pacific America*. New York: Oxford University Press. 21–42.

(2009b). From stance to style: Gender, interaction, and indexicality in Mexican immigrant youth slang. In Alexandra Jaffe, ed., *Stance: Sociolinguistic perspectives*. New York: Oxford University Press. 146–170.

Bucholtz, Mary, Nancy Bermudez, Lisa Edwards, Victor Fung, & Rosalva Vargas (2007). Hella Nor Cal or totally So Cal?: The perceptual dialectology of California. *Journal of English Linguistics* 35(4): 325–352.

Bucholtz, Mary, & Kira Hall (2004). Theorizing identity in language and sexuality research. *Language in Society* 33(4): 501–547.

(2005). Identity and interaction: A sociocultural linguistic approach. *Discourse Studies* 7(4–5): 585–614.

(2008). All of the above: New coalitions in sociocultural linguistics. *Journal of Sociolinguistics* 12(4): 401–431.

Buchstaller, Isabelle (2003). The co-occurrence of quotatives with mimetic performances. *Edinburgh Working Papers in Applied Linguistics* 12: 1–9.

(2006a). Diagnostics of age-graded linguistic behaviour: The case of the quotative system. *Journal of Sociolinguistics* 10(1): 3–30.

(2006b). Social stereotypes, personality traits and regional perception displaced: Attitudes towards the "new" quotatives in the U.K. *Journal of Sociolinguistics* 10(3): 362–381.

Bulmer, Martin, & John Solomos, eds. (2004). *Researching race and racism*. London: Routledge.

Bush, Melanie E. L. (2004). *Breaking the code of good intentions: Everyday forms of whiteness*. Lanham, MD: Rowman & Littlefield.

Butler, Judith (1990). *Gender trouble: Feminism and the subversion of identity.* New York: Routledge.

Butters, Ronald R. (1980). Narrative *go* 'say'. *American Speech* 55: 304–307.

(1982). Editor's note. *American Speech* 57: 149.

(2000). Conversational anomalies in eliciting danger-of-death narratives. *Southern Journal of Linguistics* 24(1): 69–81.

Campbell-Kibler, Kathryn (2007). Accent, (ING) and the social logic of listener perceptions. *American Speech* 82(1): 32–64.

Chafe, Wallace L. (1982). Integration and involvement in speaking, writing, and oral literature. In Deborah Tannen, ed., *Spoken and written language: Exploring orality and literacy.* Norwood, NJ: Ablex. 35–53.

Childs, Becky, & Christine Mallinson (2006). The significance of lexical items in the construction of ethnolinguistic identity: A case study of adolescent spoken and online language. *American Speech* 81(1): 3–30.

Christian-Smith, Linda (1990). *Becoming a woman through romance*. New York: Routledge.

Chun, Elaine W. (2001). The construction of white, black, and Korean American identities through African American Vernacular English. *Journal of Linguistic Anthropology* 11(1): 52–64.

(2007). "Oh my god!": Stereotypical words at the intersection of sound, practice, and social meaning. Paper presented at the annual conference on New Ways of Analyzing Variation, Philadelphia, October.

Clifford, James, & George E. Marcus, eds. (1986). *Writing culture: The poetics and politics of ethnography.* Berkeley: University of California Press.

Collins, Patricia Hill (2005). *Black sexual politics: African Americans, gender, and the new racism*. New York: Routledge.

Connell, R. W. (1995). *Masculinities*. Berkeley: University of California Press.

Cooper, Robert (1996). Detracking reform in an urban California high school: Improving the schooling experiences of African American students. *Journal of Negro Education* 65(2): 190–208.

Coupland, Nikolas (2001). Dialect stylization in radio talk. *Language in Society* 30(3): 345–375.

(2007). *Style: Language variation and identity.* Cambridge: Cambridge University Press.

Crenshaw, Kimberlé W. (1991). Mapping the margins: Intersectionality, identity politics, and violence against women of color. *Stanford Law Review* 43(6): 1241–1299.

Cukor-Avila, Patricia (2002). She say, she go, she be like: Verbs of quotation over time in African American Vernacular English. *American Speech* 77(1): 3–31.

Cutler, Cecelia A. (1999). Yorkville crossing: White teens, hip hop, and African American English. *Journal of Sociolinguistics* 3(4): 428–442.

(2003a). "Keepin' it real": White hip-hoppers' discourses of language, race, and authenticity. *Journal of Linguistic Anthropology* 13(2): 211–233.

(2003b). The authentic speaker revisited: A look at ethnic perception data from white hip hoppers. *University of Pennsylvania Working Papers in Linguistics* 9(2): 49–60.

Dailey-O'Cain, Jennifer (2000). The sociolinguistic distribution of and attitudes toward focuser *like* and quotative *like*. *Journal of Sociolinguistics* 4(1): 60–80.

Daley, Mike (2003). "Why do whites sing black?": The blues, whiteness and early histories of rock. *Popular Music and Society* 26(2): 161–167.

D'Arcy, Alex (2007). *Like* and language ideology: Disentangling fact from fiction. *American Speech* 82(4): 386–419.

De Fina, Anna (2000). Orientation in immigrant narratives: The role of ethnicity in the identification of characters. *Discourse Studies* 2(2): 131–157.

(2003). *Identity in narrative: A study of immigrant discourse*. Amsterdam: John Benjamins.

Derrida, Jacques (1976). *Of grammatology*. Baltimore: Johns Hopkins University Press.

Devine, John (1995). Can metal detectors replace the panopticon? *Cultural Anthropology* 10(2): 171–195.

Domínguez, Virginia R. (1986). *White by definition: Social classification in Creole Louisiana*. New Brunswick, NJ: Rutgers University Press.

Du Bois, John W. (2007). The stance triangle. In Robert Englebretson, ed., *Stancetaking in discourse: Subjectivity, evaluation, interaction*. Amsterdam: John Benjamins. 139–182.

Dyer, Richard (1997). *White*. London: Routledge.

Dyson, Michael Eric ([1996] 2004). We never were what we used to be: Black youth, pop culture, and the politics of nostalgia. In *The Michael Eric Dyson reader*. New York: Basic Civitas Books. 418–440.

Eble, Connie (2004). Slang. In Edward Finegan & John R. Rickford, eds., *Language in the USA: Themes for the twenty-first century*. Cambridge: Cambridge University Press. 375–386.

Eckert, Penelope (1989). *Jocks and Burnouts: Social categories and identity in the high school*. New York: Teachers College Press.

(1996). Vowels and nail polish: The emergence of linguistic style in the preadolescent heterosexual marketplace. In Natasha Warner, Jocelyn Ahlers, Leela Bilmes, Monica Oliver, Suzanne Wertheim, & Melinda Chen, eds., *Gender and belief systems: Proceedings of the fourth Berkeley Women and Language Conference*. Berkeley: Berkeley Women and Language Group. 183–190.

(2000). *Linguistic variation as social practice*. Oxford: Blackwell.

(2003). The meaning of style. In Wai Fong Chiang, Elaine Chun, Laura Mahalingappa, & Siri Mehus, eds., *SALSA XI: Proceedings of the eleventh annual*

Symposium about Language and Society – Austin (*Texas Linguistic Forum* 47). Austin: University of Texas Department of Linguistics. 41–53.

(2004). Sound change and gendered personae on the preadolescent social market. Paper presented at the third meeting of the International Gender and Language Association, Cornell University, June.

(2008). Variation and the indexical field. *Journal of Sociolinguistics* 12(4): 453–476.

Eder, Donna, Catherine Colleen Evans, & Stephen Parker (1995). *School talk: Gender and adolescent culture*. New Brunswick: Rutgers University Press.

Edley, Nigel, & Margaret Wetherell (1997). Jockeying for position: The construction of masculine identities. *Discourse and Society* 8(2): 203–217.

Ehrlich, Susan, & Jack Sidnell (2006). "I think that's not an assumption you ought to make": Challenging presuppositions in inquiry testimony. *Language in Society* 35(5): 655–676.

Eng, David L. (2000). *Racial castration: Managing masculinity in Asian America*. Durham, NC: Duke University Press.

Erman, Britt (1997). "Guy's just such a dickhead": The context and function of *just* in teenage talk. In Ulla-Britt Kostsinas, Anna-Brita Stenström, & Anna-Malin Karlsson, eds., *Ungdomsspråk i Norden*. Stockholm: Institutionen för Nordiska Språk. 82–95.

Espiritu, Yen Le (1997). *Asian American women and men: Labor, laws, and love*. Thousand Oaks, CA: Sage.

Essed, Philomena (1990). *Everyday racism: Reports from women of two cultures*. Claremont, CA: Hunter House.

Evaldsson, Ann-Carita (2005). Staging insults and mobilizing categorizations in a multi-ethnic peer group. *Discourse and Society* 16(6): 763–786.

Fairclough, Norman (2003). "Political correctness": The politics of culture and language. *Discourse and Society* 14(1): 17–28.

Feagin, Joe R., & Hernán Vera (1995). *White racism: The basics*. New York: Routledge.

Fenstermaker, Sarah, & Candace West, eds. (2002). *Doing gender, doing difference: Social inequality, power, and resistance*. New York: Routledge.

Ferguson, Ann Arnett (2000). *Bad boys: Public schools in the making of black masculinity*. Ann Arbor: University of Michigan Press.

Ferrara, Kathleen, & Barbara Bell (1995). Sociolinguistic variation and discourse function of constructed dialogue introducers: The case of *be + like*. *American Speech* 70(3): 265–290.

Fischer, John L. (1958). Social influences on the choice of a linguistic variant. *Word* 14(1): 47–56.

Foster, Michèle (1996). As California goes, so goes the nation. *Journal of Negro Education* 65(2): 105–110.

Foucault, Michel (1977). *Discipline and punish: The birth of the prison*. New York: Vintage.

Frankenberg, Ruth (1993). *White women, race matters: The social construction of whiteness*. Minneapolis: University of Minnesota Press.

(2001). The mirage of an unmarked whiteness. In Birgit Brander Rasmussen, Eric Klinenberg, Irene J. Nexica, & Matt Wray, eds., *The making and unmaking of whiteness*. Durham, NC: Duke University Press. 72–96.

Gallagher, Charles A. (1994). White construction in the university. *Socialist Review* 1(2): 167–187.

(2003). Color-blind privilege: The social and political functions of erasing the color line in post race America. *Race, Gender and Class* 10(4): 22–37.

Garrett, Peter, Nikolas Coupland, & Angie Williams (2004). Adolescents' lexical repertoires of peer evaluation: *Boring prats* and *English snobs*. In Adam Jaworski, Nikolas Coupland, & Dariusz Galasinski, eds., *Metalanguage: Social and ideological perspectives*. Berlin: Mouton de Gruyter. 193–226.

Gaudio, Rudolf P. (2001). White men do it too: Racialized (homo)sexualities in postcolonial Hausaland. *Journal of Linguistic Anthropology* 11(1): 36–51.

Gaudio, Rudolf P., & Steve Bialostok (2005). The trouble with culture: Everyday racism in white middle-class discourse. *Critical Discourse Studies* 2(1): 51–69.

Georgakopoulou, Alexandra (2007). *Small stories, interaction and identities*. Amsterdam: John Benjamins.

Gilman, Jonathon, Matthew Igoe, & Nell Lamb (1999). Quotatives: The progressive grammaticalization of BE + LIKE and introduction of BE + ALL. Paper presented at the annual meeting of the New Ways of Analyzing Variation conference, Toronto, October.

Goodwin, Marjorie Harness (1990). *He-said-she-said: Talk as social organization among black children*. Bloomington: Indiana University Press.

(2002). Exclusion in girls' peer groups: Ethnographic analysis of language practices on the playground. *Human Development* 45: 392–415.

(2006). *The hidden life of girls: Games of stance, status, and exclusion*. Malden, MA: Blackwell.

Gordon, Avery, & Christopher Newfield (1995). White philosophy. In Kwame Anthony Appiah & Henry Louis Gates, Jr., eds., *Identities*. Chicago: University of Chicago Press. 380–400.

Gramsci, Antonio (1971). *Selections from the prison notebooks*. Trans. and ed. by Quintin Hoare and Geoffrey Nowell Smith. New York: International Publishers.

Green, Lisa (1998). Remote past and states in African-American English. *American Speech* 73(2): 115–138.

(2002). *African American English: A linguistic introduction*. Cambridge: Cambridge University Press.

Guerin, Bernard (2003). Combating prejudice and racism: New interventions from a functional analysis of racist language. *Journal of Community and Applied Social Psychology* 13(1): 29–45.

Gumperz, John J. (1982). *Discourse strategies*. Cambridge: Cambridge University Press.

Hafner, Katie (1993). Woman, computer nerd – and proud. *New York Times* August 29.

Hall, Perry A. (1997). African-American music: Dynamics of appropriation and innovation. In Bruce Ziff & Pratima V. Rao, eds., *Borrowed power: Essays on cultural appropriation*. New Brunswick: Rutgers University Press. 31–51.

Halliday, M. A. K. (1976). Anti-languages. *American Anthropologist* 78(3): 570–584.

Hartigan, John (1999). *Racial situations: Class predicaments of whiteness in Detroit*. Princeton: Princeton University Press.

Hatala, Eileen (1976). Environmental effects on white students in black schools. Unpublished master's essay, University of Pennsylvania, Department of Linguistics.

Heath, Shirley Brice (1983). *Ways with words: Language, life, and work in communities and classrooms*. Cambridge: Cambridge University Press.

Hebdige, Dick (1979). *Subculture: The meaning of style*. London: Methuen.

Heller, Monica (1999). *Linguistic minorities and modernity: A sociolinguistic ethnography*. London: Longman.

Heritage, John, & Geoffrey Raymond (2005). The terms of agreement: Indexing epistemic authority and subordination in talk-in-interaction. *Social Psychology Quarterly* 68(1): 15–38.

Hewitt, Roger (1986). *White talk black talk: Inter-racial friendship and communication amongst adolescents*. Cambridge: Cambridge University Press.

Hill, Jane H. (2008). *The everyday language of white racism*. Malden, MA: Blackwell.

Holland, Dorothy, & Margaret Eisenhart (1990). *Educated in romance: Women, achievement, and college culture*. Chicago: University of Chicago Press.

Irvine, Judith T. ([1974] 1989). Strategies of status manipulation in the Wolof greeting. In Richard Bauman & Joel Sherzer, eds., *Explorations in the ethnography of speaking*. Cambridge: Cambridge University Press. 167–191.

(2001). "Style" as distinctiveness: The culture and ideology of linguistic differentiation. In Penelope Eckert & John R. Rickford, eds., *Style and sociolinguistic variation*. Cambridge: Cambridge University Press. 21–43.

Irvine, Judith T., & Susan Gal (2000). Language ideology and linguistic differentiation. In Paul V. Kroskrity, ed., *Regimes of language: Ideologies, polities, and identities*. Santa Fe, NM: School of American Research Press. 35–84.

Jackson, Ronald L., II (2006). *Scripting the Black masculine body: Identity, discourse, and racial politics in popular media*. Albany: SUNY Press.

Jacobs-Huey, Lanita (1996). Is there an authentic African American speech community?: Carla revisited. Unpublished M.A. thesis, University of California, Los Angeles, Department of Anthropology.

Jefferson, Gail (1984). On the organization of laughter in talk about troubles. In J. Maxwell Atkinson & John Heritage, eds., *Structures of social action: Studies in conversation analysis*. Cambridge: Cambridge University Press. 346–369.

Johnstone, Barbara (1995). Sociolinguistic resources, individual identities, and public speech styles of Texas women. *Journal of Linguistic Anthropology* 5(2): 183–202.

Jones, Simon (1988). *Black music, white youth: The reggae culture from JA to UK*. Basingstoke: Macmillan.

Joseph, John E. (2004). *Language and identity: National, ethnic, religious*. New York: Palgrave Macmillan.

Kakutani, Michiko (1997). Common threads: Why are homeboys and suburbanites wearing each other's clothes? *New York Times Sunday Magazine* (February 16):18.

Kang, M. Agnes (2004). Constructing ethnic identity through discourse: Self-categorization among Korean American camp counselors. *Pragmatics* 14(2/3): 217–233.

Kennedy, Randall (2002). *Nigger: The strange career of a troublesome word*. New York: Vintage.

Kiesling, Scott (1997). Power and the language of men. In Sally Johnson & Ulrike Hanna Meinhof, eds., *Language and masculinity*. Oxford: Basil Blackwell. 65–85.

(1998). Men's identities and sociolinguistic variation: The case of fraternity men. *Journal of Sociolinguistics* 2(1): 69–99.

(2001). Stances of whiteness and hegemony in fraternity men's discourse. *Journal of Linguistic Anthropology* 11(1): 101–115.

(2004). Dude. *American Speech* 79(3): 281–305.

(2005). Variation, stance and style: Word-final *-er*, high rising tone, and ethnicity in Australian English. *English World-Wide* 26(1): 1–42.

(2006). Hegemonic identity-making in narrative. In Anna De Fina, Deborah Schiffrin, & Michael Bamberg, eds., *Discourse and identity.* Cambridge: Cambridge University Press. 261–287.

Kinney, David A. (1993). From nerds to normals: The recovery of identity among adolescents from middle school to high school. *Sociology of Education* 66(1): 21–40.

Kitzinger, Celia (2007). Is "woman" always relevantly gendered? *Gender and Language* 1(1): 39–49.

Labov, Teresa (1990). Ideological themes in reports of interracial conflict. In Allen D. Grimshaw, ed., *Conflict talk: Sociolinguistic investigations of arguments in conversations*. Cambridge: Cambridge University Press. 139–159.

Labov, William (1972a). The study of language in its social context. In *Sociolinguistic patterns*. Philadelphia: University of Pennsylvania Press. 183–259.

(1972b). *Language in the inner city: Studies in the Black English Vernacular.* Philadelphia: University of Pennsylvania Press.

(1972c). Hypercorrection by the lower middle class as a factor in linguistic change. In *Sociolinguistic patterns*. Philadelphia: University of Pennsylvania Press. 122–142.

(1972d). The isolation of contextual styles. In *Sociolinguistic patterns*. Philadelphia: University of Pennsylvania Press. 70–109.

(1972e). The transformation of experience in narrative syntax. In *Language in the inner city: Studies in the Black English Vernacular.* Philadelphia: University of Pennsylvania Press. 354–396.

(1980). Is there a creole speech community? In Albert Valdman & Arnold Highfield, eds., *Theoretical orientations in creole studies*. New York: Academic Press. 369–388.

(1994). *Principles of linguistic change.* Volume 1*: Internal factors*. Oxford: Blackwell.

Labov, William, & Wendell A. Harris (1986). De facto segregation of black and white vernaculars. In David Sankoff, ed., *Diversity and diachrony.* Philadelphia: John Benjamins. 1–24.

Lakoff, Robin Tolmach (2000). *The language war.* Berkeley: University of California Press.

Laversuch, I. M. (2007). The politics of naming race and ethnicity: Language planning and policies regulating the selection of racial ethnonyms used by the US Census 1990–2010. *Current Issues in Language Planning* 8(3): 365–382.

Lee, Jung-Eun Janie (2009). "She's hungarious so she's Mexican but she's most likely Indian": Negotiating ethnic labels in a California junior high school. *Pragmatics* 19(1): 39–63.

Lee, Margaret G. (1999). Out of the hood and into the news: Borrowed black verbal expressions in a mainstream newspaper. *American Speech* 74(4): 369–388.

Leeman, Jennifer J. (2004). Racializing language: A history of linguistic ideologies in the U.S. Census. *Journal of Language and Politics* 3(3): 507–534.

Le Page, R. B., & Andrée Tabouret-Keller (1985). *Acts of identity: Creole-based approaches to language and ethnicity.* Cambridge: Cambridge University Press.

Lévi-Strauss, Claude (1966). *The savage mind.* Chicago: University of Chicago Press.

Lewis, Amanda E. (2004). "What group?": Studying whites and whiteness in the era of "color-blindness." *Sociological Theory* 22(4): 623–646.

(2005). *Race in the schoolyard: Negotiating the color line in classrooms and communities*. New Brunswick: Rutgers University Press.

Llamas, Carmen, & Dominic Watt, eds. (2010). *Language and identities*. Edinburgh: Edinburgh University Press.

Long, Jeffrey C. (2003). Human genetic variation: The mechanisms and results of microevolution. Paper presented at the annual meeting of the American Anthropological Association, Chicago, November.

Lopez, David, & Yen Le Espiritu (1990). Panethnicity in the United States: A theoretical framework. *Ethnic and Racial Studies* 13: 198–224.

Macaulay, Ronald (2001). *You're like "why not?"*: The quotative expressions of Glasgow adolescents. *Journal of Sociolinguistics* 5(1): 3–21.

Martin, Judith N., Robert L. Krizek, Thomas L. Nakayama, & Lisa Bradford (1999). What do white people want to be called?: A study of self-labels for white Americans. In Thomas L. Nakayama & Judith N. Martin, eds., *Whiteness: The communication of social identity.* Thousand Oaks, CA: Sage. 27–50.

Matthews, Tanya L. (2005). From category labels to discourse strategies: Girls' categorization practices at Millcreek High. Unpublished Ph.D. dissertation, Cornell University, Department of Linguistics.

McElhinny, Bonnie (2001). See no evil, speak no evil: White police officers' talk about race and affirmative action. *Journal of Linguistic Anthropology* 11(1): 65–78.

McIntyre, Alice (1997). *Making meaning of whiteness: Exploring racial identity with white teachers*. Albany: State University of New York Press.

McMichael, Robert K. (1998). "We insist – freedom now!": Black moral authority, jazz, and the changeable shape of whiteness. *American Music* 16(4): 375–416.

Mehan, Hugh (1991). The school's work of sorting students. In Deirdre Boden & Don H. Zimmerman, eds., *Talk and social structure: Studies in ethnomethodology and conversation analysis*. Berkeley: University of California Press. 71–90.

Mendoza-Denton, Norma (1997). Chicana/Mexicana identity and linguistic variation: An ethnographic and sociolinguistic study of gang affiliation in an urban high school. Unpublished Ph.D. dissertation, Stanford University, Department of Linguistics.

(2002). Language and identity. In J. K. Chambers, Peter Trudgill, & Natalie Schilling-Estes, eds., *The handbook of language variation and change*. Oxford: Blackwell. 475–499.

(2008). *Homegirls: Language and cultural practice among Latina youth gangs*. Malden, MA: Blackwell.

Miller, Laura (2004). Those naughty teenage girls: Japanese Kogals, slang, and media assessments. *Journal of Linguistic Anthropology* 14(2): 225–247.

Mishler, Elliot G. (1986). *Research interviewing: Context and narrative*. Cambridge, MA: Harvard University Press.

Mitchell-Kernan, Claudia (1971). *Language behavior in a black urban community.* Berkeley: Language Behavior Research Laboratory.

Modan, Gabriella (2001). White, whole wheat, rye: Jews and ethnic categorization in Washington, DC. *Journal of Linguistic Anthropology* 11(1): 116–130.

Moore, Emma (2004). Sociolinguistic style: A multidimensional resource for shared identity creation. *Canadian Journal of Linguistics/Revue canadienne de linguistique* 49(3/4): 375–396.

Moore, Robert L. (2004). We're cool, Mom and Dad are swell: Basic slang and generational shifts in values. *American Speech* 79(1): 59–86.

Morgan, Marcyliena (1994). The African-American speech community: Reality and sociolinguists. In Marcyliena Morgan, ed., *Language and the social construction of identity in creole situations*. Los Angeles: Center for Afro-American Studies, University of California, Los Angeles. 121–148.

(1998). More than a mood or an attitude: Discourse and verbal genre in African American culture. In Salikoko Mufwene, John Rickford, Guy Bailey, & John Baugh, eds., *African-American English: Structure, history, and use*. New York: Routledge. 251–281.

(2001). "Nuthin' but a G thang": Grammar and language ideology in hip hop identity. In Sonja L. Lanehart, ed., *Sociocultural and historical contexts of African American English*. Amsterdam: John Benjamins. 187–209.

Morris, Edward (2006). *An unexpected minority: White kids in an urban school*. New Brunswick: Rutgers University Press.

Myers, Greg (2006). "Where are you from?": Identifying place. *Journal of Sociolinguistics* 10(3): 320–343.

Myers, Kristen (2005). *Racetalk: Racism hiding in plain sight*. Lanham, MD: Rowman & Littlefield.

Nayak, Anoop (2003). *Race, place and globalization: Youth cultures in a changing world*. Oxford: Berg.

Nugent, Benjamin (2008). *American nerd: The story of my people*. New York: Simon & Schuster.

Oboler, Suzanne (1995). *Ethnic labels, Latino lives: Identity and the politics of (re)presentation in the United States*. Minneapolis: University of Minnesota Press.

Ochs, Elinor (1992). Indexing gender. In Alessandro Duranti & Charles Goodwin, eds., *Rethinking context: Language as an interactive phenomenon*. Cambridge: Cambridge University Press. 335–358.

Ochs, Elinor, & Lisa Capps (2001). *Living narrative: Creating lives in everyday storytelling*. Cambridge, MA: Harvard University Press.

Olivo, Warren (2001). Phat lines: Spelling conventions in rap music. *Written Language and Literacy* 4(1): 67–85.

Omi, Michael, & Howard Winant (1994). *Racial formation in the United States*. 2nd edn. New York: Routledge.

Omoniyi, Tope, & Goodith White, eds. (2007). *Sociolinguistics of identity*. London: Continuum.

Perry, Pamela (2001). White means never having to say you're ethnic: White youth and the construction of "cultureless" identities. *Journal of Contemporary Ethnography* 30(1): 56–91.

(2002). *Shades of white: White kids and racial identities in high school*. Durham, NC: Duke University Press.

Peshkin, Alan (1991). *The color of strangers, the color of friends: The play of ethnicity in school and community*. Chicago: University of Chicago Press.

Phoenix, Ann (1997). "I'm white! So what?": The construction of whiteness for young Londoners. In Michelle Fine, Lois Weis, Linda C. Powell, & L. Mun Wong, eds., *Off white: Readings on race, power, and society*. New York: Routledge. 187–197.

Podesva, Robert J., Sarah J. Roberts, & Kathryn Campbell-Kibler (2002). Sharing resources and indexing meanings in the production of gay styles. In Kathryn Campbell-Kibler, Robert J. Podesva, Sarah J. Roberts, & Andrew Wong, eds., *Language and sexuality: Contesting meaning in theory and practice*. Stanford, CA: CSLI Publications. 175–190.

Pollock, Mica (2005). *Colormute: Race talk dilemmas in an American school*. Princeton: Princeton University Press.

Pomerantz, Anita (1984). Agreeing and disagreeing with assessments: Some features of preferred/dispreferred turn shapes. In J. Maxwell Atkinson & John Heritage, eds., *Structures of social action: Studies in conversation analysis*. Cambridge: Cambridge University Press. 57–101.

(1986). Extreme case formulations: A way of legitimizing claims. *Human Studies* 9(2–3): 219–229.

Potter, Jonathan (1996). *Representing reality: Discourse, rhetoric and social construction*. London: Sage.

Prescott, Brian (2008). *Knocking at the college door: Projections of high school graduates by state and race/ethnicity, 1992–2022*. Boulder, CO: Western Interstate Commission for Higher Education.

Preston, Dennis R. (1992). Talking black and talking white: A study in variety imitation. In Joan H. Hall, Nick Doane, & Dick Ringler, eds., *Old English and new: Studies in language and linguistics in honor of Frederic G. Cassidy*. New York: Garland. 327–355.

Puckett, Anita (2001). The Melungeon identity movement and the construction of Appalachian whiteness. *Journal of Linguistic Anthropology* 11(1): 131–146.

Rahman, Jacquelyn (2007). An *ay* for an *ah*: Language of survival in African American narrative comedy. *American Speech* 82(1): 65–96.

Rampton, Ben (1995). *Crossing: Language and ethnicity among adolescents*. London: Longman.

(1999). Styling the other: Introduction. *Journal of Sociolinguistics* 3(4): 421–427.

(2006). *Language in late modernity: Interaction in an urban school*. Cambridge: Cambridge University Press.

Reyes, Angela (2005). Appropriation of African American slang by Asian American youth. *Journal of Sociolinguistics* 9(4): 509–532.

(2007). *Language, identity, and stereotype among Southeast Asian American youth: The other Asian*. Mahwah, NJ: Lawrence Erlbaum Associates.

Rickford, John R. (1975). Carrying the new wave into syntax: the case of Black English BIN. In Ralph Fasold & Roger Shuy, eds., *Analyzing variation in language*. Washington, DC: Georgetown University Press. 162–183.

Rickford, John R., Isabelle Buchstaller, Thomas Wasow, & Arnold Zwicky (2007). Intensive and quotative *all*: Something old, something new. *American Speech* 82(1): 3–31.

Rickford, John R., & Russell John Rickford (2000). *Spoken soul: The story of Black English*. New York: Wiley.

Riggle, William Harry (1965). The white, the black, and the gray: A study of student subcultures in a suburban California high school. Unpublished Ph.D. dissertation, University of California, Berkeley, School of Education.

Riley, Philip (2007). *Language, culture and identity: An ethnolinguistic perspective.* London: Continuum.

Rogin, Michael (1996). *Blackface, white noise: Jewish immigrants in the Hollywood melting pot.* Berkeley: University of California Press.

Romaine, Suzanne, & Deborah Lange (1991). The use of *like* as a marker of reported speech and thought: A case of grammaticalization in progress. *American Speech* 66(3): 227–279.

Ronkin, Maggie, & Helen E. Karn (1999). Mock Ebonics: Linguistic racism in parodies of Ebonics on the Internet. *Journal of Sociolinguistics* 3(3): 360–380.

Sacks, Harvey (1984). On doing "being ordinary." In J. Maxwell Atkinson & John Heritage, eds., *Structures of social action: Studies in conversation analysis.* Cambridge: Cambridge University Press. 413–429.

([1972] 1986). On the analyzability of stories by children. In John J. Gumperz & Dell Hymes, eds., *Directions in sociolinguistics: The ethnography of communication.* Oxford: Blackwell. 325–345.

(1995). *Lectures on conversation.* 2 vols. Oxford: Blackwell.

Santa Ana, Otto (2002). *Brown tide rising: Metaphors of Latinos in contemporary American public discourse.* Austin: University of Texas Press.

Schegloff, Emanuel A. (2007). A tutorial on membership categorization. *Journal of Pragmatics* 39(3): 462–482.

Schiffrin, Deborah (1993). "Speaking for another" in sociolinguistic interviews: Alignments, identities, and frames. In Deborah Tannen, ed., *Framing in discourse.* New York: Oxford University Press. 231–263.

(1997). Stories in answer to questions in research interviews. *Journal of Narrative and Life History* 7(1–4): 129–137.

Schilling-Estes, Natalie (2004). Constructing ethnicity in interaction. *Journal of Sociolinguistics* 8(2): 163–195.

Schourup, Lawrence (1982). Quoting with *go* 'say'. *American Speech* 57(2): 148–149.

Schwartz, Adam (2006). The teaching and culture of household Spanish: Understanding racist reproduction in "domestic" discourse. *Critical Discourse Studies* 3(2): 107–121.

Scott, James C. (1990). *Domination and the arts of resistance: Hidden transcripts.* New Haven: Yale University Press.

Sebba, Mark (2003). Spelling rebellion. In Jannis K. Androutsopoulos & Alexandra Georgakopoulou, eds., *Discourse constructions of youth identities.* Amsterdam: John Benjamins. 151–172.

Shankar, Shalini (2008). *Desi land: Teen culture, class, and success in Silicon Valley.* Durham, NC: Duke University Press.

Shek, Yen Ling (2006). Asian American masculinity: A review of the literature. *Journal of Men's Studies* 14(3): 379–391.

Shenk, Petra Scott (2007). "I'm Mexican, remember?": Constructing ethnic identities via authenticating discourse. *Journal of Sociolinguistics* 11(2): 194–220.

Shuman, Amy (1986). *Storytelling rights: The uses of oral and written texts by urban adolescents.* Cambridge: Cambridge University Press.

Silverstein, Michael (1976). Shifters, linguistic categories, and cultural description. In Keith H. Basso & Henry A. Selby, eds., *Meaning in anthropology.* Albuquerque: University of New Mexico Press. 11–55.

(2003). Indexical order and the dialectics of sociolinguistic life. *Language and Communication* 23(3–4): 193–229.

Simmons, Rachel (2002). *Odd girl out: The hidden culture of aggression in girls*. San Diego: Harcourt.

Sinclair, John, & Malcolm Coulthard (1975). *Towards an analysis of discourse*. Oxford: Oxford University Press.

Singler, John Victor (2001). Why you can't do a VARBRUL study of quotatives and what such a study can show us. In Tara Sanchez & Daniel Ezra Johnson, eds., *Papers from NWAV 29* (*University of Pennsylvania Working Papers in Linguistics* 7(3)). Philadelphia: University of Pennsylvania Department of Linguistics. 256–278.

Smitherman, Geneva (1991). "What is Africa to me?": Language, ideology, and *African American*. *American Speech* 66(2): 115–132.

(1994). *Black talk: Words and phrases from the hood to the amen corner.* Boston: Houghton Mifflin.

Spears, Arthur K. (1998). African-American language use: Ideology and so-called obscenity. In Salikoko S. Mufwene, John R. Rickford, Guy Bailey, & John Baugh, eds., *African-American English*. London: Routledge. 226–250.

Staiger, Annegret (2006). *Learning difference: Race and schooling in the multiracial metropolis*. Stanford, CA: Stanford University Press.

Stenström, Anna-Brita, Gisle Andersen, & Ingrid Kristine Hasund (2002). *Trends in teenage talk: Corpus compilation, analysis and findings*. Amsterdam: John Benjamins.

Stokoe, Elizabeth, & Derek Edwards (2008). "Did you have permission to smash your neighbour's door?": Silly questions and their answers in police-suspect interrogations. *Discourse Studies* 10(1): 89–111.

Sweetland, Julie (2002). Unexpected but authentic use of an ethnically-marked dialect. *Journal of Sociolinguistics* 6(4): 514–536.

Tagliamonte, Sali A. (2008). So different and pretty cool!: Recycling intensifiers in Toronto, Canada. *English Language and Linguistics* 12(2): 361–394.

Tagliamonte, Sali A., & Alex D'Arcy (2004). He's like, she's like: The quotative system in Canadian youth. *Journal of Sociolinguistics* 8(4): 493–514.

(2007). Frequency and variation in the community grammar: Tracking a new change through the generations. *Language Variation and Change* 19: 199–217.

Tagliamonte, Sali, & Rachel Hudson (1999). *Be like* et al. beyond America: The quotative system in British and Canadian youth. *Journal of Sociolinguistics* 3(2): 147–172.

Tannen, Deborah (1989). *Talking voices: Repetition, dialogue, and imagery in conversational discourse*. Cambridge: Cambridge University Press.

Thorne, Barrie (1993). *Gender play: Girls and boys in school*. New Brunswick: Rutgers University Press.

Thornton, Sarah (1995). *Club cultures: Music, media and subcultural capital*. Hanover, NH: Wesleyan University Press.

Tochluk, Shelly (2007). *Witnessing whiteness: First steps toward an antiracist practice and culture*. Lanham, MD: Rowman & Littlefield.

Tracy, Karen (2002). *Everyday talk: Building and reflecting identities*. New York: Guilford Press.

Trechter, Sara (2001). White between the lines: Ethnic positioning in Lakhota discourse. *Journal of Linguistic Anthropology* 11(1): 22–35.

Trechter, Sara, & Mary Bucholtz (2001). White noise: Bringing language into whiteness studies. *Journal of Linguistic Anthropology* 11(1): 3–21.

Twine, France Winddance, & Charles Gallagher (2008). The future of whiteness: A map of the "third wave." *Ethnic and Racial Studies* 31(1): 4–24.

Twine, France Winddance, & Jonathan W. Warren, eds. (2000). *Racing research, researching race: Methodological dilemmas in critical race studies*. New York: New York University Press.

Underhill, Robert (1988). *Like* is, like, focus. *American Speech* 63(3): 234–246.

van den Berg, Harry, Margaret Wetherell, & Hanneke Houtkoop-Steenstra, eds. (2004). *Analyzing race talk: Multidisciplinary perspectives on the research interview*. Cambridge: Cambridge University Press.

van Dijk, Teun A. (1987). *Communicating racism: Ethnic prejudice in thought and talk*. Newbury Park, CA: Sage.

(1992). Discourse and the denial of racism. *Discourse and Society* 3(1): 87–118.

(1993a). *Elite discourse and racism*. Newbury Park, CA: Sage.

(1993b). Stories and racism. In Dennis K. Mumby, ed., *Narrative and social control: Critical perspectives*. Newbury Park, CA: Sage. 121–142.

Vogelman, Lawrence (1993). The Big Black Man Syndrome: The Rodney King trial and the use of racial stereotypes in the courtroom. *Fordham Urban Law Journal* 20: 571–580.

von Eye, Alexander (1990). *Introduction to Configural Frequency Analysis: The search for types and antitypes in cross-classifications*. Cambridge: Cambridge University Press.

Waksler, Rachelle (2000). A HELLA new specifier. In Sandy Chung, Jim McCloskey, & Nathan Sanders, eds., *Jorge Hankamer WebFest*. <http://ling.ucsc.edu/Jorge/waksler.html>

(2001). A new *all* in conversation. *American Speech* 76(2): 128–138.

Walters, Keith (1996). Contesting representations of African American language. In Risako Ide, Rebecca Parker, & Yukako Sunaoshi, eds., *SALSA 3: Proceedings of the third annual Symposium about Language and Society – Austin* (*Texas Linguistic Forum* 36). Austin: University of Texas Department of Linguistics. 137–151.

Warren, John T. (2003). *Performing purity: Pedagogy, whiteness, and the reconstitution of power*. New York: Peter Lang.

Warren, Jonathan W., & France Winddance Twine (1997). White Americans, the new minority?: Non-blacks and the ever-expanding boundaries of whiteness. *Journal of Black Studies* 28(2): 200–218.

Waters, Mary C. (1990). *Ethnic options: Choosing identities in America*. Berkeley: University of California Press.

Wee, Lionel (2002). When English is not a mother tongue: Linguistic ownership and the Eurasian community in Singapore. *Journal of Multilingual and Multicultural Development* 23(4): 282–295.

Wellman, David T. (1993). *Portraits of white racism*. 2nd edn. Cambridge: Cambridge University Press.

Wetherell, Margaret, & Jonathan Potter (1992). *Mapping the language of racism: Discourse and the legitimation of exploitation*. New York: Columbia University Press.

Whitehead, Kevin A., & Gene H. Lerner (2009). When are persons "white"?: On some practical asymmetries of racial reference in talk-in-interaction. *Discourse and Society* 20(5): 613–641.

Widdicombe, Sue, & Robin Wooffitt (1995). *The language of youth subcultures: Social identity in action*. New York: Harvester Wheatsheaf.

Williams, Brackette F. (1989). A class act: Anthropology and the race to nation across ethnic terrain. *Annual Review of Anthropology* 18: 401–444.

Williams, Todd (2004). *The N-word*. Los Angeles, CA: UrbanWorks Entertainment.

Willis, Paul (1977). *Learning to labor: How working class kids get working class jobs*. New York: Columbia University Press.

Winter, Joanne (2002). Discourse quotatives in Australian English: Adolescents performing voices. *Australian Journal of Linguistics* 22(1): 5–21.

Wiseman, Rosalind (2002). *Queen bees and wannabes: Helping your daughter survive cliques, gossip, boyfriends, and other realities of adolescence*. New York: Random House.

Wodak, Ruth, & Martin Reisigl (1999). Discourse and racism: European perspectives. *Annual Review of Anthropology* 28: 175–199.

Wolfram, Walt, & Natalie Schilling-Estes (2006). *American English: Dialects and variation*. 2nd edn. Malden, MA: Blackwell.

Wolfson, Nessa (1976). Speech events and natural speech: Some implications for sociolinguistic methodology. *Language in Society* 5: 189–209.

Woolard, Kathryn A. (1998). Introduction: Language ideology as a field of inquiry. In Bambi B. Schieffelin, Kathryn A. Woolard, & Paul V. Kroskrity, eds., *Language ideologies: Practice and theory*. New York: Oxford University Press. 3–47.

(2008). Why *dat* now?: Linguistic-anthropological contributions to the explanation of sociolinguistic icons and change. *Journal of Sociolinguistics* 12(4): 432–452.

Wray, Matt, & Annalee Newitz, eds. (1997). *White trash: Class, race and the construction of an American identity*. New York: Routledge.

Wulff, Helena (1995). Introducing youth culture in its own right: The state of the art and new possibilities. In Vered Amit-Talai & Helena Wulff, eds., *Youth cultures: A cross-cultural perspective*. London: Routledge. 1–18.

Index